THE ROUGH G

Nelson Mandela

Max du Preez

www.roughguides.com

Credits

The Rough Guide to Nelson Mandela
Editing & picture research: Joe Staines
Layout: Ajay Verma
Proofreading: Kate Berens
Cartography: Katie Lloyd-Jones
Cover design: Diana Jarvis
Production: Rebecca Short

Rough Guides Reference
Director: Andrew Lockett
Editors: Kate Berens, Tom Cabot,
Tracy Hopkins, Matthew Milton,
Joe Staines

Front cover: Mandela at an election rally © Per-Anders Pettersson/Getty Images
Back cover: Mandela mural in Soweto © Frédéric Soltan/Corbis

Publishing Information

This first edition published November 2011 by
Rough Guides Ltd, 80 Strand, London, WC2R 0RL
375 Hudson Street, New York 10014, USA
Email: mail@roughguides.com

Distributed by the Penguin Group:
Penguin Books Ltd, 80 Strand, London, WC2R 0RL
Penguin Group (USA), 375 Hudson Street, NY 10014, USA
Penguin Group (Australia), 250 Camberwell Road, Camberwell,
Victoria 3124, Australia
Penguin Group (New Zealand), 67 Apollo Road, Rosedale,
Auckland 0632, New Zealand

Rough Guides is represented in Canada by Tourmaline Editions Inc.,
662 King Street West, Suite 304, Toronto, Ontario, M5V 1M7

Printed in Singapore by Toppan Security Printing Pte. Ltd.

288pp; includes index

A catalogue record for this book is available from the British Library.

ISBN: 978-1-40538-236-6

135798642

Contents

Introduction

I often think how lucky I am to have been born a South African and doubly lucky to have witnessed – even played a bit part in – the demise of apartheid and the creation of an open democracy on the southern tip of the continent. My fortune increased when I got to know Nelson Mandela, whose life story is so intricately woven into these events.

I am a journalist by trade, so when I was asked to write a book about Mandela I knew that I was going to have to address the man's flaws and weaknesses as well as his strengths. This is not something most South Africans would want to do: we prefer our Madiba to be pure and strong; it suits us to believe in Mandela the myth. Mandela doesn't really have feet of clay, but perhaps a few toes. And yet, the more shortcomings I discovered, the more real he became to me and the more strongly I felt that he is indeed an extraordinary human being.

I first met Mandela just five days after his release in February 1990. I was then the editor of a left-wing weekly newspaper, *Vrye Weekblad*, and in early 1989 had written an open letter to him as an opinion piece, but also knowing he was a subscriber. I told him that in order to help the country make the transition from apartheid to democracy he would have to become South Africa's Solomon, Moses and David all in one, and I warned him that he would have to drag the "hard-assed Boers" with him into the post-apartheid future.

On 15 February 1990 he phoned me and invited me to his Soweto home. As he poured the tea he apologized for not responding to my letter, explaining that the prison authorities wouldn't allow it. He chuckled at being compared to Biblical figures, but was very serious when he said one of his main tasks would be to assure white South Africans that democracy was also in their interest. We had a number of telephone conversations, a few subsequent brief meetings, and I interviewed him four times – twice on live television. Television interviews with politicians are usually robust and confrontational, but Mandela stared me down, like an African king, every time I wanted to jump in with a question.

My emphasis in *The Rough Guide to Nelson Mandela* has been to try and help readers understand and make sense of the man. How did a rural boy from the Western Cape become the global leadership icon of the last decades? His childhood as a Xhosa aristocrat, his education and his relatively late exposure to the cruelty of apartheid were all important, as was the role of his first friends – especially Walter Sisulu – when he moved to the city. I follow his transformation into a revolutionary and would-be guerrilla leader, and his development from narrow African nationalist to a leader who embraced all South Africans. I look at his personal life, in particular his relationship with his second wife, Winnie, and the impact it had on him when she went off the rails. I was initially surprised at how little Mandela has spoken or written about his 27 years of imprisonment, but although the struggle continued, most days in prison are the same as the one before and only those occasions when something out of the ordinary happens are worth mentioning.

As a journalist I had a front row seat from where I could observe the process of Mandela's release, the difficult years of negotiations with the apartheid government and his five years as South Africa's first democratic president. These events are covered but it also seemed appropriate to review his life after he left office and the state of the country entrusted to his successors, a chapter I didn't write with much joy. Some readers may not agree with all my conclusions – all I can say is that I have been honest.

During the whole process of researching and writing this book, I was constantly and painfully aware that Mandela's life was nearing its end. His place in history is assured: this is a very special human being with rare gifts of leadership, integrity and vision who will not be forgotten, not for many generations to come.

Acknowledgements

I am indebted to all the Mandela biographers, each of whom has had a different take on the subject, to friends and colleagues for their advice and to the Nelson Mandela Foundation for documentation of Mandela's life. My wife, partner and adviser-in-chief, Angela Tuck, deserves my thanks for her patience and wisdom. Thanks are due also to Rough Guides' Joe Staines and Andrew Lockett.

PART ONE

THE NELSON MANDELA STORY

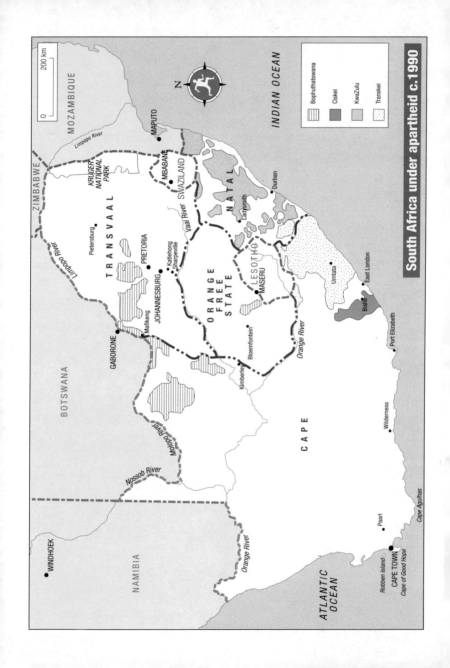

South Africa under apartheid c.1990

Legend:
- Bophuthatswana
- Ciskei
- KwaZulu
- Transkei

1 Early years

"Many years ago, when I was a boy brought up in my village in the Transkei, I listened to the elders of the tribe telling stories about the good old days, before the arrival of the white man. Then, our people lived peacefully under the democratic rule of their kings and moved freely and confidently up and down the country without let or hindrance."

Nelson Mandela, courtroom statement, 1962

Nelson Mandela was born on 18 July 1918 in the village of **Mvezo** in the Transkei region in the present Eastern Cape province of South Africa, the son of **Henry Gadla Mphakanyiswa** and his third wife, Nosekeni (also known as Fanny). Both parents were of the Thembu people, part of the Xhosa-speaking group that still dominates the Eastern Cape, having migrated from further north in Africa and established themselves in the region more than four hundred years ago.

Mandela's paternal DNA, analysed in 2004, indicates that he is a descendant of the sub-Saharan African ironworkers and agriculturalists from the Great Lakes region of East Africa, while mitochondrial DNA links him to the original peoples of southern Africa, the **Khoisan**. DNA tests have shown that living descendants of the Khoisan have the oldest genetic markers ever found, which makes them closer to the first members of our species than any other population group in the world.

WHAT'S IN A NAME?

Nelson Mandela should really be known as **Rolihlahla Dalibunga Mphakanyiswa**. Imagine millions of admirers worldwide trying to get their tongues around that. "Free Rolihlahla Mphakanyiswa" on a protest poster in London wouldn't have had the same impact as "Free Nelson Mandela". Rolihlahla literally means "to pull a branch of a tree" but is more commonly translated as "troublemaker", while Dalibunga was the name Mandela received after his traditional teenage initiation ceremony (see p.6). **Nelson** was his "Western name", provided by the first mission school he attended, and his surname, Mandela, was his grandfather's first name. Later in life he preferred to use his clan name, **Madiba**.

In the middle of the seventeenth century **Dutch settlers**, followed by a number of Germans and French Huguenots, established themselves at the Cape of Good Hope and a century later the first white farmers, called Trekboers, started encroaching on Xhosa land and competing for good grazing for their cattle. With **British colonization** of the Cape in 1806, the Xhosa people's life of peace, freedom and independence was over. Several Xhosa chiefs and resistance leaders were imprisoned on Robben Island off Cape Town by the colonial authorities – the same island where Mandela was later jailed by the apartheid government. When South Africa became a Union under the British crown in 1910, black South Africans were denied the franchise, with the exception of a small number in the Cape Province.

Family background

Henry Mphakanyiswa's grandfather was the Thembu regent **Ngubengcuka**, who died in 1832, but Henry was not regarded as proper royalty because his grandmother was the regent's third wife. Members of this minor "left-hand house" of the king could only

Daily life in the village of Qunu, where Nelson Mandela grew up.
(© Per-Anders Pettersson/Getty Images)

aspire to be chiefs and senior counsellors – a position Mandela was supposed to inherit. Henry Mphakanyiswa was himself a senior counsellor to the Thembu regent of the time; according to Mandela, this was almost the equivalent of the king's prime minister.

Mandela himself has retold the story many times of how his father had a showdown with the local colonial magistrate about a stray ox and was unceremoniously relieved of his duties as a chief when he refused to accept the white man's jurisdiction over him. Researchers have subsequently found the court records of 9 July 1926, which indicate that he was charged with corruption and abuse of his powers as a headman. Mphakanyiswa defended himself and contested the evidence of several witnesses, but he was found guilty and dismissed, a decision ratified by the chief magistrate. Mandela was only eight years old at the time and was probably only told the version he gave later. He writes in his autobiography that his father "possessed a proud rebelliousness, a stubborn sense of fairness, that I recognize in myself".

As Mandela tells the story, his father, having lost his title and livelihood, moved his family to the tiny village of **Qunu**, where, some seventy years later, Mandela built himself a home after he became president. In fact, Mandela's mother had moved to Qunu well before her husband's dismissal as chief: each of Henry Mphakanyiswa's four wives lived in her own *kraal* or homestead, some of them up to 30km apart. The young Rolihlahla spent most of his time playing in the veld, practising stick fighting with friends when his duties as a herdboy allowed him. "It was in the fields that I learned how to knock birds out of the sky with a slingshot, to gather wild honey and fruit and edible roots, to drink warm, sweet milk straight from the udder of a cow, to swim in the clear, cold streams, and to catch fish with twine and sharpened bits of wire."

When he turned seven, he was sent to the nearby missionary school where a teacher decided that he should also have an English name and called him Nelson, almost certainly after the famous British admiral, Lord Nelson. Until then, he only wore a blanket over one shoulder, pinned at the waist. Now his father told him he had to dress properly for school. Henry took a pair of his own trousers, cut them off at the knee and tied them at the waist with string. "I have never owned a suit I was prouder to wear," Mandela later declared.

When Mandela's father died of tuberculosis two years later, the young man's life changed completely. He had never been very close to his father and said later he didn't feel grief so much as "cut adrift", and that he mourned more for the world he was leaving behind than for the loss of his father: "Although my mother was the centre of my existence, I defined myself through my father." With his father gone, his mother decided he should grow up in the household of the Thembu regent, **Chief Jongintaba Dalindyebo**, at Mqhekezweni – the Great Place. Jongintaba would be his guardian for the next ten years and Mandela was brought up almost as a prince himself, alongside the king's son, Justice. Although Mandela's mother was a Christian, religion meant little to him. But when he went to live at the Great Place, which had a Methodist mission station nearby, he had no choice but to accompany Jongintaba and his family to church services every Sunday.

Growing up at the Great Place

Mandela has very happy memories of the time he spent at the royal kraal, a new exciting world into which he was quickly absorbed. Instead of the mud huts of Qunu, the Great Place had large white-washed buildings with tin roofs, gardens and fruit orchards. The inhabitants wore Western clothes: suits for the men and long skirts and high-necked blouses for the women, like the white missionary wives. Mandela himself was given smart new trousers, shirts and jackets. The regent drove a huge, shiny car, a Ford V8, and his new home was, according to Mandela, a "vision of wealth and order beyond my imagination".

For the first time, the young Mandela started believing that he could one day be more than just another country boy. He had seen little of his father while he was still alive – Henry Mphakanyiswa had thirteen children and four wives – and once he had moved to the Great Place, contact with his mother was discouraged. Chief

The thatched rondavel at Mqhekezwini where Mandela lived with the family of Jongintaba. (© Eva-Lotta Jansson/Africa Media Online)

Jongintaba's family became his family. Mandela later treated his comrades in the struggle against apartheid as his family, and – it's been argued – had a better relationship with some of them than he did with his own children.

Mandela's famous love of good clothes and personal neatness can also be traced to his childhood at the royal court. He tells the story that one of his favourite jobs he did for his foster father was to press his suits: "He owned half a dozen Western suits, and I spent many an hour carefully making the creases in his trousers." Mandela was made painfully aware in his new surroundings of his lack of social graces, his inadequate table manners and his poor English and he worked hard at improving himself and fitting into this more sophisticated environment.

Thembu governance

Although Mandela's interest in politics only really took off in early adulthood, as a young boy he showed a keen interest in the political structures, leadership and decision making of the traditional **Thembu chieftaincy**. He later stated that his own notions of leadership were "profoundly influenced" by observing the regent and his court. At regular intervals, the Thembu men would arrive at the Great Place for discussions on matters concerning the people: drought; orders given by the magistrate; matters regarding cattle; or serious disputes among members of the community. The young Mandela would sit quietly in a corner and take it all in. Senior counsellors, chiefs and headmen would surround Jongintaba, who would welcome all present and explain why he had asked them to gather. He would then not say another word until all who wanted to speak had spoken. Mandela describes the process as "democracy in its purest form". Everyone, regardless of social status, had the right to say exactly what he liked. To the young Mandela's astonishment, some of them, even people with little social standing, launched into vehement attacks on the regent himself. Jongintaba would merely listen, hour after hour.

The meetings did not stop until some form of consensus was reached, even if it was an agreement to disagree. "Democracy meant all men were to be heard, and a decision was taken as a people. Majority rule was a foreign notion. A minority was not to be crushed by a majority," Mandela later explained.

At the end of a meeting Jongintaba would rise to summarize the views and formulate the consensus reached. His view was that a leader was like a shepherd, staying behind the flock, letting some race ahead, others follow slowly, all the while being directed from behind. This stuck with Mandela: "As a leader, I have always followed the principles I first saw demonstrated by the regent at the Great Place. I have always endeavoured to listen to what each and every person in a discussion had to say before venturing my own opinion. Oftentimes, my own opinion will simply represent a consensus of what I heard in the discussion."

There was another side to Jongintaba that Mandela was either oblivious of, or preferred not to mention in his later reminiscences. Researchers have dug up material from the local magistrate's archives relating to the regent's problems with women, alcohol and money. One magistrate recorded that these issues arose from the "gross extravagance of his style of living" and mentions that Jongintaba was "unable to resist buying as long as credit is extended to him".

After the formal proceedings at the Great Place the chiefs and other elders would normally socialize, sitting around telling stories of the past, mostly about heroes and great kings. These stories often centred on Thembu history, but there were also tales of other prominent African leaders such as the legendary Xhosa chiefs Hintsa and Sandile, and the impressive "war doctor" and indigenous theologian **Makhanda**, who was jailed on Robben Island as a political prisoner 142 years before Mandela. At first, the older men would order the young upstart to leave their gatherings, but he was hooked and came back every time, sitting quietly in the corner. After a time they just let him be. Mandela was fascinated to learn that his country's history did not, as he was taught at school, start when the first European settlers arrived in 1652; that his ancestors were not primitive savages who needed the white man to "uplift" them; that the black peoples of southern Africa had had complex social, legal and religious beliefs and structures for many centuries before they met the first Europeans.

He was particularly impressed with the stories told by the oldest living Thembu chief, **Zwelibhangile Joyi**, who knew more about Thembu history than anyone else. Tatu Joyi, as everyone called him, was an angry man and he regularly railed against the white people who had taken Thembu land, and failed to understand that it should be shared and not owned by individuals. He was particularly bitter about the British queen who was so disrespectful and arrogant that she proclaimed herself the regent of the Thembu and other Xhosa groups. It was this white queen, he said, who had used witchcraft disguised as papers to trick the black people out of their land and freedom, and set tribe against tribe. Mandela later discovered that Tatu Joyi's version of history was in many respects flawed. But it left him with a sense of anger at the injustices perpetrated against his people, and he seemed to retain some of the old chief's romanticized views of Xhosa history.

Coming of age

When he was sixteen, Mandela underwent the traditional, elaborate Xhosa initiation ceremony (see box overleaf), which among other things meant he was circumcised by an old man with a sharp *assegai* or spear. His initiation name was **Dalibunga**, which means "founder of the Bunga", and refers to his destined role as a counsellor – the Bunga being the administrative body of the Transkei. At the end of his initiation ritual, he and his fellows were addressed by a senior chief who provided a grim analysis of the future awaiting the young Thembu men. The Xhosa people and all other black South Africans were slaves in their own country, he said, a people conquered by the white settlers. These young men would have no say over their own destiny. They would live in shacks

Xhosa initiates in the Western Cape. (© Gallo Images/CORBIS)

XHOSA INITIATION

It is still a strict rule in Xhosa culture, as it has been for many generations, that a boy must be **circumcised** and undergo an initiation ceremony before he can be viewed as a man, get married, hold office or plough his own field. In notes he kept in prison, now in the care of the Nelson Mandela Foundation, Mandela wrote: "I still remember well my first reaction, and even revulsion, at Fort Hare when I discovered that a friend had not observed the custom."

When he was sixteen years old, it was Mandela's turn. Prince Justice, son of the Thembu regent, led the twenty-five boys to two huts on the Mbashe River known as Tyhalarha, the traditional place where Thembu royals were circumcised. Here they were isolated from society for a few days in order to bond as initiates. Tradition demanded that the initiates had to perform an act of bravery before the circumcision. In the distant past this could have been a daring cattle raid on an unfriendly neighbouring chiefdom or the killing of a lion or leopard. In 1934 these were not options open to Mandela's initiation mates, so instead they stole a pig from a local farmer and cooked it over a fire. For Mandela "No piece of pork has ever tasted as good before or since."

The night before the circumcision ceremony, women from the area came to the huts and the boys danced to their singing and clapping. At dawn the initiates bathed in the river to purify themselves and at midday lined up before the assembled relatives, chiefs and counsellors. At the moment of circumcision each boy had to shout "ndiyindoda!" (I am a man). Mandela remembers: "Without a word, he [the *ingcibi* or circumcision expert] took my foreskin, pulled it forward, and then, in a single motion, brought down his assegai. I felt as if fire was shooting through my veins; the pain was so intense that I buried my chin in my chest. Many seconds seemed to pass before I remembered to cry, and then I recovered and called out, 'ndiyindoda!'"

Each man's foreskin was tied to a corner of his blanket and healing plant leaves applied to the wound. Their naked, shaved bodies were painted in **white ochre** and, that night, the severed foreskins were buried in ant hills, so the insects could devour them before witchdoctors could get hold of them. When the initiates re-emerged from their seclusion, they washed the white ochre off their bodies and replaced it with **red ochre** that was supposed to be rubbed off on the body of a woman during intercourse, although Mandela simply wiped his off with fat. A great party followed with singing, speeches and gifts. Mandela was given two heifers and four sheep, the first property he ever owned apart from clothes. "I felt strong and proud that day. I remember walking differently on that day, straighter, taller, firmer."

in the cities because the whites had stolen their land. They would get sick in the white man's mines and toil so that the white man could become even more prosperous. Their talents and intelligence would be wasted because they would do mindless jobs for whites. Perhaps God was asleep, the old man concluded.

Up to this point in his life, Mandela had had very little contact with **white people**. He occasionally saw the white magistrate or a white policeman, but they were peripheral to his life as a Thembu prince and he had had no personal experiences of racism or humiliation. Psychologists have suggested this as the reason why when Mandela was confronted with the harsh realities of apartheid and white oppression in his early twenties, he was able to deal with them so rationally, and that the absence of early scars caused by racism helped to make him the inclusive leader he later became.

Mandela recalls that he was angry and annoyed at the chief's harsh words and thought him ignorant, ungrateful and prejudiced because he did not appreciate the benefits the white man had brought to Africa, such as education and technology. To the young Mandela, whites were benefactors more than oppressors and he could not understand why the chief was so aggressive. But the words remained in Mandela's mind; they were a seed that eventually started growing. "Later I realized that the ignorant man that day was not the chief but myself."

The Clarkebury Institute

Young Mandela's life took a major shift when he graduated from primary school and was sent to the prestigious **Clarkebury Institute** at Engcobo for the last five years of his schooling. To mark the event, Chief Jongintaba had a sheep slaughtered for a big party of singing and dancing at the Great Place, and gave the boy his first pair of proper shoes – boots which he polished and shined at every occasion. His arrival at the school was equally momentous: driven by the Thembu regent himself in his impressive V8 Ford – one of very few cars in Thembuland at the time – Mandela walked tall among the other new boys; he was a prince, after all, even though both his parents were illiterate.

Clarkebury was a Methodist school with a British graduate, the reverend **Cecil Harris**, as its principal, and with well-qualified teachers. Some sceptics in the Xhosa-speaking world at the time called the school a "little corner of England" where "black Englishmen" were being trained. Most members of Thembu high society, including Jongintaba himself, were Clarkebury graduates, but wealthy parents from other regions and language groups also sent their children there. It was Mandela's first social interaction with young people of non-Thembu extraction.

Despite his years at the royal Thembu court, Mandela was still very much a country boy and he was painfully reminded of that on his first day at Clarkebury. When he walked into class, he heard an attractive girl called **Mathona** remark to her giggling friends that "the country boy is not used to wearing shoes" and walked "like a horse in spurs". Mandela remained sensitive about his English accent and his country manners for years afterwards, but he did get to know Mathona better and she became a close friend and confidante.

The teenage Mandela's closest friends were all female, despite the virtual absence of his mother in his life and his time in the strictly patriarchal Jongintaba household. He confessed later that he found it easier to "let my hair down" with women and show fears and weaknesses he wouldn't reveal to another man. During his adult years (before he went to jail) many of his closest personal friends were women.

Mandela respected and liked Reverend Harris and corresponded with his daughter Mavis while he was in jail, but his favourite teacher was the senior black teacher **Ben Mahlasela**. It struck Mandela and his friends that Mahlasela treated Harris like an equal, unlike other black teachers who were intimidated by the white principal.

Clarkebury was the end of schooling for many of Mandela's school-mates, but a boy destined to become a royal counsellor had to go to a senior secondary school to prepare him for university. When Mandela passed his Standard 8 exams, his foster father organized another traditional celebration and took the young man shopping for white shirts, a black blazer and the maroon and gold tie of **Healdtown**, one of the prime black schools in South Africa. Jongintaba's son Justice was already enrolled as a student there.

Healdtown

Healdtown and the nearby Lovedale College and St Matthew's School, like other Christian mission schools during the first half of the twentieth century, played a very important role in producing a new, educated black elite and intellectual class – crucial participants in the shaping of South Africa up to liberation. After 1950 successive apartheid governments saw these schools as subversive, closing some of them down and making it difficult for others to operate. The white authorities preferred to control the education of blacks through the system of "Bantu Education", designed to confine them to the working class. Ironically, the missionary schools were later criticized for being too Eurocentric and neglecting indigenous African culture and history.

Healdtown (later Healdtown Comprehensive School), in the small town of Fort Beaufort, was another English-style institution run by Methodists, with elegant Victorian buildings covered in ivy, set in a complex of large trees and cool courtyards. The headmaster, the reverend **Arthur Wellington**, claimed to be a descendant of the Duke of Wellington. According to Mandela, he also told them that Napoleon's defeat at the hands of Wellington had rescued civilization for the natives of Africa as well as for Europe. The pupils had to raise the Union Jack every week and sing "God Save the King" after which they were also allowed to sing "Nkosi Sikelel' i Afrika" (God Save Africa), which became the hymn of the black liberation movement and, eventually, the national anthem of South Africa.

By all accounts Mandela was a diligent and disciplined though not outstanding student. He liked sport and at Healdtown he became a competitive long-distance runner, enjoying the solitude the sport brought. His main gripe at Healdtown was the poor food. While other privileged pupils could use their pocket money to make their daily meals more palatable, Jongintaba thought it inappropriate to supply his son and foster son with a monthly allowance.

Early political influences

Researching Mandela's early life, one inevitably looks for influences that would explain his political philosophy later in life. The proceedings of the Thembu royal court certainly had an effect, as did his two years at Healdtown. His fellow pupils there included children from other regions of South Africa as well as the British Protectorates of Swaziland, Bechuanaland (now Botswana) and Basutholand (now Lesotho). Ethnic chauvinism was rife in those days and the Thembu and other Xhosa-speaking groups were no exceptions. Up to this point most of Mandela's companions were Thembu, but now he made friends with a Sotho-speaking pupil, Zachariah Molete. His Thembu schoolmates did not approve. The reverend **Seth Mokitimi**, Mandela's housemaster, was also a Sotho-speaker and Mandela came to admire him for fighting for a better diet for the pupils and for standing up to the school's white principal.

Mandela himself recognizes that these experiences had an impact on his thinking. His time at Healdtown "loosened the hold of tribalism that still imprisoned me". Unlike most liberation movements in sub-Saharan Africa, the African National Congress (ANC), of which

Mandela became the greatest leader, had a strong policy of discouraging tribal divisions, a feature that partly explains the political stability of South Africa in the post-apartheid era.

Another significant influence was the visit in 1938 by the great Xhosa writer, poet and *imbongi* (praise singer) **Krune Mqhayi**. It was Mandela's final school year and he later described the experience as "like a comet crossing the sky". A great poet was meant to be someone like Keats or Tennyson, and here was a man dressed in full Xhosa traditional dress – leopard skin, spear and all – entering the stage of their assembly hall ahead of the headmaster. Mqhayi recited a poem he had written thirteen years earlier, when Edward, Prince of Wales, had visited South Africa:

> "Hayi, O mighty Great Britain!
> You arrive on our shores with a Bible and a bottle.
> You arrive in pairs, a missionary escorted by a soldier.
> You bring gunpowder, rifles and cannons.
> Excuse me, O my father, but which of these gifts are we to accept?"

The sentiment was reminiscent of the often-repeated South African political adage that when the white man arrived in Africa he had the Bible and the black man had the land. Now the black man has the Bible and the white man has the land.

Mqhayi moved to the front of the stage, raised his spear and touched the curtain rod with it. The spear was a symbol of the African as artist and warrior, he said, it represented the glory and magnificence of African history. The curtain rod was a symbol of European industry, clever, but cold and soulless. Gazing intently at the pupils he continued: "We have been kneeling too long before the false gods of the white man." He added, prophetically, that the time would come when black Africans would regain their freedom and dignity. The Healdtown pupils were electrified and the applause was thunderous.

It made a deep impression upon Mandela's young mind: "It seemed to turn the universe upside down," he wrote later.

Mandela was now beginning to view himself as an African and a South African, rather than a Thembu or a Xhosa-speaker. But he was still struggling to fully comprehend his place in the clash between the modern and the traditional, between the Western and the African way of thinking and being.

In 1937 Mandela passed his final school exams with flying colours and there was no doubt in the mind of Chief Jongintaba that his young charge should be one of the privileged few black South Africans to go to university. And the obvious institution – the Cambridge or Yale of black South Africans – was the South African Native College, right next door to Healdtown at Fort Hare in the town of Alice. Later renamed the University of Fort Hare, this was the factory of political and intellectual leaders of the subcontinent. The majority of the students were not Xhosa speaking.

Life at Fort Hare

Mandela was still socially insecure when he started at **Fort Hare**. Despite a new tailor-made grey suit and his aristocratic background, he was intimidated by the students from urban elite families, and remembers the pain of being called a "backward fellow from the countryside". At school his jovial foster brother, Justice, was his protection, but he was still a pupil at Healdtown. At Fort Hare Mandela attached himself to his cousin, **Kaizer Mantanzima**, a descendant of the Great House of King Ngubengcuka and thus a true prince.

Mantanzima, a senior student, was a prominent figure on campus and became Mandela's mentor; he also shared his monthly allowance with his cousin, as Jongintaba had continued his tight-fistedness. Mantanzima was known as KD by most people, but he and Mandela

KAIZER MANTANZIMA

Mandela's cousin, **Kaizer Mantanzima**, later became one of his bitterest political enemies. In 1975, when Mandela was in jail for promoting violent resistance to white minority rule, Mantanzima argued in his book *Independence My Way* that a federation of black "homelands" was the right way to black liberation, rather than the armed struggle waged by the African National Congress. In 1976 he became the first traditional leader to support the ruling National Party's scheme of only providing black South Africans with political and property rights within ethnic "homelands", or **Bantustans**. Mantanzima became the president of a nominally "independent" Transkei but he was a corrupt dictator who banned all opposition parties. He even tried to jail the new Thembu regent, Sabata Dalindyebo, who fled to Zambia and joined the exiled ANC.

Mandela did not cut Mantanzima off completely during these years. He corresponded with him from jail and Mantanzima visited him on Robben Island more than once. In 1984 he even tried to convince Mandela to accept a release from jail on condition he went "into exile" in Transkei. Mandela told him in a letter that his plan was "highly disturbing" and urged him "not to continue pursuing a course which will inevitably result in an unpleasant confrontation between you and ourselves". Mantanzima was forced to retire in 1986 and was succeeded by his brother George. After his death in 2003, Mandela praised his former university companion as a Thembu elder.

called each other by their initiation names, Daliwonga ("Maker of Majesty") and Dalibunga. The two **Thembu aristocrats** made a strong impression at Fort Hare, both being very tall, well-dressed, courteous and princely, but less arrogant than other students from royal families. Mantanzima told one of Mandela's earliest biographers, Fatima Meer, that they were "handsome young men and all the women wanted us". The two attended church, joined the Students' Christian Association together and both were teetotal. They also taught at Sunday School classes in the villages around Alice, along with another student, **Oliver Tambo**, who would one day form a law firm with Mandela and become an important ANC colleague.

Mandela is remembered as being a thoughtful, responsible and reserved student, popular among the women on campus. He boxed, continued his long distance running and even played a bit of football. He also enjoyed ballroom dancing (especially foxtrots and waltzes), and was a fan of Victor Sylvester – the then world ballroom champion. A member of the drama society, Mandela particularly enjoyed a play in which he played Abraham Lincoln's assassin, John Wilkes Booth.

The college's principal, **Dr Alexander Kerr**, had a passion for English literature that rubbed off on Mandela, who became something of an Anglophile while at Fort Hare. He followed the events of World War II on BBC radio with interest and was a great admirer of Winston Churchill. When Mandela attended a speech by South Africa's deputy prime minister, **Jan Smuts**, who was campaigning for South Africa's entry into the war on the side of Britain, he gave the controversial Afrikaner general a standing ovation. Mandela admitted later that he felt an affinity with Smuts because, despite being a brilliant man, he too spoke English with a heavy accent.

Nelson Mandela aged 19, around the time he was a student at Fort Hare. (UWCRIM Mayibuye/Link)

Mandela never graduated from **Fort Hare**. The model student was expelled – a crucial event that led to his entering militant politics. His conflict with the university authorities didn't start as a political issue but as an argument about the poor food. When the students demanded that the powers of their **Representative Council** be extended in order to deal with such grievances, a majority (including Mandela) voted to boycott forthcoming council elections if this didn't happen. But Mandela had already been nominated as a candidate, and was one of six members to be elected to the new council by the handful of students who voted.

When all six subsequently resigned, Principal Kerr decided to have another vote at supper time the next day, when all students would

FORT HARE UNIVERSITY

The university was founded in 1916 at the site of a British fort built during the wars against the Xhosa in the mid-nineteenth century. Originally called the **South African Native College**, it became the most prominent institution for black tertiary education in sub-Saharan Africa. Between 1951 and 1960 it was affiliated with Rhodes University and renamed the **University College of Fort Hare**, before being separated off as a college for Xhosa students only. This was in line with the Extension of University Education Act (1959), which effectively prevented black students from attending white universities. Fort Hare was instrumental in creating a **new black elite**, supplying leaders to liberation movements and governments across Africa.

Among Fort Hare's distinguished alumni were many key figures in the struggle against apartheid. These included Davidson "DDT" Jabavu, who was the first black professor at Fort Hare and, from 1936, president of the All-Africa Convention, which campaigned against segregation legislation; the influential academic Professor Z.K. Matthews, who lectured during Mandela's years as a student and whose son, Joe Matthews, became a deputy minister in Mandela's post-1994 cabinet; Dr Archibald Campbell Jordan, teacher, author and father of ANC theoretician and cabinet minister Pallo Jordan; Govan Mbeki, jailed with Mandela in 1964 and father of Thabo Mbeki; Robert Sobukwe, founder of the Pan Africanist Congress; Oliver Tambo, leader of the ANC in exile; Mangosuthu Buthelezi, leader of the Inkatha Freedom Party and a minister in Mandela's cabinet; Desmond Tutu, Anglican Archbishop and Nobel Peace Prize recipient; Chris Hani, liberation hero and leader of the South African Communist Party; and John Hlophe, the first black judge in the Cape High Court and later Judge President.

be present. Once again, the same twenty-five students voted for the same candidates and this time five of them accepted to serve on the council. But not Mandela, who resigned for a second time. Kerr then confronted him with the stark choice of either serving or being expelled. It shouldn't have been a difficult decision: graduate from a prestigious tertiary institution and embark on a life of leadership, success and financial security, or leave under a cloud and face an uncertain future.

Mandela told the principal he would rather face expulsion than go against his **conscience**. Kerr asked Mandela to reconsider during the summer holidays, adding that he would be welcome to finish his degree the following year, if he agreed to serve on the student council. Mandela writes in his memoirs that he was as surprised by his response as Kerr was. "I knew it was foolhardy for me to leave Fort Hare, but at the moment when I needed to compromise, I simply could not do so. Something inside would not let me."

Cutting loose

Mandela has never indicated whether he might have reconsidered, especially after being bluntly ordered to do so by Chief Jongintaba, because another life-changing event intervened. The Thembu regent informed his son, Justice, and his foster son, Mandela, that he had chosen **brides** for them both and that the marriages must take place right away. Justice was to marry the daughter of a Thembu aristocrat, and Rolihlahla, as Jongintaba always called Mandela, the daughter of a local priest. Arrangements had already been made for *lobola*, the bride price, to be paid to the two family patriarchs. Jongintaba told the young men that he wanted them to be settled before his own health deteriorated.

While Mandela acknowledged that, according to Thembu law and custom, the regent had the right to choose his bride and force him to marry her, now it was about to happen to him he couldn't go through with it. Justice, who was by this time living in Cape Town, felt the same.

Mandela later observed that at this stage of his life he was more advanced socially than politically, and while he would never have dreamed of opposing the political system of the white rulers, he was prepared to "rebel against the social system of my own people". But he also blamed his foster father for his predicament: sending him to missionary schools and university had helped him grow out of his tribal skin. What is more, he had already had quite a few love affairs, and regarded himself as something of a romantic. A further complication was that the bride chosen for Mandela was actually in love with Justice, who married her a few years later.

Though Mandela came to regret not trying to engage with the regent through intermediaries, at the time all he and Justice could think of was that a young man could not oppose the leader of the Thembu, and so they decided to run away. For Mandela, this option may also have been attractive because it meant he no longer had to decide whether to return to Fort Hare or stick to his principles.

There was only one place the two wanted to go – **Johannesburg**. To finance their escape they stole two of the regent's prize oxen and sold them to a trader, and with the money paid someone to take them to the railway station. But Chief Jongintaba had anticipated their move and had told the station manager to expect two runaways, giving him strict orders not to allow them on the train. Mandela and Justice then rushed to the next station, but the train from there only went as far as Queenstown.

In Queenstown, being black, they needed documents to travel outside their own district. While they succeeded in conning a brother of Jongintaba into organizing their documents with the local magistrate, the official needed to inform the magistrate of **Umtata** (the biggest town in Transkei) as a matter of courtesy. Unfortunately, when the call was made, Jongintaba was sitting in the Umtata office, and

Mandela and Justice could hear him screaming that the two young men should be arrested. Mandela's legal studies at Fort Hare enabled him to explain that though they may have lied to the magistrate, they had done nothing that would justify arrest. The magistrate reluctantly let them go, and in the end the two paid a white woman who was travelling to Johannesburg almost all their remaining money to give them a lift.

Johannesburg or **eGoli** ("city of gold") had been built on rich gold deposits and was South Africa's biggest city. As the two young men drove into it on 16 April 1941, the lights and the cars mesmerized Mandela. Like most country boys, he had dreamed about Johannesburg all his young life, as a place of opportunity, tall buildings, gangsters, music, sophisticated women and danger. "I had reached the end of what seemed like a long journey," Mandela wrote in his memoirs, "but it was actually the very beginning of a much longer and more trying journey that would test me in ways that I could not then have imagined."

2 City slicker

"...during the whole of this period I studied under very difficult and trying conditions. I was a part-time student and resided ... in a noisy neighbourhood. In the absence of electric light I was compelled to study in the evenings with a paraffin lamp and sometimes with candle light."

Nelson Mandela, letter to the University of the Witwatersrand, 1949

Mandela was so excited about being in Johannesburg that not even the daily hordes of dirty and dog-tired **mineworkers** he saw returning to their meagre accommodation could put him off. His foster brother Justice's status as a Thembu prince had secured them both soft jobs on the mine. As a Crown Mines night watchman, Mandela was armed with a torch, a stick and a whistle. Unfortunately, Chief Jongintaba soon found out about the deceit and ordered the two youngsters to be sacked and sent home.

Mandela was determined not to give up and his doggedness paid off. He told his cousin **Garlick Mbekeni**, with whom he had found a temporary room, that he would take any job to stay alive, but that he actually wanted to become a lawyer. Mbekeni was impressed and took him to meet an estate agent in the city centre, a man known for his wide connections in black Johannesburg and reputation as a community leader. This was the break Mandela was hoping for and a meeting that would change his life profoundly.

Meeting Sisulu

The man was **Walter Sisulu**, who was six years older than Mandela, also from the Transkei but from a very different background. The son of a black domestic worker, Alice Sisulu, and a white official, Victor Dickenson, Sisulu had little formal education and had moved to Johannesburg when he was fifteen. On meeting Mandela, he was impressed by the bright, idealistic young man sitting across the table. The country urgently needed black professionals and leaders, and he sensed that this man could become one of them. Sisulu went to see **Lazar Sidelsky**, of the law firm Witkin, Sidelsky and Eidelman, and asked if he would employ Mandela. Sidelsky, a progressive and open-minded man, was struck by the young man's demeanour and background and agreed to give him a job as a paid clerk. At the same time Mandela was completing his Bachelor of Arts degree through correspondence at the University of South Africa. Mandela and Sidelsky quickly developed a good working relationship, but his first white friend was **Nat Bregman**, a colleague at the firm and a member of the Communist Party. Bregman invited Mandela to party meetings, and Mandela later remarked that he was surprised to see, for the first time in his life, how blacks, whites, coloureds and Indian South Africans mixed socially and interacted as equals. Through Bregman he met **Michael Harmel**, an academic at the University of the Witwatersrand and a prominent communist intellectual, and the two struck up a long-lasting friendship.

But it was another employee at the law firm, **Gaur Radebe**, who took the still largely apolitical Mandela to his first **ANC meetings**. Radebe was a suave, streetwise and outspoken black man in his early thirties with a reputation (among whites) as a radical political agitator connected to the Communist Party, the ANC and the trade union movement. Mandela's then rather timid attitude towards political matters is illustrated by a story involving Radebe. When the firm's white secretary bought two new teacups for Mandela and Radebe, the implication was that they shouldn't share cups with white employees. Radebe intentionally took a different cup when tea was served, but couldn't persuade Mandela to do the same – he preferred to miss the tea ritual altogether rather than offend the secretary or alienate his black friend.

Though he was largely spared personal humiliation or intimidation by whites or the authorities at this point, Mandela did get a real taste of what it was like to live in a black Johannesburg township. **Alexandra** was a chaotic, unhygienic slum with no electricity or paved roads, over-populated and riddled with violent crime. His tiny room, at the back of the Xhoma family's property, had a dirt floor and a tin roof that made it hot in summer and cold in winter. His wages were just two pounds a month, which didn't quite cover the cost of his rent of thirteen shillings per month, his bus fare, candles for studying and food. His only suit, a gift from Sidelsky, had to be patched many times and Mandela often went hungry, and sometimes had to walk the fifteen kilometres to work.

Mandela's political consciousness soon moved beyond being simply formative. He passed his final exams in 1942 and received his **BA degree** from Fort Hare early the next year, wearing a new suit given to him by Walter Sisulu. Despite pressure from Kaizer Mantanzima (see p.19) and his family to establish himself in Transkei, he returned to Johannesburg and enrolled at the mostly white **University of Witwatersrand** (popularly known as Wits) for a post-graduate law degree, an LL.B.

A widening circle of friends

Mandela was the only black student in the law faculty but quickly befriended a number of white and leftwing Indian students who would have a strong influence on his thinking. Many of these new

CITY OF GOLD

The richest gold reef in the world was discovered in 1886 about 50km from Pretoria, then the capital of the old Boer Republic of Transvaal. A huge **gold rush** followed, attracting people from all over the world. Within ten years, more than a hundred thousand people were living in and around the mining town that had been named **Johannesburg**, probably after the surveyor, Johannes Rissik. The region's first inhabitants were the San or Bushmen, the original hunter-gatherers of the subcontinent. After the twelfth century they were joined by black farmers and ironworkers migrating from further north, with the white Afrikaner settlers or Boers arriving in the mid-eighteenth century.

After the discovery of gold, the **Transvaal Republic**, or the Zuid-Afrikaansche Republiek (ZAR) as it was officially known, suddenly appeared very desirable to British imperialists. Following a failed coup attempt, involving associates of the Cape prime minister and mining magnate Cecil Rhodes, Britain turned up the heat, and in 1899 engaged in a war against the ZAR and its Boer ally, the Orange Free State.

Johannesburg kept on growing, and attracting more and more black South Africans to work in the mines. One slum settlement after another sprang up around the town. The authorities made it clear that these would be tolerated only because the white bosses needed cheap labour, and strict measures were applied to control black people's movements. In the 1930s some of these slums were bulldozed and the inhabitants moved to an area southwest of the town, which was named **Orlando** after a white local government politician. Still the influx of black people from rural areas continued unabated: Johannesburg had become the city of opportunity where rural boys became "real men". Twenty years later the apartheid government laid out more townships along tribal lines, and in 1963 the conglomerate of townships was called **Soweto**, from SOuth WEstern TOwnships.

friends became political associates for life. Notable among them was **Joe Slovo**, a future leader of the Communist Party and later a minister in Mandela's 1994 cabinet. Among his Indian student friends was **Ismail Meer**, prominent Communist Party and Indian Congress leader, whose wife Fatima became Mandela's first biographer in 1988. It was also at Wits that Mandela came into contact with **Bram Fischer**:

Johannesburg photographed in 1935. Today the city is still the commercial and financial capital of South Africa: a sprawling metropolis popularly known as Jozi, eGoli or Jo'burg. Some ten million people live in the greater Johannesburg metropolitan area. (Hulton-Deutsch Collection/CORBIS)

law lecturer, barrister and a leading member of the Communist Party. Fischer was also a member of one of the most influential Afrikaner families in South Africa and a sufficiently talented rugby scrum-half to have played against the New Zealand All Blacks.

Fischer and Ismail Meer were both involved in one of Mandela's very first brushes with racist aggression. One day Mandela and Meer, along

GANDHI IN AFRICA

From 1860, successive shiploads of Indian indentured labourers arrived in South Africa to work in the sugar plantations of Natal in the east of the country. Most of them were low-caste Hindus from Madras who had been recruited on five-year contracts with the agreement that their passages home would be free after ten years. Despite the appalling working conditions, rough treatment and low wages, most stayed on.

Then, from the late 1870s a smaller number of so-called "passenger Indians", people who paid their own passage, arrived in Durban. These mostly Gujarati-speaking Muslims became traders and shopkeepers, first in Natal but soon all over South Africa. In 2009 there were about 1.3 million Indian South Africans, as most prefer to be called, in a population of about 49 million.

In 1893, an Indian businessmen, Dada Abdulla, who was involved in a large commercial court case, asked a young London-trained Indian lawyer, Mohandas Gandhi, for his help. When Gandhi arrived in Durban he immediately came into conflict with white officials who regarded him as a "coolie". Outraged at the way Indians were treated in South Africa, he decided to stay on, instigating a mass defiance campaign called Satyagraha ("soul force") and launching a newspaper called *Indian Opinion*.

In 1894 he formed the Natal Indian Congress, which remained at the forefront of Indian political resistance and eventually played a key role in the African National Congress. Gandhi was jailed several times by the white authorities and when he finally left South Africa in 1914, prime minister Jan Smuts declared: "The saint has left our shores, I sincerely hope forever!"

The father of peaceful resistance he may have been, but Gandhi didn't care much about the plight of black Africans. In September 1896, Gandhi said this about the struggle of Indian South Africans: "Ours is one continued struggle against degradation sought to be inflicted upon us by the European, who desire to degrade us to the level of the raw Kaffir [the derogatory name for black South Africans], whose occupation is hunting and whose sole ambition is to collect a certain number of cattle to buy a wife with, and then pass his life in indolence and nakedness."

In February 1905, Gandhi protested against the fact that blacks had been allowed to settle in an Indian residential area: "About this mixing of the Kaffirs with the Indians I must confess I feel most strongly. I think it is very unfair to the Indian population, and it is an undue tax on even the proverbial patience of my countrymen."

with their friends Jaydew Singh and Ahmed Bhoda, were on their way from the university to Meer's flat, which he shared with **Ruth First** (Joe Slovo's future wife) and where many activists regularly gathered. After they boarded a tram, in which Indians were permitted but not blacks, the white Afrikaans-speaking conductor began shouting at Meer and his friends that they had brought a "kaffir" with them. When they asked him what he meant, he pointed a finger at Mandela and said in broken English, "That kaffir there, you cannot carry him." Their response was to ask the conductor why he was using such a derogatory word, while Mandela, who was much taller than his friends, sarcastically wondered what made him think these little guys could "carry" him. The conductor lost his temper, stopped the tram and the four of them were arrested. At the police station the police tried to get Mandela to make a statement against his Indian friends in exchange for his release, but he refused.

The next morning the four appeared in court, represented by Bram Fischer. Such was Fischer's status that the white magistrate felt honoured to have him in court, and mentioned that he had recently had a meeting with Bram's father Percy, the Judge President of the Free State Province. He was in excellent health, the magistrate told Bram, before acquitting the accused without further ado. That kind of reverence for Fischer on the part of his fellow Afrikaners did not last long and he soon became a much-hated figure.

In August 1943 Gaur Radebe persuaded Mandela to perform his first public act of political resistance when he took part in the **Alexandra bus boycott** which Radebe had helped to organize. Walter Sisulu, meanwhile, had maintained contact with Mandela and did his bit in pulling him closer into the ANC sphere. Sisulu turned out to be a double kingmaker, Mandela's fellow Fort Hare student befriending Oliver Tambo when he arrived in Johannesburg in 1942, and helping get him a position as an articled clerk at a law firm. Like Mandela, Tambo had been expelled from the university because of his political activism. These three men would have a profound effect on the

WALTER SISULU: IN THE SHADOW OF MANDELA

Walter Sisulu and Oliver Tambo were Mandela's two best friends and liberation legends in their own right, but to a large extent their achievements have been overshadowed by his. Sisulu was a few years older than both Tambo and Mandela and acted as their mentor, identifying them as potential leaders, getting them jobs and drawing them into the ANC.

He could instead have built his own political empire, but his one disadvantage was that, in a time of fervent African nationalism and white oppression, his father, **Victor Dickenson**, was a white man: an assistant magistrate who never married Walter's mother, **Alice Sisulu**, a Xhosa-speaking domestic worker from the Transkei. In race-obsessed South Africa, that made their son, technically speaking, a "coloured", even though he had a traditional Xhosa upbringing and never saw himself as anything other than a black African.

Walter Sisulu only had a few years of formal education before leaving home for Johannesburg at the age of fifteen. Self-educated thereafter, he ended up a good writer and an excellent strategist, becoming the ANC's **secretary general** in 1949. The veteran anti-apartheid activist Mary Benson remembers interviewing him in 1952: "…it struck me that his early experiences as a miner, as a kitchen boy and a factory worker meant that he, more than any other leader, knew just what it meant to be regarded by whites as a 'native.'"

Sisulu was jailed and his movements restricted several times, and in 1964 he was sentenced to life imprisonment with Mandela. He became the wise father figure to many young political prisoners in Robben Island and Mandela relied heavily on his advice and support. He was released in 1989. At Sisulu's funeral in 2003 Mandela said: "We have lost a remarkable man. He has not been honoured in the way some of us have been honoured. Nevertheless, he stood head and shoulders above all of us."

fortunes of the ANC, becoming the most respected and influential figures in the liberation struggle.

Sisulu was probably the most politically astute, best connected and visionary of the three, but he thought that having a white father and a light complexion disqualified him from being the leader of a black liberation movement. Instead he chose to become the "power

Walter Sisulu (1912–2003) greeting old friends at a reunion of political prisoners on Robben Island in 1996. His wife Albertina, who he married in 1944, was also a significant figure in the ANC and was frequently jailed for her political activities. She died in 2011. (Gideon Mendel/CORBIS)

behind the throne" and groomed Mandela and Tambo as new young leaders. He was probably right; it is known that in those early years some of his black opponents mocked his mixed-blood heritage, one ANC leader saying he wasn't "a real Xhosa" and shouldn't try leading them. Even so, he played a critical role in the revival of the ANC in the 1940s and was elected its secretary general in 1949.

The impact of Lembede

Another young man who had a decisive influence on Mandela's thinking during the 1940s was **Anton Muziwakhe Lembede**. The son of a Free State farm worker, he was fascinated by the successful mobilization of Afrikaner nationalism in the rural areas where he lived and worked during his early twenties. By the time he met Mandela, he had a masters degree in philosophy and an LL.B, and was serving articles with **Pixley Ka Seme**, one of the co-founders of the ANC (see box opposite). Lembede, who was four years older than Mandela, had strong beliefs about blackness and **African solidarity** – to him, whites and Indians would always remain settlers in Africa and all foreign ideologies such as communism had to be rejected as un-African. "Africa is the black man's country. Africa belongs to him," he declared.

This rather romanticized view of being African appealed to Mandela with his proud, traditional Xhosa roots and he declared himself an **African nationalist**. But he wasn't very convincing – or convinced. As his old friend and biographer Fatima Meer has written: "… his personal friendships were modifying his position; he was taking in the different worlds and learning to live in all of them, and they were challenging his African exclusivism and preparing him for that international humanism that upholds him today." Lembede's influence on Mandela, Sisulu and Tambo continued, almost until his death of a heart attack in 1947. He was only 33 years old.

The rebirth of the ANC

In 1940 **Dr Alfred Xuma**, a medical doctor trained in the US, Hungary and Britain, was elected president of an almost dormant **ANC** and immediately began injecting new life into the movement. He realized that it would have little impact if it continued to be dominated by conservative, older middle-class black leaders and asked younger ANC

A CLUB OF GENTLEMEN

South Africa's main liberation movement and ruling party since 1994, the **African National Congress** was formed in 1912 under the leadership of conservative urban intellectuals as a body that would cut across all black ethnic and language groups. The stimulus was the creation of the Union of South Africa as a dominion of the British Empire that brought together the colonies of the Cape and Natal and the two Boer Republics in one state. Apart from a small number of black property owners in the Cape, black citizens were disenfranchised.

The main initiator of the South African Native National Congress, as it was called until 1923, was **Pixley Ka-Isaka Seme**, a Johannesburg lawyer who had studied at Columbia, Oxford and the Middle Temple; he was also the organization's treasurer. **John Dube**, a newspaper editor who had studied in the US, was the first president, **Sol Plaatje**, another editor and writer, its chief secretary, while the distinguished theologian and writer **Dr Walter Rubusana** was made honorary president. Photographs of the time show men formally dressed in dark suits, waistcoats and top hats carrying rolled up black umbrellas.

Their core aim was to fight for black rights and to oppose racial discrimination, but the new body's constitution also stated that it wanted to improve relations between black South Africans and the white government, and between black and white citizens.

The new party's first campaign was against the **Native Land Act** of 1913 that had imposed a policy of territorial segregation and severely restricted black South Africans' access to land. A delegation was sent to the minister of Native Affairs and when the response was negative, a delegation (including Dube, Plaatje and Rubusana) went to speak to the Secretary of State in London, Lewis Harcourt. According to Plaatje, Harcourt didn't even make notes or ask questions. The ANC's essentially polite and peaceable style never made much of an impression on the white establishment, and it wasn't until the 1940s, when Mandela and his group of young firebrands began agitating for a new approach, that the ANC started becoming a real factor in effecting change.

members like Sisulu to help recruit new members and leaders among the youth. He got more than he bargained for. Under Lembede's leadership, impatient young intellectuals known as "the graduates" – Mandela and Tambo among them – met regularly at Sisulu's house and started pushing for a separate ANC youth structure that would promote a new Africanist agenda. When they took the proposal to Xuma for his endorsement, he eventually accepted it after failing to convince them that the proposal was too ambitious. It was formally ratified by the ANC's national annual conference in December 1943.

On Easter Sunday, 9 April 1944, the **Congress Youth League** was formally constituted. The only woman present was Albertina Thethiwe, who married Sisulu that same year. Mandela was voted on to the executive committee, Tambo became the first secretary and Sisulu the treasurer. Lembede, as the first president, pushed hard to get membership limited to black Africans, but eventually the constitution was softened so that the League was open "to all African men and women between the ages of twelve and forty" but also to "other sections of the community who live like and with Africans and whose general outlook on life is similar to that of Africans".

The League's **manifesto**, however, contained no such compromise. It positioned the League as a "brains trust and power-station" of African nationalism that recognized only the leadership of the masses and took its tactics from spontaneous popular militancy. It declared that Africa was "a black man's country" and that there was a unity of all Africans "from the Mediterranean to the Indian and Atlantic Oceans". It warned against communist ideology because it cloaked white paternalism and misled people by focusing on class oppression, while Africans were oppressed as a group. The manifesto also criticized the ANC leadership for lacking in organization, representing a privileged few and for being reactive rather than assertive. Xuma and other senior ANC leaders were incensed at both the militancy and the criticism. Xuma called their proposed programme of action "rash" and even threw a delegation of Lembede, Mandela, Sisulu and Tambo out of his house when they refused to back down. But it was the Youth League and the trio of Mandela, Tambo and Sisulu that would revive the ANC in the years ahead, and in 1949 they won a motion of no confidence in Xuma at the ANC conference and had him replaced by **Dr James Moroka**.

It is clear from interviews later given by all three men that while Mandela wasn't a prominent ideologue of the Youth League at the time, he nevertheless actively supported its racially exclusive and anti-communist positions. On more than one occasion Mandela tried to break up Communist Party meetings and once even roughed up his friend Yusuf Cachalia on stage. It was after one of these incidents that an Indian teenager angrily confronted Mandela and challenged him to debate. His name was **Ahmed Kathrada** and not only did he spend a large part of his life with Mandela on Robben Island, he also became one of his closest friends and confidantes. In 1945 Mandela co-sponsored a conference motion that members who belonged to other organizations (meaning the Communist Party) be expelled from the ANC. Asked about this time in his life and his reaction to the cry "Hurl the white man into the sea", Mandela later said: "While I was not prepared to hurl the white man into the sea, I would have been perfectly happy if he had climbed aboard his steamships and left the continent of his own volition."

ANC executive

Mandela was voted on to the executive of the **Transvaal ANC** in 1947. He used his position to lobby against a "Votes for All" campaign jointly organized by the ANC, the Communist Party and the Indian Congress. Not even Sisulu and Tambo shared his enthusiasm on this point. Reflecting on this period, Sisulu later said that Mandela was essentially "a moderate, reasonable man in his approach ... But then there is this contradiction of stubbornness. When it comes to the final point, he can become very stubborn, very arrogant. His anger becomes extreme. It is not in argument

AFRICAN COMMUNISTS

The International Socialist League, formed in 1915 in Johannesburg by British-born socialists, was a forerunner of the **Communist Party of South Africa**, founded in 1921, four years after the Russian Revolution. The party immediately affiliated to the Moscow-based Communist International.

For the first few years, whites dominated the party: British socialists, Jewish immigrants and their children mostly from Lithuania and Latvia, and some radical Afrikaner workerists. The party supported a strike by white mineworkers a few months after its formation and, notoriously, one placard read "Workers of the World Fight and Unite for a White South Africa". After 1924 the party started recruiting black members, who quickly became the majority, but the leadership remained mostly white for some years. Still, for many decades it was the only political party in South Africa where black and white South Africans could freely mix.

In 1928, the party, at the insistence of the Comintern, declared that it was campaigning for an "independent native republic". This led to years of infighting, cost the party many white members, and was abandoned as a policy by 1948. The **Suppression of Communism Act** made the party an illegal organization in 1950 (it was only legalized in 1990) and drove it underground. Renamed the South African Communist Party (SACP), it started working more within the ANC itself and was instrumental in the formation of the ANC's armed wing, **Umkhonto we Sizwe** (Spear of the Nation) in 1961.

When the ANC was itself declared illegal in 1960, with many leaders going into exile, the SACP's influence grew, in part because the Soviet Union was the movement's main benefactor. The SACP leadership was always fiercely loyal to Moscow, even embracing Stalinism and endorsing the Soviet invasions of Czechoslovakia in 1968 and Afghanistan in 1979.

It was long an unspoken rule that one had to be a SACP member to make it through the ranks of the ANC, because the SACP was regarded as the "vanguard" of the liberation movement and home to the leading theoreticians. This practice ended after the party was legalized in 1990. The SACP is today in a formal alliance (the "Tripartite Alliance") with the ANC and the Congress of South African Trade Unions, and does not take part in elections under its own flag.

that he becomes angry. It is when he suspects people's motives – as he did with the communists."

But Mandela's – and the Youth League's – enthusiasm for the militant Africanist and anti-communist stance was beginning to wane, particularly after Lembede's death in 1947. Black, white and Indian communists were proving their commitment and efficiency as activists, and the Indian Congress was very successful in its anti-apartheid campaigns. Personal friendships across the divides also softened attitudes. **Peter Mda**, a teacher who took over from Lembede as Youth League leader, published a Basic Policy document in 1948 rejecting the "Africa for Africans" concept, stating: "We of the Youth League take account of the concrete situation in South Africa, and realize that the different racial groups have come to stay. But we insist that a condition for interracial peace and progress is the abandonment of white domination …"

Seven years after arriving in Johannesburg, Nelson Mandela was a political leader and public figure of note. Everyone who was someone in South African resistance politics – as well as the security police – knew who he was and expected him to become a national leader. That in itself is unusual, since he was neither a great mobilizer of the masses, nor a formidable orator, organizer or theoretician, and in the heady ideological discourses of the time he was a follower rather than a leader.

How this came about derives from a combination of factors. His **aristocratic background** must have played some role. Despite the fact that most of the political activists of the time were educated, urbanized, largely detribalized people, it made a difference that he was the grandson of a Thembu king and grew up as the foster-son of the reigning Thembu regent in the royal kraal. Even today royal roots count in sophisticated black South African society, as they do in many other societies around the world.

More important was what his background and upbringing as a Xhosa prince brought to his personality. It must have given him a sense of belonging and a natural confidence, despite confessing that he sometimes felt intellectually inferior to men such as Anton Lembede. This background also shielded him from the worst experiences of racism when he was young and helped him to view whites and Indians as his equals. It is true he had a temper and could be stubborn, but he was also known as someone who would listen, who cared about people, was respected and who had impeccable, almost old-world, manners. Charisma, regal bearing and warmth are the words most used by people who knew him during those years. It no doubt helped that, at six foot four inches, he was much taller than most and that he was in good physical shape (he exercised regularly, never smoked and rarely drank alcohol). He was a handsome man, and since his student days, had a very particular way of dressing and grooming himself. His old friend Joe Mathews, whom he appointed as a deputy minister in 1994, said of Mandela's famous dark suits: "You know the two best-dressed chaps in the movement were Madiba and Cachalia on the Indian side. You would look at a suit that Madiba was wearing and you would go all over and say, 'I want a suit like that one'. The tailors would tell you, 'There's no such suit.' He was really a great dresser." Some, of course, say simply that Mandela was a natural leader.

Family man

His first seven years in the big city not only transformed Mandela from an apolitical country boy to a prominent political operator, he also became a husband and father. From Alexandra, Mandela moved to a room in a mining compound and then lived for a time in Sisulu's house in **Orlando** (now part of Soweto). This was a popular gathering place for young people, and Sisulu's mother Alice's food was even more popular. Members of the extended Sisulu family arriving from Transkei also often stayed there. His cousin Sam Mase was one of them, and when his sister **Evelyn** arrived, she also stayed. The Mases' parents died when Evelyn was very young and her brothers took care of her, sending her to Johannesburg to be educated. When Sam married and got his own house, Evelyn went to live with him while she was studying to be a nurse.

It was during one of the social gatherings at Orlando that Sisulu introduced his attractive cousin to his handsome friend. Evelyn told Fatima Meer: "I think I loved him the first time I saw him. There was something special about Nelson." They started a relationship almost immediately. "Everyone we knew said that we made a very good couple," said Evelyn, adding: "I thought he was beautiful."

The two got **married** on 5 October 1944 at the Native Commissioner's Court in Johannesburg. There was no traditional Xhosa wedding, no *lobola* (bride price) paid, no permission asked of her brothers, and nor could the couple afford a wedding reception. It wasn't a good start. In a way Mandela was already married – to the ANC and the struggle against racial oppression. He and Evelyn were very poor: she earned little as a student nurse and he even less as an articled clerk, with university fees to be paid on top of living expenses. They lived in a small room in her sister's house.

In February 1946 the Mandelas had a son, **Thembekile**. The next year they were allocated a house at 8115 Orlando West, exactly the same as hundreds of other matchbox houses in the township, with no electricity, a bucket toilet, and a monthly rent of seventeen shillings and sixpence. But it was a home, Mandela's first since he left Jongintaba's Great Place, and as he wrote in his memoir: "It was the opposite of grand but it was the first true home of my own and I was mightily proud. A man is not a man until he has a house of his own." A young priest, **Desmond Tutu**, later the Archbishop of Cape Town,

Nelson Mandela married Evelyn Mase, a cousin of his friend Walter Sisulu, in 1944. (UWCRIM Mayibuye/Link)

moved into a house a little further down the same street – the only street in the world with two Nobel Laureates as former residents.

Many years later Evelyn told an interviewer that Mandela was "very regular in his habits". He got up very early every morning and went for a jog before eating a light breakfast. He sometimes bathed the babies. A daughter **Makaziwe** had been born in 1947 but died of meningitis a year later. Soon Mandela's mother Nosekeni, with whom he had had very little contact since infancy, and his sister Leabie both came to live with him and Evelyn.

Apart from being active as a trade unionist in the Nursing Union, Evelyn was not a political animal and didn't fit in with Mandela's sophisticated circle of political activists. The couple steadily grew apart, although they had another daughter, **Pumla Makaziwe**, in 1954. Mandela's political activities didn't just undermine his marriage, they also ruined his studies. He spent seven years studying for his LL.B, borrowed money from the Bantu Welfare Trust to pay for it, and failed his final exams three times. In December 1949 he wrote to the dean of the law faculty for permission to take a supplementary exam. Explaining his serious financial problems and the difficulties of commuting to the university, the letter concluded: "It is my candid opinion that if I had done my work under more suitable conditions I would have produced a better result." There was not a word about his political activities. The dean refused permission. Mandela abandoned his LL.B and instead completed a **law diploma** that enabled him to practice as a lawyer. According to Evelyn, Mandela was devastated that he could not become a barrister and

> "My devotion to the ANC and the struggle was unremitting. This disturbed Evelyn... I patiently explained to her that politics was not a distraction but my lifework, that it was an essential and fundamental part of my being."
>
> Nelson Mandela, from *Long Road to Freedom*

blamed the white academics for it. She even claimed that it radicalized him politically.

Mandela's political career was just beginning. In 1948 the political vehicle of Afrikaner nationalism, the **National Party**, defeated the more liberal government of General Jan Smuts at a whites-only election and formed a new government. For the first time the word **apartheid** was being used: racial separation as ideology taken to absurd lengths. The liberation movement needed a new champion.

3 Lawyer and volunteer

"We know that there are many people and even educated
Africans who are telling people that you are backwards and that
the police and army will crush you if you rise against them...
There is nothing superior about the white man. He can be fought
as he has been fought before. If we can stand together we can
sweep everything before us."

Nelson Mandela, at a Sophiatown meeting, 1954

Nelson Mandela eventually qualified as a lawyer in 1952 and soon
afterwards started his own practice in partnership with **Oliver Tambo**.
At the time, it was the only black-owned law firm in South Africa and
managed to thrive despite the myriad apartheid regulations passed
by the National Party government. The waiting room of Mandela
and Tambo in **Chancellor House** near the Johannesburg magistrates
court was almost always full of black clients with problems regarding
residential segregation, racial classification, or with the permits and
passes regulating black people's movements outside the traditional
"black" areas.

The pair also did a lot of civil law work for the black elite of
Johannesburg, which did wonders for their social status. On most
days, the two partners had lunch at the nearby **Kapitan's Oriental
Restaurant** in Diagonal Street, owned by Madanjit Ranchod. The
rather run-down restaurant remained famous for its former clients

until Ranchod's death in 2007; he liked to boast that he had served, among others, the King of Kuwait, the Shah of Iran, Jackie Onassis and Eva Peron, all of whom came to eat in "Mandela's favourite restaurant". The two partners did well financially and at last Mandela could afford tailor-made suits, from the outfitter who looked after

Nelson Mandela in his Johannesburg office. The sign on the window reads "MANDELA & TAMBO Attorneys". (© Jürgen Schadeberg)

Johannesburg's wealthy white elite, and a two-tone green Oldsmobile with lots of chrome and white-walled tyres.

Lawyers who worked with Mandela during those days remember him as a competent legal mind, an imposing figure in court and someone who liked to play to the gallery. Policemen called as witnesses in cases he defended often simply didn't turn up in court because they feared Mandela's aggressive cross-examination. Mandela loves to tell the story of how he defended a domestic worker accused of stealing her employer's clothes. He walked to the table with the forensic exhibits, picked up a pair of panties with his pen, held them out to the woman making the accusation and asked, "Madam, are these yours?" She was too embarrassed to make any response, and the case was thrown out of court.

Domestic strife

Mandela's success as a lawyer, and his spectacular rise as a leader in the ANC during the early 1950s, coincided with the deterioration of his marriage. The couple had had another son, **Makgatho**, in 1950, but Mandela spent very little time with his family. In 1952 Evelyn went to Durban for a course in midwifery and when she returned several months later, she discovered that Mandela was having an affair with his married secretary, **Ruth Mompati**. Evelyn told the story that she was so angry about the obvious intimacy between them and the fact that Mompati had "pursued" her husband into their home in an "unseemly manner" that she threatened to pour boiling water over her. Mandela was livid and started sleeping in the sitting room. He grew "increasingly cold and distant", Evelyn said later.

It is widely believed in Mandela's social and political circles that Mompati had a child with Mandela. The author of *Young Mandela*, David James Smith, says he has reliable testimony that she used to boast about this while in exile in Zambia. Smith believes their son was born in 1955 and that his name was Mompati Neo Matsoane. His death was announced by the ANC in 1998. When Smith interviewed Ruth Mompati in 2008, she told him: "Mandela was my boss, my leader, my friend." She knew that people believed she had had a child with him, but said that it was disrespectful to her then husband and was not true. Mompati went on to become a prominent ANC leader, an MP in 1994, and later South Africa's ambassador to Switzerland.

Love affairs

Mandela had several other affairs during the 1950s, even though he and Evelyn had had another daughter, Makaziwe, in 1954. He had a fling with the popular singer, actress and *Drum* magazine pin-up, **Dolly Rathebe**, who was heart-broken when he lost interest in her. One affair that became rather public was with **Lilian Ngoyi**, a powerful leader of the ANC Women's League and member of the ANC's Executive Committee. Evelyn said she liked and admired Ngoyi but when the rumours of an affair persisted, she confronted her husband. Mandela told her Ngoyi was an important ANC leader which was why he had to see her so often. He accused his wife of asking more questions than the police. When Evelyn asked Walter Sisulu to intervene, Mandela angrily accused her of "broadcasting" their problems and stopped eating at home. Kaizer Mantanzima tried to help, but Mandela told him he didn't love Evelyn any more. Some of her friends tried to console her by maintaining her husband was bewitched. After Mandela's release from jail in 1990, Evelyn told the British reporter Fred Bridgland that people who compared the event to the second coming of Christ were silly: "How can a man who has committed adultery and left his wife and children be Christ? The whole world worships Nelson too much. He is only a man."

There have been many rumours in South Africa over the years that Mandela may have fathered children with other women. In 2010 **Mpho Pule** went public with her claim that she was Mandela's

OLIVER TAMBO: LEADER IN EXILE

Oliver Reginald Tambo, also known as OR, was a bright university graduate who became Mandela's partner in his Johannesburg law firm after the two became close friends during their time as leaders of the ANC's Youth League. The pair of them were so close that Mandela described Tambo as "…a man who is tied to me by an umbilical cord which cannot be broken."

Tambo played a leading role in the re-activation of the ANC during the 1940s and 1950s, but his most important contribution came as the leader of the ANC in exile after Mandela and many other senior leaders were jailed. His quiet and pragmatic leadership held the movement together in spite of sharp differences and serious crises. **The Organisation for African Unity** recognized him as South Africa's head of state in exile and he become a driving force within the international anti-apartheid movement working to isolate the white minority regime.

Tambo returned to South Africa after the ban on the ANC was lifted in 1990, but his health deteriorated after a stroke and he died exactly a year before the country's first democratic elections in April 1994. For Mandela he was "a great giant who strode the globe like a colossus". South Africa's main airport, outside Johannesburg, was named after him in 2006.

Oliver Tambo (left) arriving in Addis Ababa in 1961. (© Drum Social Histories/BAHA/Africa Media Online)

love child and had been trying for twelve years to see her father. A month after Mandela's office wrote to her promising to examine her claim, she died. A few weeks after Pule's claim, **Onicca Nyembezi Mothoa** also claimed she was Mandela's daughter and the Nelson Mandela Foundation promised her that they would investigate the matter. Mandela's health scare in January 2011 prompted Mothoa to rush to the hospital demanding to meet her father before he died. When a reporter on Johannesburg newspaper *The Star* asked the foundation to comment, a spokesperson said they had handed things over to the Mandela family, claiming it was a private matter. Mothoa told the reporter: "There is an iron door. They don't want to allow me to see him. If they can remove that iron door everything will be okay."

Mothoa said she would like to take a DNA test to prove her claim. She was born in Atteridgeville outside Pretoria in 1947and claims that her mother, Sophie Majeni, was working as a domestic worker when she met Mandela, but was forced to go into hiding by her family when it became known that she was carrying his child. They were afraid to be associated with a politician who had been targeted as an enemy by the white government. Mbamatshe Majola, headman of Mandela's village of Qunu, confirmed that Mothoa had visited him several times. He believed her when she said she was Mandela's daughter. "The minute I saw her, I knew she was a Mandela." Most people who have seen Mothoa, or pictures of her, comment on the remarkable resemblance between the two.

The end of a marriage

Mandela has always been very reluctant to talk about his estrangement from Evelyn and has never mentioned his extramarital relationships. The only explanation he's ever given for the failure of his marriage was that Evelyn became very religious and was unhappy about the time and energy he committed to politics. She became a devout **Jehovah's**

Witness after the birth of Makaziwe in 1954, even getting their children to distribute *Watchtower* pamphlets in the neighbourhood and trying to convert Mandela. He, in turn, was instructing their children in politics and placed photographs of his political heroes – Churchill, Joseph Stalin and Gandhi – next to her religious pictures. Evelyn filed court papers in 1956 in a petition for **separation**, alleging that Mandela had abandoned her in February 1955 and after that had assaulted her on three occasions by hitting her with his fists and knocking her to the ground. She alleged that he gave her a week to leave the house in February 1956 and, when she refused, he "maliciously assaulted her by hitting her with his fists and choking her and attempted to kill her by strangling her".

Mandela strongly denied these allegations in an answering affidavit and the matter never came before a court. Evelyn withdrew her case in November 1956 and never subsequently talked about Mandela assaulting her. Friends of the couple later expressed surprise at the allegations, saying if there had been physical altercations they would certainly not have been as violent as suggested in the court papers. While some friends regard Mandela as an early feminist, others suggest that at the time of his first marriage he hadn't outgrown his traditional patriarchal background. Mandela's sister Leaby, who lived with the Mandelas at the time, told Fatima Meer that it was hard for her to live with the conflict, "the two people we respected, suddenly turning on each other. We all depended on them and when they went on like that it was as if the ground below us was breaking and we were falling. It was black magic, that's what it was." The two finally got divorced in 1958. Evelyn claimed she only learned of the **divorce order** when it appeared in the newspaper. Makaziwe was two, Makgatho was five and Thembi was eight. Both parents agreed that Thembi took it the hardest: Evelyn said he "suffered intensely", Mandela wrote later that the boy started wearing his clothes for "some attachment to his too often distant father".

Mandela and the Indian Congress

The 1950s was undoubtedly the most important decade in Mandela's political life before he was released from prison in 1990. On top of being a busy lawyer and having to provide for his family, he became the linchpin of the revival of the ANC and the escalation of the resistance to the apartheid regime. No wonder his personal life was in such a mess. After the Young Turks outmanoeuvred Alfred Xuma as president of the ANC and had him replaced by James Moroka, Sisulu was elected secretary general and in February 1950 Mandela was co-opted onto the ANC's National Executive. But while Sisulu had by this time become convinced that cooperation with the Communist Party and the **Indian Congress** was essential, Mandela and Tambo were still on their Africanist mission – Mandela even accused Sisulu of "selling out" to Indians.

Two explanations were offered for Mandela's position, which flew in the face of his social friendships with Indian South Africans. He himself said cooperation with Indians would be unpopular among black people because they viewed Indian businessmen as exploitative. Others believe he was afraid that Indian leaders, with their sophisti-cated city manners, fluency in English and often superior education, would overshadow the black leadership. He gave credence to this theory in a later interview when he remarked that joint campaigns with Indians when blacks had few literate leaders and little money or influence "could give to minorities enjoying these advantages an influence out of all proportions to their numbers". But the efficiency and commitment of both the Indian Congress and the Communist Party were hard to ignore, and by the early 1950s Mandela's posi-tion was no longer shared by most other ANC leaders. Influenced by his old friend Michael Harmel and a new friend, Moses Kotane, the Communist Party general secretary, he started reading the works of **Karl Marx** and **Friedrich Engels**. He was impressed by their analysis and conceded privately that a revolution "needed theory"; he even started using typical communist phrases and arguments in his speeches. Ironically, it was a national campaign of civil disobedience supported by the ANC, the Natal Indian Congress, the Communist Party and coloured organizations that finally identified Mandela as the undisputed leader of the resistance against apartheid – despite his initial opposition to the inclusive approach.

In July 1951 the ANC leadership concluded an agreement with the Indian Congress to launch joint mass campaigns against discriminatory laws. At the end of that year, the ANC announced that the **Defiance Campaign** against Unjust Laws was to be launched in April 1952. It was a seminal moment in the resistance to apartheid. The wording of the announcement was significant. It stated among other things that "All people, irrespective of the national group they belong to and irrespective of the colour of their skin, who have made South Africa their home, are entitled to live a full and free life." And: "The struggle which the national organisations of the non-European people are conducting is not directed against any race or national group. It is against the unjust laws which keep in perpetual subjection and misery vast sections of the population."

The Defiance Campaign

Mandela claimed that it was Sisulu who first mentioned the idea of a campaign of disobedience and that it immediately appealed to him, and most historians credit both of them for the initiative. Sisulu confirmed this version of events, but there is evidence that the initial idea for the campaign came from the **Franchise Action Committee** (FRAC) in Cape Town, which was formed to fight the removal of coloured people from the voters' roll. FRAC organized huge demonstrations and strikes in Cape Town in March 1951.

A Defiance Campaign rally with (from left to right) Yusuf Cachalia, Walter Sisulu and Dr J.S. Moroka. (© Drum Social Histories/BAHA/ Africa Media Online)

The first step of the campaign was a letter from the ANC to Prime Minister **D.F. Malan**, drafted by Mandela, Sisulu and others. It demanded the repeal of repressive legislation, failing which a campaign would be launched during which these laws would be defied. Malan was so angry at the tone of the letter that he refused to respond in person, instead having his private secretary write that his government would "deal adequately with those responsible for inciting any subversive activities whatsoever". The letter also claimed the racial laws referred to were "of a protective nature" and justified because there were "permanent and not man-made differences between Africans and Europeans". The ANC responded in another letter saying, "The question at issue is not one of biological differences, but one of citizenship rights which are granted in full measure to one section of the population, and completely denied to the other by means of man-made laws artificially imposed, not to preserve the identity of Europeans as a separate community, but to perpetuate the systemic exploitation of the African people."

Sisulu and four others formed the **Joint Planning Council** and did most of the planning work for the campaign, while Mandela, appointed chairman of the Action Committee Joint Volunteer Board and, significantly, National Volunteer-in-Chief, did a lot of mobilization work while also continuing to run a law firm. Mandela's personal philosophy was revealed in part of the oath he asked volunteers to swear: "It shall be my duty to keep myself physically, mentally and morally fit."

Support for the campaign was mobilized during mass rallies and speeches on 6 April 1952, when white South Africans were celebrating 300 years of European settlement in the country. Chief Albert Lutuli, who became the president of the ANC at the end of that year, remarked: "while they celebrated 300 years of white domination, we looked back over 300 years of black subjugation". Mandela made a controversial speech during this time, one that is probably indicative of how his own confidence and indeed ambitions had grown. At a dinner held for **Professor Z.K. Matthews**, who was leaving for the US to take up a visiting professorship at Columbia University, Mandela said he was looking forward to becoming South Africa's first black president. For some of the ANC old guard it was preposterous that a Youth League leader should make such a statement in their presence.

The campaign begins

The Defiance Campaign officially started on 26 June 1952, a date now remembered in South Africa as **Freedom Day**. Considering that few black people had telephones at the time, and the ANC had no support from radio stations or mainstream newspapers in communicating its message, the campaign was a dramatic success. Volunteers refused to carry the notorious **pass books** or dompas, ignored the "whites only" signs in public places and violated the curfew on blacks. More than eight thousand volunteers who defied these and other trace laws were convicted during the course of the campaign. Things intensified after the government had many ANC leaders arrested in September, and in November the action spread to smaller towns, leading to riots in Port Elizabeth and East London. In December forty volunteers were arrested when they entered a Germiston township without permits. Prominent among these were Manilal Gandhi, son of Mahatma Gandhi (who had overcome his initial resistance to the campaign), Patrick Duncan, son of the previous South African governor general, and six other whites. They were all jailed.

Early in 1953 the government instituted heavy punishment, including stiff fines and prison sentences of up to five years, for politically motivated law-breaking. With most of the campaign's leadership either jailed or served with banning orders (which restricted an individual's movements and only allowed meetings with two people at a time), the campaign petered out and was formally ended in March. Mandela and his fellow leaders viewed the campaign as a huge success, despite the fact that the racial laws targeted were not repealed. The black population had been mobilized and radicalized like never before and the ANC's membership had grown to a record one hundred thousand. Mandela pointed out that the campaign was most successful in the Eastern Cape, where there were no Indians – he was clearly slower in ridding himself of his anti-Indian prejudice than he would later admit.

Mandela was **arrested** in June, subsequently acquitted, and then arrested again in November (two weeks after he launched his legal practice) and charged with twenty others under the new

Suppression of Communism Act. He was sentenced to twenty months in prison, which was suspended for nine months. More seriously, Mandela and 51 other ANC leaders were served with banning orders for six months from December, and so were

AFRICA'S FIRST NOBEL PEACE PRIZE LAUREATE

Albert John Lutuli (often spelled Luthuli) was the most revered leader of the ANC before Mandela. He was a deeply moral man and a devout Christian, and yet embraced the ANC's new militancy of the 1950s. Lutuli was a teacher before he was persuaded to become the tribal chief of a Zulu clan at Groutville in 1935. He was also a lay preacher of the Methodist Church and active in missionary work.

Lutuli became an ANC provincial leader in 1951 and when he joined the **Defiance Campaign** of 1952, the government stripped him from his position as chief. In a statement entitled "The Road to Freedom is via the Cross" he declared: "Who will deny that thirty years of my life have been spent knocking in vain, patiently, moderately, at a closed and barred door? What have been the fruits of my moderation? Has there been any reciprocal tolerance or moderation from the Government, be it Nationalist or United Party? No!" He added, significantly, since the talk in the ANC was increasingly about violent resistance: "I have embraced the non-violent passive-resistance technique in fighting for freedom because I am convinced it is the only non-revolutionary, legitimate and humane way that could be used by people denied, as we were, effective and constitutional means to further aspirations."

Lutuli was elected **ANC president** in 1952 and re-elected in 1955 and 1958. He was a popular leader respected for his inclusive, tolerant style and for championing the cause of non-racialism, but banning orders restricted him to his remote rural village for most of his presidency and he wasn't able to involve himself in the day-to-day running of the movement. Still, he continued to influence the leadership's policies and decisions through his writing and occasional speeches.

Shortly after the **Sharpeville massacre** of 1960, when police killed 69 black protestors (see p.89), Lutuli burned his pass book in public and was detained for five months. Under pressure, the apartheid government allowed him to travel to Oslo in December 1961 to receive the **Nobel Peace Prize**. He died in 1967 when he was struck by a train near his home.

unable to leave the Johannesburg district or meet without official permission. Mandela wrote that these **banning orders** "imprison one's spirit" and induced "a kind of psychological claustrophobia" so that "at a certain point one began to think that the oppressor was not without but within."

His banning did not stop the ANC from electing Mandela as its **deputy president** at the end of 1952. The president was Chief Albert Lutuli, who in 1960 became the first African, and the first person outside Europe and the Americas, to be awarded the Nobel Peace Prize (see box on p.57). Lutuli replaced Moroka, who had fallen into disfavour after seeking his own legal counsel during the trial with Mandela and dissociating himself from the Communists in the group.

Implementing apartheid

The white **National Party** government, meanwhile, was steadily implementing its grandiose scheme to completely separate all races in South Africa. From 1950 onwards this ideology had a new champion, the Dutch-born Minister of Native Affairs **Hendrik Frensch Verwoerd**, a former sociology professor and newspaper editor. As a young man Verwoerd refused an Abe Bailey bursary to study at Oxford because "Bailey was a British imperialist", preferring instead to study in Germany, and during World War II he demonstrated strong pro-German sentiments. As editor of *Die Transvaler*, he famously ordered his journalists to completely ignore the British Royal Family's visit of 1947, although in the end, the visit did receive the following sentence: "The presence of certain visitors will cause some dislocation to the traffic."

In his ministerial capacity, Verwoerd steered five notorious apartheid laws through parliament, laws that became the foundation of

---

APARTHEID

Apartheid is the only word in the Afrikaans language (spoken by minority groups in South Africa and Namibia) that is recognized all over the world. Its literal meaning is "separateness". The white Afrikaner **National Party** first used the word to describe its policies of racial segregation while campaigning in the election of 1948, from when it went on to govern South Africa until 1994. But the idea of apartheid in South Africa was nothing new: racial segregation and oppression by the white minority had been practised from the earliest days of Dutch and later British colonialism; the National Party merely gave it its name and turned it from practice into ideology. Apartheid's aim was a complete political and social separation of race groups divided into whites, Coloureds (people of mixed race), Indians and blacks. Several **Bantustans** were created – areas where blacks could own property and exercise political rights – but their movement in "white" South Africa was severely restricted and tightly controlled. A host of laws enforced **racial segregation** in residential areas, public amenities, education and the labour market, while sexual relationships between black and white were punishable by law. Most of these laws were relaxed from the 1980s onwards and finally abolished just before the country became a democracy in 1994.

"grand apartheid". These were the **Population Registration Act** of 1950, which forced every South African to be classified according to a specific race group; the **Group Areas Act** of 1950, enforcing residential segregation; the **Pass Laws Act** of 1952 that refined the practice of forcing blacks to carry a "reference book" at all times; the **Preservation of Separate Amenities Act** of 1953; and the **Bantu Education Act** of 1953, which devised a separate and inferior education system for blacks. Of this last measure, Verwoerd declared: "There is no place for the Bantu in the European Community above the level of certain forms of labour. What is the use of teaching the Bantu child mathematics when it cannot use it in practice? That is quite absurd." This Act led to the closing down of most of the church schools at which nearly all the black elite and middle class of the time had been educated.

Sophiatown campaign

During the 1940s and 1950s a situation developed on the western edge of Johannesburg that deeply offended the disciples of apartheid. A vibrant suburb, **Sophiatown**, inhabited by blacks, coloureds, Indians and some whites had developed in size and was almost encircled by white suburbs. It was home to several senior ANC figures, like Dr Alfred Zuma and Robert Resha of the Youth League, and popular artists and entertainers – and to a firebrand British priest of the Church of England, Father **Trevor Huddleston**.

In June 1953 the apartheid government announced that it was going to remove all the black inhabitants of Sophiatown to an area called **Meadowlands**, near the black township of Orlando where Mandela lived. The community was outraged and the ANC and the Indian Congress organized a protest meeting in the Odin cinema. Huddleston was the first speaker and as he finished, the second speaker, Yusuf Cachalia, was grabbed by policemen and removed from the hall. Huddleston stormed after them to where some hundred armed policemen were standing outside the cinema hall. "I had seen and felt, in those moments, the terrifying spectre of the police state," he wrote later. Mandela defused a potentially explosive situation by jumping on the stage and starting a popular protest song.

The ANC was very confident that its resistance to the removal of the people of Sophiatown was going to be successful – Lutuli promised it was going to be

> "We cherished Sophia-town because it brought together such a great concentration of people, we did not live in it, we were Sophiatown. It was a complex paradox which attracted opposites; the ring of joy, the sound of laughter, was interposed with the growl and the smell of insult..."
>
> Bloke Modisane, from his autobiography *Blame Me On History* (1963)

THEY CALLED IT A TRIUMPH

Sophiatown and the ideology of apartheid could not exist in the same country. Unlike other black townships at the time, the people of this township on the edge of "white" Johannesburg could own their properties, which brought a different spirit to the place. It also meant that the suburb did not have row upon row of identical matchbox houses like other state-built townships, but an eclectic mix of brick houses, big and small, and shacks made of corrugated iron, wood and cardboard. A good mix of blacks, coloureds, Indians and a number of Chinese and even a few white families called the narrow, overcrowded streets and alleyways home. It was an apartheid-free zone.

By the 1940s a rich, pioneering culture had developed. Every night the sounds of African jazz and *mbaqanga* music could be heard from the many shebeens (illegal drinking houses) and nightclubs like the Thirty-Nine Steps. On weekends popular musicians like the "songbird" Dolly Rathebe and the lead singer of the Manhattan Brothers, performed at the **Odin cinema**. Gangs like the Americans and the Berliners – who claimed they mostly stole from rich whites – copied US movie gangsters and set the style: two-tone shoes, stylish hats, double-breasted suits and flashy American cars. Sophiatown was the cultural home of the black Johannesburg elite: professional people, exciting new writers, journalists, artists and political activists. This vibrant culture was captured best by the magazine *Drum* where writers like Can Themba, Lewis Nkosi, Nat Nakasa and Alex la Guma became famous, and where photographers like Peter Magubane, Alf Kumalo and Jürgen Schadeberg made their name. Nelson Mandela was *Drum*'s favourite politician and public figure, and most of the iconic photographs of Mandela of this era were taken by Magubane, Kumalo and Schadeberg.

Sophiatown was living, vibrant proof that "separate development", as the government often euphemistically called apartheid, was nonsense. In 1955 the government started removing the black people of Sophiatown to a faraway township and had working-class white Afrikaners move in – they then renamed the township **Triomf**, Afrikaans for triumph.

apartheid's "Waterloo". Week after week militant speeches were made at protest meetings in the township and the cry "Asihambi!" (We will not move!) reverberated every night. Robert Resha mobilized a group of volunteers to assist families threatened with **forced removal**.

Mandela was an active participant in the campaign and for the first time in his political career he was making statements that were close to promoting an armed resistance. One such speech was later used against him in court. He now felt that non-violence was a "useless strategy" and could never overthrow the government; only violent tactics would destroy apartheid and the ANC had to prepare to start using that strategy in future.

And yet on more than one occasion it was Mandela who had to step in and defuse a potentially violent conflict with the authorities when the actual removals from Sophiatown started. He was beginning to prepare the ground for what he now thought was inevitable, although he knew his followers were not yet ready to take on the iron fist of the apartheid state. Ultimately the ANC's Sophiatown campaign was a failure. When, in February 1955, the first trucks started transporting the families away to Meadowlands and the bulldozers moved, there was no resistance, not even demonstrations. Soon after, Sophiatown became Triomf – an Afrikaner suburb.

A tactical rethink

In his autobiography Mandela states that the lesson from the Sophiatown campaign was clear: speeches, demonstrations, strikes and marches did nothing to move the National Party government, only **violent resistance** was going to be effective. But it would take several years and a lot of debate and political intrigue before that became the official policy of the ANC. As it happened, the ANC's national executive reprimanded Mandela for his statements. And in September 1953, the government served another banning order on Mandela, preventing him from attending meetings and restricting him to the district of Johannesburg for two years. This was a major blow to his political plans and limited him to clandestine involvement

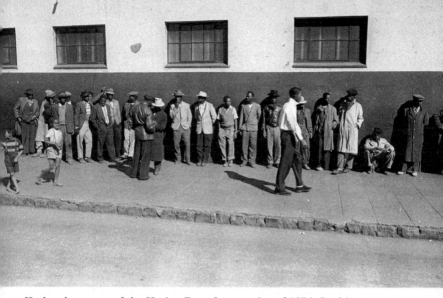

Under the terms of the Native Resetlement Act of 1954, Sophiatown residents were forced out of their homes and resettled. (© Drum Social Histories/BAHA/Africa Media Online)

in the ANC's activities. He later admitted that he had "overstepped the line" in his Sophiatown speech. Despite his ban, he continued to "lecture small study groups" in the townships.

Mandela wasn't the only ANC figure to have thoughts of armed struggle. In 1953 Sisulu had an invitation to a student festival in Romania and also visited China and the Soviet Union. According to both men's recollections, they had agreed that Sisulu should ask the **Chinese** to supply the ANC with arms for an uprising against the apartheid regime. Sisulu did put the request to his Chinese hosts, but they advised him that an armed struggle was premature and were not eager to get involved.

The severe restrictions on leaders and the narrow margins of manoeuvrability dictated by new legislation made Mandela and other ANC tacticians rethink their strategies. The fear that the government could actually ban the ANC as a party became real after the Communist Party was declared illegal in 1950. The result was a restructuring of the ANC and a new strategy for political action and mobilization called the **M Plan**. The "M" stood for Mandela, but did not use his name because of the restrictions already imposed on him. The ANC was broken down into cells – one cell per street. Each cell would have blocks of seven households, seven cells would make up a zone, and four zones would make a ward with a branch secretariat. Mandela explained to the ANC leadership that the new structures would be more suited to the "new methods" that would be essential in the time ahead when activists would have to work behind the scenes or even underground. In the end the M Plan was only implemented in parts of the Eastern Cape, mostly because local organizers thought it would undermine their authority and would take up too much of their time. A form of "street committee" system was, however, revived during the heated struggle against the white government in the 1980s.

A widening opposition

The ANC leadership at the time – Mandela included – was slow to take notice of the fundamental shift in white politics after the Nationalist Party's election victory in 1948. They were too preoccupied with mobilizing the black majority and questioning whether they should cooperate with Indians, coloureds and communists to spend time thinking about the potential role of white opponents of apartheid. This started changing in 1953 with the launch of two opposing parties (mainly aimed at white South Africans) who rejected apartheid: the **Liberal Party** and the **Congress of Democrats**. The Liberal Party was clear in its rejection of white rule and advocated political rights for all citizens, but preferred a qualified franchise (voters had to be "suitably qualified") and proclaimed themselves against boycotts, strikes and other forms of resistance. They were also vehemently anti-communist. The party's first leader was the novelist **Alan Paton**, author of the seminal 1948 novel *Cry the Beloved Country*.

Mandela angrily dismissed the Liberals as "subordinate henchmen of the ruling circles" and refused any cooperation with the party. "They believe in criticising and condemning the government for its reactionary politics but they are afraid to identify themselves with the people and to assume the task of mobilising that social force capable of lifting the struggle to higher levels." This jaundiced view of white liberals would persist in the ANC until after the liberation of South Africa in 1994. The Congress of Democrats was a completely different animal. It was the brainchild of white communists and intended to form the white arm of the ANC alongside the Indian Congress. The leaders – almost all prominent communists – included Mandela's friends Bram and Molly Fischer, Joe Slovo, Ruth First and Michael Harmel. The party, whose membership never grew beyond a few hundred, was vehemently opposed not only by the Liberal Party (who called it a communist front) but also by the Africanists in the ANC. However, by now Mandela's own resistance to working with communists had more or less disappeared and Chief Lutuli himself declared he would work with anyone who stood for the liberation of South Africans, adding that ideological differences could be sorted out after liberation. Walter Sisulu secretly became a Communist Party member in 1955.

Freedom Charter

With the formation of the **South African Coloured People's Organisation** in 1953, the ANC's "Congress Alliance" with the three parties representing the country's minority groups was in place. It was now time for a bold move: a **Freedom Charter** for all South Africa's people "which will inspire all the people of South Africa with fresh hope for the future" and provide "a positive programme

THE FREEDOM CHARTER

The Freedom Charter, adopted at the Congress of the People on June 26, 1955, remains the source document of all policies of the ruling African National Congress. The Preamble stated:

"We, the People of South Africa, declare for all our country and the world to know, that South Africa belongs to all who live in it, black and white, and that no government can justly claim authority unless it is based on the will of all the people; that our people have been robbed of their birthright to land, liberty and peace by a form of government founded on injustice and inequality; that our country will never be prosperous or free until all our people live in brotherhood, enjoying equal rights and opportunities; that only a democratic state, based on the will of all the people, can secure to all their birthright without distinction of colour, race, sex or belief; and therefore, we, the people of South Africa, black and white together equals, countrymen and brothers adopt this Freedom Charter; and we pledge ourselves to strive together, sparing neither strength nor courage, until the democratic changes here set out have been won."

of freedom in our lifetime", as an ANC memorandum of December 1953 worded it. The four bodies constituting the Congress Alliance formed the National Action Council and started preparing for a "Congress of the People", a gathering at which the charter would be formally accepted. Some fifty thousand volunteers criss-crossed the country to whip up support for the event and gather proposals for what should be in the charter. Despite his banning orders, Mandela took an active part in the campaign attending many clandestine meetings. He was also the convenor of a **Resolutions Committee** that tried to streamline the process.

Thousands of proposals were received, covering everything from major ideological questions to local issues such as housing. In early 1955, all these demands were given to a small committee of mostly white communists to draft into a charter. Their job was to find middle ground between often-conflicting demands and to soften extreme positions. A demand that all mines should be nationalized, for instance, was changed to the nationalization of the mineral wealth beneath the soil. About three thousand people delegated from all over the country started convening on an open piece of land at **Kliptown**, a township outside Johannesburg, on 25 June 1955. Some seven hundred of them were from the minority groups, making it the first big **multiracial political rally** in South Africa's history. There were more whites present than the 112 delegates: a number of security policemen mingled with the crowd and took notes as the meeting went ahead. Mandela's banning orders prevented him from taking part, but he was determined to be a part of it and stood, disguised, at the edge of the crowd on that first day.

Piet Beyleveld, a white trade unionist and president of the Congress of Democrats, was the chairman. Every single clause of the proposed Freedom Charter was approved by a show of hands and shouts of "Afrika! Mayibuye!" (Africa shall rise again). On the second day of the gathering, several policemen walked onto the stage and told Beyleveld that they were investigating a charge of **treason** and had a warrant to collect documents. The delegates insisted that the process had to go on and while the police confiscated documents and took photographs of delegates, the reading of the clauses continued to great enthusiasm.

As intended, the Freedom Charter became the core credo of the struggle against apartheid, and to this day it is seen as the guiding document of principles for the ANC. It declared "The People Shall Govern!" and demanded **full democratic rights** for all. Crucially, it cemented the principle of "non-racialism" by stating: "South Africa belongs to all who live in it, black and white." This clause caused a lot of unhappiness among the Africanists in the ANC, and their journal, *The Africanist*, declared that the delegates at Kliptown were the pawns of the Congress of Democrats whites, which it accused of being in favour of maintaining the status quo.

Mandela was very happy with the contents of the charter. In hindsight, the Congress of the People of 1955 appears to be his personal Rubicon in terms of his attitude towards the minority populations in South Africa. During and after this time he began defending the ANC's **cooperation** with "non-Africans" (as the ANC still prefers to call the minority groups) in the resistance against apartheid. His social friendships with white and Indian communists played a role, as did strategic considerations. But in his memoir, and in other writings and interviews, Mandela gave another clue as to his change of heart: personal experiences with sympathetic, or simply decent, white South Africans during the early 1950s. One example was a white magistrate who treated him fairly and courteously; another was the offer of help from Afrikaner lawyers when the Law Society tried, unsuccessfully, to remove him from the roll of attorneys in 1954; while a third was an Afrikaner police sergeant who treated him "like a gentleman".

The apartheid regime as well as the Liberals viewed the economic clauses in the charter as socialist and the work of the communists. Mandela denied that it was a "socialist blueprint", but conceded that it was a "revolutionary document" because the changes it envisaged "cannot be won without breaking up the economic and political setup of present South Africa".

It was certainly **too revolutionary** for the white government. During the following months they raided more than a thousand homes and offices of activists, collecting documents and other evidence. Early in the morning of 5 December 1956 they knocked on Mandela's door with a warrant of arrest on charges of **high treason**. His life was about to change forever.

4 Treason trial

"...before we launched the Defiance Campaign, we said that the campaign we were about to launch was not directed against any racial group. It was a campaign which was directed against laws which we considered unjust, and time without number the ANC has explained this."

Nelson Mandela, testimony at his trial, 1960

It was 5 December 1956. As Mandela, Evelyn and their three young children stood and watched, the police spent an hour rummaging through their home, collecting documents and books. The family knew the charge of **high treason** carried with it a maximum penalty of death by hanging, and the children cried when Mandela was led away by a white policeman, **Head Constable Rousseau**.

Despite the seriousness of the charge, and contrary to standard practice, Mandela was placed in the front of the car with Rousseau, rather than bundled into the back of a police van. Nor was he handcuffed. Mandela asked his captor if he wasn't afraid that he might try to escape, whereupon Rousseau responded: "Mr Mandela, you are playing with fire." Mandela retorted: "Playing with fire is my game." The two continued to exchange words until the policeman told Mandela that he was treating him with respect and deserved Mandela's respect. Mandela agreed.

This would be his way with his persecutors in the years ahead: even people "in the system" deserved to be treated with fairness and respect if they demonstrated the same in their attitude towards political activists. He once even stopped his friends from embarrassing a state prosecutor with compromising photographs from his private life because, he said, the prosecutor was a fair man in court.

Imprisonment

When Mandela arrived at the **Old Fort**, the prison in central Johannesburg, he discovered that he wasn't the only ANC leader arrested. In the largest police raid in South Africa's history, security police had swooped at dawn on the homes of activists around the country. They used military transport planes to fly those of the **140 arrested leaders** who lived far from Johannesburg to be imprisoned at the Old Fort. The cream of the ANC's leadership was now in jail, including Chief Albert Lutuli, Oliver Tambo and the acting head of Fort Hare University, Professor Z.K. Matthews. With them in the Old Fort were priests, lawyers, doctors, journalists and trade unionists, as well as female activists like Lilian Ngoyi and Helen Joseph, a leader of the Congress of Democrats who had emigrated from England in 1931.

One senior ANC leader who was not arrested was Walter Sisulu. When he heard of the arrests early that morning, he left his home, but later learnt that the police hadn't come for him. He had no explanation for his non-arrest and was even accused of being a collaborator, leading him to remark that he regretted not being among his comrades. He went to visit them in jail and was impressed with their high spirits, recording that some of the detainees met for the first time and new friendships were formed in the cells. Sisulu's turn came a week later, when he was arrested with fifteen others, including Mandela's friends Ahmed Kathrada, Rusty Bernstein and Ruth First. First's husband, Joe Slovo, was also picked up, despite the fact that he had already been appointed as one of the Old Fort detainees' lawyers. True to the fanatical commitment to racial separation, white and black detainees, charged with the same crime, were held separately.

Mandela and his co-leaders promptly organized themselves into political committees in jail – he called it the "largest and longest unbanned meeting of the Congress Alliance in years". Just as would happen a few years later on Robben Island, the activists arranged physical exercises, games, debates and history lessons among themselves. The black men in the Old Fort even formed the Accused Male Voices Choir. Meanwhile, Ambrose Reeves, the Anglican bishop of Johannesburg, and **Canon John Collins**, the head of the London-based organization Christian Action, were busy raising funds for the 156 accused and their families, and for their legal representation. Among the defence counsel was Bram Fischer (see p.28).

No Johannesburg court was big enough to accommodate all the accused, so the state turned the old **Drill Hall** into a court. When the pre-trial hearing started on 19 December, the hall was surrounded by thousands of loud, placard-waving supporters. A wire cage was erected around the area where the accused stood and some of them attached signs reading, "Dangerous! Don't feed!" When their lawyers threatened to walk out in protest – the accused were "caged like wild beasts", lawyer Maurice Franks told the magistrate – the cage was removed. On the second day, police clashed with the protestors and after that hundreds of uniformed police surrounded the hall every day. The **indictment** was 18,000 words long. It stated that the accused were guilty of high treason because they wanted to overthrow the state by force and replace it with a communist state. The evidence? Statements and speeches made between the Defiance Campaign and the Congress of the People, and the Freedom Charter itself.

Out on bail

The state unexpectedly granted the accused **bail** two days later and in line with the racial obsession of the apartheid state whites paid 250 pounds, Indians 100 pounds and blacks and coloureds 50 pounds. The accused were hugely relieved that they could spend Christmas with their families – everyone except Nelson Mandela, who went back to an empty home because Evelyn had finally decided to go her own way. It was a short-lived reprieve. The accused were back in court on 9 January 1957 for the magistrate's

Robert Sobukwe addressing a meeting, photographed by Peter Magubane. (© Drum Social Histories/BAHA/Africa Media Online)

decision on whether the state's case was strong enough to be heard in the **Supreme Court**. Rusty Bernstein remarked that it was like going back to boarding school after a holiday, "a sinking feeling of depression, mixed with pleasure at seeing the same old gang again". Joe Slovo noticed the irony that black, white, coloured and Indian sat side by side in the dock – unusually, they were seated in alphabetical order rather than separated by race – "charged, among other things, with the crime of creating hostility between black and white races in South Africa".

It was, indeed, one of the achievements of the trial that the leaders of the different structures of the ANC became much closer. Chief Lutuli, for instance, established firm friendships with the Indian Congress leaders. Sisulu remarked: "The government wanted to immobilise us and put us out of action. Instead, in some ways, we were able to do more political work than before when we had to worry about problems of communication. We were all in one place and were able to plan strategy and tactics together." Defence counsel Vernon Berrangé, himself secretly a member

SOUTH AFRICA'S RACIAL TERMINOLOGY

The racial terms used in South Africa can be confusing, especially to outsiders, and may even lead to embarrassment. Here's a short guide:

The original people of the country were the San, who were hunters and gatherers. They had no collective name for themselves, and were called San by their pastoralist cousins, the Khoikhoi, who moved down into South Africa a few thousand years ago. The word San originally meant something like vagrant, so many San descendants prefer the name they got from the first Dutch settlers, Bushmen.

Only a small number of Bushmen survive in South Africa, Botswana and Namibia, while the Khoikhoi (called the Hottentot by the Dutch settlers) have also disappeared as a group, although their descendants form part of several other groups later classified as coloureds. In South Africa, coloureds are people of mixed blood: the Khoikhoi, the Bushmen, slaves from the East Indies and Africa, and white and black South Africans. Most of them speak the language they share with white Afrikaners, Afrikaans.

The black farming groups who moved into southern Africa over a thousand years ago were originally called natives. During the middle of the twentieth century, this came to be regarded as insulting and the government started referring to them as Bantu. This was a name ethnologists had given to the large language family of black farmers and ironworkers who originated on the border of present-day Nigeria and Cameroon some four thousand years earlier, and who form the majority of people in the subcontinent today. The term Bantu was then associated with apartheid; black people preferred to be called Africans, although of the Communist Party, told the court that the trial was a battle of ideas rather than simply a prosecution of people. The overwhelming majority of South Africans, and indeed humankind, supported the ideas contained in the Freedom Charter.

Pre-trial hearing

The **preparatory examination** lasted thirteen monotonous months. It was soon clear to all that the case against the accused was weak if

this became controversial because it excluded other ethnic groups who regarded themselves as indigenous.

Portuguese seafarers called black South Africans *cafre* (from the Arabic *kafir* meaning infidel) and seventeenth-century cartographers referred to South Africa as Cafreria, while the British colonialists called a part of the Eastern Cape, British Kaffraria. Later, many white South Africans referred to black people as **kaffirs**. By the early twentieth century this was recognized as a pejorative term, and for the last fifty years the use of the word has been regarded as insulting enough to warrant a *crimen injuria* charge, as an act that seriously injures the dignity of another.

White South Africans are mainly divided between Afrikaners (descendants of the original, northwestern European settlers) who speak Afrikaans, and "the English" or **English-speakers**. Afrikaners are also sometimes called **Boers**, the Dutch word for farmers. When black and coloured people use the term Boer, they mostly mean it in a pejorative sense – the apartheid police were also called Boere. But many Afrikaners proudly refer to themselves as Boere, especially the descendants of the Voortrekkers, the pioneers who moved into the interior after 1838 and established the Boer republics of the Transvaal and the Free State.

Some older generation Afrikaners still resent "the English" because of British imperialist activity in South Africa, in particular the Anglo Boer Wars. A large number of English-speaking South Africans are descendants of the 1820 Settlers brought to the Eastern Cape by the British government. *Rooinek* ("red neck") was a term used by Afrikaners to refer to English-speakers (because British soldiers burnt easily in the African sun) but is no longer common, though still sometimes used in jest.

not unwinnable, and various theories were suggested as to why the state went ahead with it. Some put it down to arrogance, others saw it as a strategy to tie up the leadership of the Congress Alliance in court, or a way of simply intimidating the opposition. Then there was the possibility that the judges were sufficiently loyal to the apartheid state to give a guilty verdict in spite of the flimsy evidence. And at times the evidence given by policemen of the Security Branch was so ridiculous that the accused burst out laughing and were warned by the magistrate to behave. A detective who claimed to have written down everything said at a five-hour meeting had to admit under cross-examination by Joe Slovo, who defended himself, that he didn't actually understand English well. When Slovo asked him whether he agreed that his notes were "a lot of rubbish", he responded: "I don't know." Another witness, **Solomon Ngubase**, who claimed to be an ANC office bearer, a lawyer and a university graduate, said he was present when the ANC decided to send men to the Soviet Union to get arms. But under cross-examination he admitted that he had no university education, was neither a lawyer nor a member of the ANC, and had in fact served four jail terms. When Berrangé asked when he had last done "an honest day's work", Ngubase replied: "I can't remember."

Halfway through, the state called **Andrew Murray**, a professor of political science at the University of Cape Town, as their expert on communism. Berrangé read out parts of books and statements and asked Murray to say whether they were communist statements or not. First he read out a statement on the need for worker cooperation. It was "communistic", Murray replied. Berrangé then revealed the statement was made by the former prime minister and leader of the National Party, D.F. Malan. One of the passages Berrangé read was from Murray's own pen, and the professor called it "straight from the shoulder communism" before being told he was the author. Two other "communistic" statements he identified were in fact written by former presidents of the United States – Abraham Lincoln and Woodrow Wilson.

In October 1957 the state prosecutor dropped the case against 65 of the accused, including Chief Albert Lutuli and Oliver Tambo. In January 1958 the magistrate found that there were sufficient grounds to refer the case against Mandela, Sisulu and 89 others to the Supreme Court. The actual trial started in the **Old Synagogue** in Pretoria in August 1959, but shortly afterwards the case against 59 of the accused was dropped, with Mandela and Sisulu again among the remaining 30.

The trial in Pretoria

In March 1960 the government declared a **state of emergency** and at the end of that month Mandela, Sisulu and others were arrested and held without warrant. The day after his arrest a policeman at Newlands police station, where he was held, addressed Mandela as "Nelson". Mandela's fellow detainees were greatly fortified when they heard Mandela snap back: "I'm not Nelson to you, I am Mr Mandela." The Treason Trialists now in jail were driven in closed vans from jail to the Old Synagogue every day for the ongoing trial. Their defence team withdrew in protest and, for a few months, Mandela and **Duma Nokwe** formed the accused's legal team.

Mandela testified in August 1960 and was cross-examined at length. It was a great performance, a mix of assertiveness and reason – one of his lawyer friends at the time said he was an even better lawyer in the dock than when he was defending someone else. The member of the defence team assigned to Mandela, **Sydney Kentridge QC**, recalled: "He was obviously very steadfast and committed to his cause, but if you asked him a question about a political issue he would give a really thoughtful reply, not a slogan

Mandela steps from the court in the Old Synagogue, Pretoria. With him is Moses Kotane, secretary general of the SACP. (© Jürgen Schadeberg)

or cliché. He wouldn't have described himself as an intellectual but to me he was a thinker as well as a doer." Kentridge added that despite his fierce criticism of the government, Mandela was never insulting, always eloquent.

Mandela's remarkable pragmatism was demonstrated by his explanation that the ANC would even have been prepared to accept a government offer of a limited franchise for black South Africans as a starting point. "In my view," he told the court, "that would be a victory, my Lords; we would have taken a significant step towards the attainment of universal adult suffrage for Africans, and we would then for five years, say, suspend civil disobedience, we won't have any stay-at-homes, and we will then devote the intervening period for the purpose of educating the country, the Europeans to see that these changes can be brought about and that it would bring about better racial understanding, better racial harmony…" He qualified this statement by saying such a process would eventually have had to lead to **full voting rights** for blacks. According to the court record, Mr Justice Simon Bekker asked Mandela: "… as a matter of fact, isn't your freedom a direct threat to the Europeans?" Mandela: "No, it is not a direct threat to the Europeans. We are not anti-white, we are against white supremacy and in struggling against white supremacy we have the support of some sections of the European population… It is quite clear that the Congress has consistently preached a policy of race

> I do not believe, of course, that the Government was in any way sincere in saying it was part of Government policy to extend autonomy to Africans. I think they acted in order to deceive … in spite of that deception one thing comes out very clearly and that is that they acknowledged the power of the Defiance Campaign…
>
> Nelson Mandela at the Treason Trial

harmony and we have condemned racialism no matter by whom it is professed."

On 29 March 1961 the judges found the accused **not guilty** of treason and stated that the ANC's policies were clearly neither violent nor communist. Kentridge remembers: "It was pandemonium. The spectators and crowds waiting outside for the verdict cheered and some of the accused were carried shoulder high by their supporters." The celebration parties in the black townships all over South Africa were exuberant. The bitter irony of the verdict was that by the time it was delivered, the ANC was actually in the process of abandoning its strategy of non-violence and about to launch into an **armed struggle**. Between the start of the trial on 19 December 1956 and the final verdict more than four years later, the political landscape of South Africa had changed fundamentally – and not primarily because of the trial. This was also true of Mandela's personal life.

5 Courting Winnie

"I love you all the time, in the miserable and cold winter days and when all the beauty, sunshine and warmth of summer returns. My joy when you're bursting with laughter is beyond measure. This is how I always think of you ... with a smiling face whatever the circumstances."

Nelson Mandela, letter to Winnie from prison, 1979

Her first name is Nomzamo, which means "trial" or "ordeal" in Xhosa. But Nomzamo Zanyiwe Winifred Madikizela became known to the world simply as Winnie – **Winnie Mandela**. And she has indeed endured many ordeals and more than one court trial, becoming one of the most controversial public figures in South Africa.

Born in 1934, Winnie – like Nelson Mandela – was from Transkei, but her parents came from the **Pondo** branch of the Xhosa people. Her father and mother, Columbus and Gertrude, were both teachers. Columbus's mother, Seyina, hated Gertrude and treated her badly, mainly because her father was a white man and she had a pale complexion, long, silky hair and blue eyes. According to Seyina, this made her a "mlungu" – a white person – and the grandson of the great Pondo chief Madikizela deserved better. Gertrude died after the birth of her ninth child when Winnie was only ten.

Winnie was a bright student and her father sent her to Johannesburg to train as a **social worker**. She shared a room at the hostel with Adelaide Tshukudu, who was the girlfriend of a young lawyer, Oliver Tambo, from Winnie's home village. Early in 1956 Tambo briefly introduced her to his law partner, Nelson Mandela, through a car window. She knew very well who he was, having seen "this towering, imposing man" in court when he was representing a colleague of hers.

Meeting Mandela

Winnie often saw Mandela when she was waiting for a bus to take her to **Baragwanath Hospital**, where she had started working. He would be dropping off or picking up someone from the bus stop. Winnie was a very beautiful young woman – her picture had by then appeared in newspapers and magazines a few times – and of course Mandela had noticed her too. Once she was late for the bus, so Mandela gave her a lift to the hospital. Winnie herself has said she was completely apolitical at this stage in her life.

It's typical of the mythology surrounding Mandela's private life that there are several different versions of how he and Winnie actually got together. She says she was shopping with Tambo and his fiancée at a delicatessen in Johannesburg when they bumped into Mandela and were formally introduced. Mandela says that the introduction took place when she visited Tambo in his law office. Friends of the Mandelas tell another story: Mandela's cousin and student friend Kaizer Mantanzima had taken a fancy to Winnie and wanted to marry her, so he arranged to see her at an address in Orlando where he was staying. It turned out to be Mandela's house, and it was a pleasantly surprised Mandela who opened the door when she knocked.

Courtship

All three versions end the same way: Mandela was smitten, and phoned her shortly afterwards to invite her for Sunday lunch – to discuss something in relation to the Treason Trial, which by then had started. Mandela didn't fetch her from her hostel himself, but instead sent his friend Joe Mathews to take her to his office. Winnie was a bit intimidated by the famous man sitting behind his impressive lawyer's desk, despite the fact that she was wearing a "sophisticated" dress she had borrowed from a friend for the occasion. After lunch they went for a walk when, Mandela says, he told Winnie he wanted to marry her – Winnie only remembers that he unexpectedly kissed her. Mandela was clearly trying to impress: he briefed her about the prospects of success in the Treason Trial and took her to a fancy curry restaurant, which Winnie found agonizing because she had never eaten curry before. The next day he took her to the gym to watch him exercise and shadow box.

When Mandela and Kaizer Mantanzima discovered they were interested in the same woman they had a serious confrontation. Mantanzima, who already had other wives, reluctantly stepped back but remained resentful for a long time. This incident made Mandela realize just how desirable Winnie was and he started courting her with greater enthusiasm. He brought her with him to the Treason Trial hearings, introduced her to all his comrades, and took her home to meet his children and friends. One of Mandela's co-accused, Ahmed Kathrada, told him after meeting her "such beauty does not go with a revolutionary".

It was an unusual experience for the 22-year-old from Transkei to be welcomed into the homes of wealthy white people in the leafy northern suburbs of Johannesburg, but she quickly established good relations with many of them, as well as with Mandela's Indian friends, such as Fatima Meer and Amina Cachalia. Years later Winnie would remark: "Even at that stage, life with him was a life without

THE ROUGH GUIDE TO NELSON MANDELA

him. He did not even pretend that I would have some special claim to his time." She added with an apparent hint of bitterness that if people were looking for "some kind of romance" between them, they wouldn't find it.

Those close to Mandela at the time have repeatedly pointed out that he did not leave his wife for Winnie and that she did not break up his marriage to Evelyn, which was well and truly over by the time the two met. They also make the point that had Mandela not been a relatively liberated, post-tribal man, he would simply have remained married to Evelyn and taken Winnie as a second wife, as many of his peers would have done. (The present leader of the ANC and president of South Africa, Jacob Zuma, has three wives, two ex-wives and a fiancée.)

It is not hard to figure out that Mandela had, by the mid-1950s, "outgrown" Evelyn, who was a sedate, conservative and religious mother figure and conventional wife, while Mandela had become a debonair, charismatic and famous national leader and revolutionary. Winnie, with her striking physical beauty, aristocratic Xhosa background, urban sophistication, sense of fashion and vivacious personality – and newfound interest in politics – was the perfect match for him. He called her **Zami**, short for Nomzamo, and she called him by his clan name, **Madiba**. The pair quickly became the darling couple of the black elite and within the tight-knit group of Johannesburg left-wingers. They would eat in all the right places and hang out in the trendiest jazz clubs. Soon after their relationship started, Winnie became an active member of the ANC Women's League.

Proposal and marriage

In March 1958, after a romantic picnic, Mandela caught Winnie completely off-guard by telling her that Ray Harmel (wife of his old friend Michael) was going to make her **wedding dress** and asking her how many bridesmaids she wanted. She simply asked him what the

Nelson and Winnie on their wedding day, 14 June 1958. (© International Defence and Aid Fund/Handout/Reuters/CORBIS)

date was he had in mind. "That's how I was told I was getting married to him! It was not put arrogantly; it was just something that was taken for granted," she writes in her autobiography, *Part of my Soul.* "I was madly in love with him at that stage, and so was he with me in his own way. It was such a mutual feeling and understanding that we didn't have to talk about it."

Because of his banning orders, Mandela could not go to Transkei to ask Columbus Madikizela for his daughter's hand, so he sent a cousin to negotiate the *lobola* or bride price. Winnie was disappointed when her father expressed disapproval of her marrying an older man with three children, and one who was likely to be spending a lot of time in an apartheid jail. Her grandmother verbalized the feeling of many family members in Bizana, Winnie's home village: "You are going to look after that man's children. All he wants is a maid to look after his children while he's in prison."

The public got to know about the wedding plans on 25 May 1958 when the newspaper *Golden City Post* reported: "It's this week's No 1 social announcement. Attorney Nelson Mandela and social worker Miss Winnie Madikizela are holding a party today to announce their engagement. The wedding is planned for June 14."

The wedding took place in the Methodist Church in **Bizana**, and she did wear a Ray Harmel dress. The party in the town hall was attended by many of Mandela's political colleagues – those, at least, who were not restricted to their homes by banning orders, as Walter Sisulu was. Mandela received special permission from the police to attend his wedding and be away from home for six days, but he wasn't allowed to make the bridegroom's speech, since his banning orders prevented him from speaking to more than a few people. Columbus Madikizela spoke, and warned his daughter that her new husband was already married – to the struggle.

The struggle continues

It took just five months before Mandela's bride experienced the wrath of the apartheid state. In October 1958 the new Mrs Mandela, pregnant with her first child, was part of a group of about two thousand women who protested against the pass laws in Johannesburg. Over one thousand women, including Winnie, were then arrested and locked up under appalling conditions at the Old Fort jail. While inside, Winnie started to bleed, but fortunately she was in the same cell as Albertina Sisulu, a qualified midwife, whose intervention probably saved her from losing the baby.

On her release, Winnie discovered that her activism had resulted in her being fired from Baragwanath Hospital. This loss of employment coincided with a serious crisis at the law firm Mandela and Tambo: the two partners could hardly practice law when they were in court five days a week for the Treason Trial. Winnie was beginning to pay the price for marrying a political activist, who was also financially ill disciplined (he never had a bank account). She found a job with the Johannesburg Child Welfare Society and the couple had to survive on her small salary. Her father, now a successful businessman and member of Kaizer Mantanzima's Bantustan government, sent her some money to help out. In February 1958 the Mandelas' daughter **Zenani** was born and life became even harder.

By all accounts, Mandela was more devoted to Winnie and Zenani than he had been to Evelyn and his first three children. Several of his close friends at the Treason Trial tell stories of how obsessed he was with his new wife and child, and how often he talked about them. But from Winnie's accounts it is also clear that he saw very little of them. When he wasn't in jail and being driven to the treason trial by police van, he had to get up before dark and make his own way to the courtroom in Pretoria. Back late each evening after preparing for the next day's hearing, he also had to put in time at his law practice. In between all these responsibilities he was still an ANC leader, organizing, mobilizing and meeting people. For Winnie there was "never any kind of life I can recall as family life, a young bride's life", although when he was with her, Mandela was "very affectionate".

> "Your beautiful photo still stands about two feet above my left shoulder as I write this note. I dust it carefully every morning, for to do so gives me the pleasant feeling that I'm caressing you as in the old days."
>
> Nelson Mandela, letter to Winnie from prison, April 1976

At home, late at night, he sometimes told Winnie stories from the trial. One was an account of how, after coming out of court, he helped an elderly white woman whose car was stuck in traffic. After he had pushed the car and started it again, she offered him 5 cents. When he declined the offer, she got out of the car and said: "Look at this Kaffir! He wants 25 cents! Well, you won't get it from me!"

The couple's second daughter, **Zindiswa** (Zindzi for short), was born in December 1960. It was a very difficult birth and both mother and child struggled. Once again Mandela was not present: he was visiting his older children in Transkei because Makgatho was ill, and when he arrived back home he found a police raid underway.

Some three months later, at the end of the Treason Trial's final day and his acquittal, Mandela went home but remained outside the house talking to people. **Joe Modise**, a young colleague, was sent in to ask Winnie to pack a bag for her husband as he was going on a journey he could not tell her about. She handed Modise a suitcase full of clothes and then Mandela and his friends left. "That was the last time I saw my husband as a family man, legally at home," Winnie wrote later. Mandela had gone underground.

6 The Black Pimpernel

> "I have had to separate myself from my dear wife and children, from my mother and sisters, to live as an outlaw in my own land. I have had to close my business, to abandon my profession, and live in poverty and misery, as many of my people are doing ... I shall fight the government side by side with you, inch by inch, and mile by mile, until victory is won."
>
> Nelson Mandela, in a statement released in June 1961

The event that changed the face of South Africa's politics and rendered the not guilty verdict in the Treason Trial largely irrelevant was the killing of sixty-nine pass law protestors on 21 March 1960 by the police in Sharpeville township south of Johannesburg (see box on p.91).

Sharpeville

The **Sharpeville Massacre**, as it became known, was a defining moment in South African history. It was condemned in virtually every capital of the world, including Washington and London, and put the apartheid ideology in the spotlight as never before. It finally demonstrated that apartheid was a violent and racist policy, and dispelled all notions of it being a morally justifiable strategy

An image that shocked the world. Dead and wounded lying in the road at Sharpeville. (© Hulton-Deutsch Collection/CORBIS)

of "separate development" of races. The United Nations Security Council declared that apartheid was causing international friction and the General Assembly asked that action be taken against South Africa. For the international community, apartheid was no longer just an "internal affair".

Sharpeville radicalized black South Africans and sent white South Africans into a spiral of fear. Many of those with rights to UK passports left the country; others armed themselves. The property and stock markets fell sharply.

Reactions to the massacre

The massacre and its aftermath also had a profound impact on Nelson Mandela and the ANC. Mandela and his senior leadership colleagues were at the Treason Trial on that fateful Monday, only learning about the massacre late in the afternoon. That night Mandela, Walter Sisulu and others met to discuss the crisis, with

THE SHARPEVILLE MASSACRE

Keen to make its mark, the Pan Africanist Congress (the Africanist party that broke with the ANC in 1959) launched a campaign against the pass laws on 21 March 1960. Few protestors turned up in Johannesburg, Pretoria and the Eastern Cape. But in **Sharpeville**, a township near Vereeniging (south of Johannesburg), and in the Cape Town township of **Langa** thousands of demonstrators confronted the police.

What happened outside Sharpeville around lunchtime on that day has been the subject of a judicial enquiry, as well as several films, plays and songs. It was also the subject of an investigation by the Truth and Reconciliation Commission in 1998. Most sober accounts agree that thousands assembled near the police station to present themselves for arrest for not carrying passes. They were boisterous, but unarmed and peaceful. The policemen present, however, were very nervous, in part because they were not used to (or trained in) the control of large crowds, but also because nine of their number had been killed in Durban two months earlier.

Angered when military jet fighters flew low over the crowd to intimidate them, a group surged towards the fence around the police station and a panicked policeman **opened fire**. His colleagues immediately joined in and kept on shooting even after the crowd started running away. A judicial enquiry later confirmed that no order to shoot was given by the commander. Officially 69 people were killed and some 180 wounded. In Langa township, later that day, thousands of protestors also confronted the police. Three were shot dead and 47 wounded.

In 1994, 21 March was declared **Human Rights Day**, a national holiday.

Mandela accusing the PAC – the organizers of the demonstration – of "blatant opportunism" motivated "more by a desire to eclipse the ANC than to defeat the enemy". On their recommendation, ANC president Albert Lutuli announced 28 March as a national **day of mourning** to be marked by a national stay-away and a strike. On that day, Lutuli and Mandela were among many who publicly burned their pass books. The photograph of Mandela on his haunches with a wry smile holding his pass in his hands just before he set light to it became an iconic image. He was thrown in jail two days later under the emergency regulations and only released 156 days later, on 31 August.

Prime Minister Hendrik Verwoerd's reaction to both the internal and international statements of outrage was to declare the ANC and PAC unlawful organizations. They "do not want peace and order," the minister of Justice, **F.C. Erasmus**, declared, "what they want is our country." It was now a criminal offence to belong to the ANC. The government declared a national **state of emergency** and arrested thousands of people belonging to the PAC, the ANC, its sister congresses and even the Liberal Party.

This crackdown and wave of arrests marked the beginning of the ANC leadership's thirty-year **life in exile**. Oliver Tambo left first, charged with the task of mobilizing international support for the ANC. He lived in London and was the exiled president of the ANC for 28 years.

Amidst all this turmoil Mandela, Sisulu and 28 others had to go through another year of the Treason Trial. On 25 March, four days before the final judgement, Mandela's banning orders of five years expired and he made a surprise appearance at a conference (the All-In Conference) in Pietermaritzburg that the ANC had organized for all its supporting groups. Mandela made a stirring speech before 1400 delegates: his first appearance before a large audience in 5 years and the last for 31 years.

The **All-In Conference** demanded a representative national convention and a democratic, non-racial constitution for South Africa. This was in reaction to the fact that South Africa had left the Commonwealth on 15 March and would officially become a republic on 31 May 1961. The conference decided to call a three-day **national strike** from 31 May if the government didn't accede to their demand for a national convention.

By this time the working committee of the ANC had already decided that Mandela had to go underground if the Treason Trial judges found the accused not guilty, because they knew he would simply be

ASSASSINATION ATTEMPTS

Nineteen days after the Sharpeville Massacre, on 9 April 1960, Prime Minister **Hendrik Verwoerd** spoke at an agricultural show in Johannesburg. Minutes after he sat down, a white farmer in a tweed jacket with a VIP card walked right up to him and called his name. When Verwoerd looked up, the man produced a .22 pistol and shot him in the face. Before anyone could stop him, he fired another shot hitting Verwoerd in the ear. Only then did the prime minister's bodyguard reach the would-be assassin and wrestle him to the ground.

The man was identified as **David Beresford Pratt**, a 54-year-old cattle and trout farmer from the Johannesburg district who was born in England and educated at Cambridge University. The court sent him for psychological evaluation and in September he was declared mentally disturbed and unfit to stand trial. He told friends and family that he had seen black prisoners being bundled into a police van the day before the shooting. Already an obsessive with a hatred of Afrikaner nationalism, he decided to act the next day. He hanged himself in his hospital cell in October 1961.

The two bullets were removed during a delicate operation and Verwoerd suffered no long-term damage, returning to work fifty days later. His more fanatical followers firmly believed that his miraculous survival was confirmation that God had saved him to serve his people, and the hero worship that the majority of white South Africans had for him increased as a result.

Six years later, on 6 September 1966, Verwoerd was stabbed to death in his seat in parliament by a 48-year-old parliamentary messenger, **Dimitri Tsafendas**. He too was declared mentally unfit to stand trial, and died in prison in October 1999.

jailed again. It was an important switch in ANC strategies and turned Mandela's life – and his family's – upside down.

On the night of the verdict, after a brief return home for some clothes, Mandela left for a **safe house** which had been organized by the Communist Party, an organization with considerable experience of underground activities since being made illegal eleven years earlier. From these hiding places Mandela organized the national stay-away at the end of April, but this had limited success and was called off after the first day.

A visibly angry Mandela told a British television interviewer at the time: "If the government reaction is to crush by naked force our non-violent struggle, we will have to reconsider our tactics. In my mind we are closing down a chapter on this question of non-violent policy." The ANC leadership formally rebuked him for this statement, though he knew many privately agreed with him. Shortly afterwards a warrant for his arrest was issued. He was now officially a **man on the run**.

Mandela in hiding

This was the beginning of the period that established Mandela as a popular legend, as a mythical, defiant revolutionary being hunted down by thousands of cruel apartheid policemen. Here was an educated man, a lawyer, a prominent and widely admired leader who was prepared to abandon his new wife and family and live as a fugitive from the law: constantly moving from hide-out to hide-out and risking his life in the cause of freedom for the people of South Africa. In a letter he sent to newspapers he talked about his separation from "my dear wife and children, from my mother and sisters, to live as an outlaw in my own land".

Newspapers and magazines added to the mystique with reports about the search for Mandela and called him the **Black Pimpernel**. By day he mostly read books on war and resistance: Che Guevara, Mao Zedong, Karl von Clausewitz and two accounts of guerrilla warfare – Menachim Begin's story of his fight against the British between 1945 and 1948, *The Revolt* (1951), and Deneys Reitz's 1929 book on the Anglo Boer War, *Commando*.

Ahmed Kathrada was part of a small group charged with organizing Mandela's life in hiding: finding him safe houses, arranging transport, fixing secret meetings with colleagues, as well as family and media interviews. They also helped him with various disguises. At different times he dressed as a chauffeur with a peaked cap, a gardener, a security guard and a labourer. Kathrada says they regarded as essential that he shave off his trademark beard, but Mandela refused: "He must have known how the beard enhanced his looks and personality."

Mandela actively participated in the myth-making. He would phone newspaper reporters from public call boxes and give them details of his visits to places like Durban, Cape Town and Port Elizabeth, in defiance of the police search for him. Some in the ANC later said that the Communist Party had a strategy to push Mandela as the "new Messiah" because they were impatient with the more conservative leadership of Albert Lutuli.

Staying with Kodesh

Wolfie Kodesh, a white journalist and Communist Party member, was also a member of the group looking after Mandela. On one occasion, after organizing a meeting between Mandela and other senior ANC figures in a block of flats, he noticed a white couple in the same block watching the steady trail of banned people entering the building. When he heard the man say "Quickly, go and phone", he burst into the meeting and told everyone to run away. But Mandela, dressed as a chauffeur, was stranded, because he was a long way from the township safe house where he was living at the time. Kodesh had a flat under a false name and that's where it was decided Mandela should go, but only after persuading him that – because of apartheid's forced residential segregation – a white suburb would actually be safer for him.

At 5am the next day Kodesh woke up and saw Mandela preparing for a run as he did every morning. He told him that a black man running around a white suburb would look very suspicious and refused to give him the key to the door. Kodesh later told the British journalist John Carlin in a TV interview: "Then he got up, in his tracksuit, and he started running on the spot. So that was his running. I thought, 'Oh well, if you want to run on the spot, good luck to you. I am going to sleep.' I went to sleep and about a half an hour afterwards I woke up again, and he's still running on the spot, sweating and heaving… At the end of it all, I noticed he did a few frog jumps across the flat, jumping up … that took at least an hour. So I said, 'that's all right, you can do this but not me.' He says, 'No, tomorrow you're going to join me.'" From the next day on, Kodesh joined Mandela in his early morning routine, doing an hour to Mandela's two. His fitness routing later stood Mandela in good stead when he was in jail, where he regularly ran on the spot to keep fit.

Kodesh said Mandela was "heartbroken" to be away from his family and constantly asked him to find out how Winnie was coping and how their children were. He describes Mandela as compassionate and forgiving, but also someone with a "short fuse". One day they heard the news of a police killing of black people. Mandela was fuming and paced up and down the flat. "Then he blurted out, 'Wolfie, one day, I'm telling you, it's going to be an eye for an eye and a tooth for a tooth.' And he kept on pacing. I could see this was such a situation, that I thought look, I'll read and do something. I'm not going to interfere with this man. Then about an hour afterwards, he tapped me on the shoulder, and he said, 'Wolfie, I didn't mean that at all. I could never do that.'"

Close calls

Mandela and Kodesh's problem was that there was a black man who cleaned the flats in the block who would get suspicious if he wasn't allowed into Kodesh's flat. Mandela made up a story that his name was David and he was a student who had got a grant to study overseas and was waiting to leave. The cleaner ended up befriending Mandela, even running errands for him. Two months into Mandela's stay, Kodesh went to look for the cleaner and found him with a newspaper carrying a story about the "Black Pimpernel" with several photographs of Mandela. Mandela brushed it aside, saying the man would never betray him.

NARROW ESCAPES

When hiding from the police, there were several occasions when Mandela ran the risk of being discovered. Once, dressed as a **chauffeur** with long jacket and peaked cap, he was standing at a street corner waiting to be picked up by an underground contact. A black security police officer he knew then walked in his direction and looked straight at him. Mandela was aware the man had seen him and thought he was about to be arrested, but the policeman merely winked at him, closed his fist in the ANC salute and walked past.

On another occasion, while at traffic lights, a car pulled up right next to the one Mandela was driving. He instantly recognized **Captain Spengler**, a senior security policeman who had arrested him previously. Waiting for the light to change was "the longest day I ever had", he later recalled, but in the end Spengler never looked his way.

Winnie Mandela tells the story of what happened when the car that her husband had given her started playing up. After Mandela got to hear about it, he instructed her – via an ANC underground operative – to drive to a specific street corner and wait. She did so and as she stopped a tall man in a blue uniform opened the door and asked her to move over. It was Mandela, who proceeded to drive the vehicle to a dealer and trade it for a new one before driving back to the city centre and getting out. It was the last time she saw him for many weeks.

Mandela's love of the traditional drink **amasi** (sour milk) nearly gave him away. He always left a bottle of milk on the windowsill of the flat to sour, but one day overheard two black workers wondering why it was there, since only black people drink amasi and there were no black people living in the flats. When the two men decided to investigate, Mandela though it best to move to another white suburb where he pretended to be a gardener.

When rumours started spreading that Mandela was dead or had left the country, the small committee looking after him decided to have a fresh picture taken to give to the media. Another white communist, the photographer **Eli Weinberg**, was smuggled in to his hideout to take the picture, which caused quite a stir when it was published.

In October 1961 Mandela was moved to what seemed like the perfect hideaway: a small farm in a semi-rural area north of Johannesburg that had been bought by the Communist Party through a dummy company set up by Michael Harmel and Harold Wolpe. The farm was **Liliesleaf** and the area **Rivonia** – names that would later become famous. The Communist Party member and artist **Arthur Goldreich** lived with his family in the homestead, and Mandela, taking the name **David Motsamayi**, occupied the outbuildings, posing as a cook and a gardener. Because of its rural setting, leaders of the ANC and the Communist Party were able to

An aerial police photograph of Liliesleaf showing the farmhouse where the Goldreich family lived and the farm buildings where Mandela hid out. (Historic Papers, University of the Witwatersrand)

visit the farm undetected for regular planning meetings. The farm was also deemed safe enough for Winnie and the children to visit Mandela occasionally, although this was done with great circumspection as Winnie was under constant security police surveillance.

Launching the armed struggle

By the time Mandela went to live at Liliesleaf, he was doing more than just his regular ANC work. In mid-1961 he had formally proposed a plan to the ANC, which he had often discussed with Sisulu and others: the launch of a military wing for the ANC. There was strong resistance to this plan, especially from **Moses Kotane**, a senior communist who had studied at the Lenin School in Moscow and accused Mandela of wanting to resort to violence because political work had become too difficult. Kotane insisted that there was "still room for the old methods if we are imaginative and determined enough". Mandela eventually won Kotane over, and after much lobbying and arguing at two drawn-out sessions convinced the ANC's senior leadership that non-violent strategies were ineffective and armed struggle was inevitable: "If peaceful protest is met with violence, its efficacy is at an end."

Even Chief Albert Lutuli, by now in the shadow of the popular Mandela, eventually relented when assured that the new organization would be independent of the ANC, although under its political leadership. Mandela knew he was going to get opposition from Lutuli "because he believed in non-violence as a principle, whereas we believed in it as a tactic, although we couldn't so say to court [referring to the Treason Trial]". Lutuli later changed his mind and accused Mandela of going against ANC policy. Mandela dismissed this, claiming that Lutuli "… was ill and he forgot very easily."

Another argument was used to support his case for armed action. The PAC was in the process of forming its own military wing, called

Poqo ("pure"), and Mandela said ANC supporters were demanding more militant action. Poqo concentrated on killing white civilians and what they called "collaborators" in the Transkei Bantustan.

Mandela was supported strongly by the South African Communist Party, who became the *de facto* co-sponsor of the new guerrilla movement and would play a dominant role in the armed struggle for three decades. The movement was named **Umkhonto we Sizwe**, the Spear of the Nation, more commonly referred to as **MK**. Nelson Mandela became its first commander-in-chief, with Joe Slovo, of the Communits Party's Central Committee, as its Chief of Staff. Liliesleaf Farm became MK's first headquarters.

The decision to launch an armed struggle would have far-reaching consequences for the ANC and for South (and Southern) Africa, and the debate as to whether this was a disastrous decision or an inevitability continues in South Africa to this day.

Sabotage strategy

It is clear from Mandela's own statements, and the versions of those around him, that for him a violent strategy meant sabotage: attacks on government buildings and infrastructure. In the months before he proposed the new strategy, he read a lot about other **sabotage campaigns**. Such a campaign would be a tool to force the apartheid government to talk to the ANC about abolishing apartheid and establishing a democracy, and a way to mobilize the people against the government. "Sabotage did not involve loss of life and it offered the best hope for race relations," Mandela said. "Bitterness would be kept to a minimum and, if the policy bore fruit, democratic government could become a reality."

Mandela could not have foreseen then that in years to come, MK would be based in camps in Angola and Zambia and embrace a doctrine committed to the violent overthrow of the regime, or that its tactics would include the bombing of civilians and the use of landmines on civilian roads; that there would be gross violations of human rights in those camps, including arbitrary detentions, executions and torture. And it's unlikely that he would have pushed the ANC so hard to embark on armed struggle had he known that the military campaign would be completely ineffective. In the end, it was **mass mobilization** and **international isolation** – especially during the 1980s – that forced the apartheid state to its knees, not violence.

Later, several ANC and Communist Party strategists, including Mandela, would state that the decision was perhaps a mistake, or at least premature, and that all the options for a non-violent resistance had not been exhausted. For Yusuf Cachalia of the Indian Congress, "It was pure adventurism. It was impractical. They had not worked out the consequences." Neither did the sabotage campaign have the desired effect of mobilizing the people into action. Some of the most talented activists were drawn from the ANC, its sister congresses and the trade union movement to be part of MK, in the process weakening these other bodies. With the energies shifting to military options, the ANC started neglecting the work needed to be done in a political organization. And it was soon clear that the militarization of resistance politics evoked a renewed and increasingly severe repression that all but paralysed the ANC.

> **"To the people and the world the uprising must assume the character of a popular revolutionary movement. To the enemy it must appear as an uprising of a few only. We must seek the support of the entire population with a perfect balance of social classes."**
>
> Nelson Mandela, from a notebook of 1962

But at the time, Mandela genuinely believed that his new course would shorten the lifespan of the apartheid state with very limited loss of life and he poured all his energies into recruiting young men to become saboteurs. He was especially successful in the Eastern

Cape, where his old M Plan had been more effectively implemented than elsewhere.

White communists became the driving force behind MK. When it came to the training of new recruits, Mandela had no one else to ask. By this time the communists had not only been preparing to establish their own sabotage units, they also had a few men with military experience. These included Arthur Goldreich, who had fought in the 1948 Israeli-Arab War as a member of Palmach, the elite strike force of the Haganah (the Jewish military underground), and **Jack Hodgson**, who fought for the British in North Africa during World War II and had picked up some knowledge of explosives while working in the copper mines. The communists also had connections with China and were able to arrange for a handful of recruits to be trained there.

Hodgson started making bombs using Condy's crystals (potassium permanganate) – a commonly available disinfectant – combined with aluminium powder and acid. The timing device was made from the plastic tube inside a ballpoint pen. A sympathetic pharmacist supplied the nitroglycerine. Wolfie Kodesh's brother owned a brickworks east of Johannesburg, which is where Hodgson, Kodesh and an excited Mandela tried out their home-made devices. They threw a few **Molotov cocktails** to see if those were put together properly, and then planted the bomb, which exploded spectacularly.

The first attacks

The new MK High Command was now eager to launch its first sabotage attack, but in October 1961 an event occurred that forced them to hold back. The irony could not have been greater: the president of the ANC, Chief Albert Lutuli, was announced as the winner of the **Nobel Peace Prize** for his role in advancing black South Africans' political rights through non-violent means. He was due to receive the prize in Oslo on 11 December and to have exploded the first bombs before then would have seriously embarrassed both him and the ANC.

The date for the first attack was switched to 16 December. This was a day laden with symbolism, celebrated as a sacred day of remembrance by Afrikaners as the **Day of the Covenant** or Dingane's Day, commemorating the Afrikaner settlers' victory over Zulu king Dingane's army at Blood River in 1838. In the run up to the day, the formation of MK was announced publicly. Leaflets distributed countrywide stated: "The time comes in the life of any nation when there remain only two choices: submit or fight. That time has now come to South Africa."

During the early hours of Saturday 16 December bombs exploded at **government buildings** and **electric substations** in Johannesburg, Port Elizabeth and Durban. As intended, this struck fear into the hearts of white South Africans. However, Mandela and his colleagues had completely misread the mindset of the white government, which simply became more repressive and more resolute, using the violence as an argument to scare its white voters into a **laager**, or siege mentality. There was more and more talk of "Die Swart Gevaar" – the black danger.

Most bomb attacks were successful, but there were some mishaps. The incendiary device given to **Ben Turok** caught fire and he had to rewrap it using a paper bag. In the end it never exploded but Turok was incriminated by his fingerprints on the wrapping and sent to jail. Another bomb exploded prematurely and killed the MK recruit, Petrus Molefe. Mandela did not plant any bombs himself.

Early in January 1962 the ANC decided to accept an invitation to a conference in Addis Ababa of the **Pan-African Freedom Movement** for East, Central and Southern Africa. As well as being nominated to speak on behalf of the ANC, Mandela was also asked to use the opportunity to raise funds and request the help of independent African governments with military training and arms for MK.

Travelling for the cause

On 11 January 1962 Mandela was smuggled over the border with Bechuanaland, now Botswana, on a trip that would last for six months. While on his travels, Mandela was frequently shocked at the reserved reception he received in some countries. This was a result of the PAC having got to Africa before the ANC and spread suspicion about the ANC's cooperation with whites, Indians and communists. The Sharpeville Massacre had put the PAC on a pedestal in Africa and the party's simple message of fighting for black rule, as opposed to the ANC's more complex ideal of a non-racial government, was more easily digestible.

His first meeting was with Tanzanian president **Julius Nyerere**, to whom Mandela expressed reservations about Nyerere's ideas on a

Mandela standing outside Westminster Abbey in 1962, a few yards from where his statue would be erected 45 years later. (Gamma-Rapho/Getty Images)

traditional communal socialism – Nyerere called it *ujamaa*, family-hood, a policy that would eventually ruin Tanzania's economy. From Tanzania he went via Sudan to Nigeria, where he was met by Oliver Tambo, who seriously questioned the decision to engage in armed struggle. Mandela then flew to **Addis Ababa** for the conference ,where he upset many sub-Saharan delegates with his statement that Arabs could also call themselves Africans. He received a warm reception in Tunisia and Morocco, and spent several fruitful hours talking to the leaders of the Algerian National Liberation Front which was fighting French colonialism. Mandela recorded in his diary that their army commander, **Houari Boumedienne**, told him that the objective of most liberation movements was seldom military victory, but rather to force governments to negotiate.

Mandela also visited Egypt, Guinea, Sierra Leone, Liberia, Ghana and Senegal and met thirteen African heads of state. Some of these governments gave him money – the total amount was just over 20,000 pounds – which was sent on to Oliver Tambo in London. Mandela joined Tambo in London in June where he had a "most cordial" meeting with **David Astor**, the influential editor of *The Observer* newspaper, who arranged for him to meet with the leaders of the Liberal and Labour parties. Importantly, he also met with Canon John Collins of St Paul's Cathedral, who had previously raised funds for the ANC's legal battles. Collins also had questions about the new military direction and Mandela had to go out of his way to explain that this was a "purely defensive action". Collins had founded the International Defence and Aid Fund for Southern Africa (IDAF) in 1956, which over the following decades proved crucial in raising funds to cover the legal costs of anti-apartheid activists in South Africa.

The trip to London wasn't all work. Tambo also took him sight-seeing, including a boat ride on the Thames, and he met many old friends by then in exile in Britain. One of these was **Esme Matshikiza**, wife of the playwright Todd Matshikiza, who urged him not to go back to South Africa where he was bound to face arrest. According to her, Mandela replied: "I see myself as a leader of the people and the leader of the people must be with the people." Tambo told the story of how, as they strolled past the statue of South African General Jan Smuts near Westminster Abbey, Mandela jokingly wondered whether his own statue would one day replace that of Smuts.

Mandela returned to Ethiopia where he was trained by an army officer in demolitions, "field craft", mortars and the use of automatic rifles and pistols. They spent hours on the shooting range and even did a "fatigue march" together, with Mandela completing the 26km march in under three hours. But the training, supposed to run for six months, was cut short after eight weeks by a message from Walter Sisulu back in Johannesburg, urging Mandela to return to South Africa. Sisulu's fear was that Mandela's long absence could lead to suspicion that he too had gone into exile and that this might well undermine the morale of the new MK recruits who were desperately trying, but with little success, to keep up the sabotage campaign. On his way home, Mandela met up with a group of 21 recruits in Dar es Salaam who were on their way for training in Ethiopia.

Back home

Back in Bechuanaland Mandela was met by a white MK member, **Cecil Williams**. Masquerading as his chauffeur, Mandela drove all the way back to Liliesleaf Farm with the semi-automatic rifle and ammunition he'd been given by the Ethiopians hidden in the car. A few hours later an anxious Winnie and her daughters arrived at the farm in an ambulance, Winnie pretending to be in labour. She was deeply concerned about his safety and told him about a new bill before parliament that sought to widen the definition of sabotage and made provision for the **death penalty**. She was feeling the pressure herself. Before Mandela's return, she told a newspaper interviewer:

"Whenever my children and I are about to sleep, Security Branch police arrive. They ask me where my husband is and sometimes search the house. Sometimes they joke and at other times they are aggressive, which frightens the children. There are rumours that Nelson is back, but I have not seen or heard from him."

That night Mandela briefed the ANC's national working committee on his trip. His travels had clearly radicalized his political outlook. To the surprise of some, he strongly proposed a new strategy of underplaying the ANC's partnership with the Communist Party, whites and Indians. He told them there was "violent opposition" in Africa to the ANC's policy of non-racialism and criticism that the organization was dominated by whites and communists. It was time that the ANC changed its image – "make adjustments in tactic, not policy" – and established itself as the vanguard of the Pan-African movement in South Africa, a position then claimed by the PAC. He sharply criticized Chief Lutuli for remarks he had made that had created "the impression of a man who is a stooge to whites".

The PAC had meanwhile started spreading the rumour that Mandela had become an Africanist during his tour of Africa and had actually joined the PAC. Mandela wanted to meet with Lutuli and the Indian Congress in Durban to deal with these rumours as a matter of urgency, and despite the warnings of colleagues, he again used Cecil Williams's car to travel there and again refused to shave off his trademark beard.

The changes in Mandela were clear for his old friends to see. When he met with senior MK members in Durban, he was dressed in an Arabic gown and greeted them with the Muslim greeting, "As-Salama Alaykum" (Peace be with you). One of those present, Billy Nair, remembers that Mandela told them that "it was not sufficient for us to engage in sabotage; we would need to train people militarily. It was not a campaign to take lives, nor was it against whites. It was to overthrow the regime, if necessary, by force."

He went on to meet with Indian Congress leaders and with Lutuli, who told him sternly that the ANC wasn't going to weaken its commitment to non-racialism simply to suit a few African politicians. Mandela's response was that he was only proposing cosmetic changes to make the ANC more palatable in Africa, but Lutuli was not convinced.

Mandela was so fired up following his African tour and military training that he became reckless. After his meeting with Lutuli he went to a party at a journalist's house, dressed in his Ethiopian **military fatigues**, and openly talked about the necessity to move toward guerrilla warfare. Fatima Meer, who attended the party, said that Mandela "cut a large military figure in khaki" and that all present were "excited by their intrigue". Billy Nair was one of those who believed that not everyone at the party had the ANC's best interests at heart.

The next morning Mandela and Cecil Williams got back in the car and started the drive back to Johannesburg. It was Mandela's last few hours of freedom for 28 years.

7 End of freedom

> **"Why is it in this courtroom I face a white magistrate, am confronted by a white prosecutor and escorted into the dock by a white orderly? Can anyone honestly and seriously suggest that in this type of atmosphere the scales of justice are evenly balanced?"**
>
> Nelson Mandela, from the opening statement of his 1962 trial

Nelson Mandela, dressed as a chauffeur, was in the passenger seat of Cecil Williams's Austin Westminster as they drove through the lush green hills from the east coast back to Johannesburg on 5 August 1962. Mandela was too pumped up about his new role as a **freedom fighter** to make small talk. Instead, the two talked about sabotage, with Mandela remarking that the main railway line between Durban and Johannesburg ran parallel to the road they were on and thus presented an easy target. Mandela clearly was not entertaining any thoughts about the risk of arrest, but was writing down his thoughts in a notebook that included references to previous conversations and meetings with other activists. He even had the Russian-made **handgun** he brought from Ethiopia with him. Just before the two men reached the town of Howick, near the village of Cedara about 100km from Durban, a police car overtook them and indicated that they should pull off the road. As they did so, another police car pulled up behind them.

Under arrest

Mandela had just enough time to hide his handgun and notebook between the front seats when a white policeman, one **Sergeant Vorster**, came to his window and asked who he was. "My name is David Motsamayi," he answered. The officer, who Mandela remembers as being very polite, immediately indicated that he knew the real identity of both men and informed them that they were under arrest. Mandela was then driven, unhandcuffed, to the police station in nearby Pietermaritzburg. Williams's car was never searched and it is a mystery to this day what happened to the handgun (see box on p.123). For the journey from Pietermaritzburg to Johannesburg, Mandela was allowed to receive food from his friend Fatima Meer, which he shared with two police officers. On his arrival he was locked up at **Marshall Square**, the police headquarters.

Mandela's colleagues in the ANC and MK were in a flat spin. Did the police know about his role in the sabotage campaign? Was the whole of MK compromised? Wolfie Kodesh went to inform Winnie, who on seeing Kodesh – "white like a ghost, his hair was standing on end" – realized immediately what he had come to tell her and simply asked: "Is it Nelson?" She knew that her husband faced a lengthy jail sentence. "Part of my soul went with him at that time," she wrote later.

Who turned him in?

It has never been established beyond doubt who had betrayed Mandela. The favourite theory in the ANC was that the **CIA** was the guilty party, and there is some evidence to support this. The agency would have been interested in Mandela because of his involvement with the South African Communist Party. In 1986, James Tomlins, a foreign correspondent reporting on South Africa, told the US television network CBS that a CIA operative, Donald C. Rickard, had admitted being stationed in the US consulate in Durban. Rickard had a source

THE MAN WHO DROVE WITH MANDELA

Cecil Williams, in whose stately Austin Westminster Mandela drove to and from Botswana and Durban posing as his chauffeur, was instrumental in influencing Mandela and the ANC in adopting the most gay-friendly position of any African liberation movement. Gay rights are enshrined in the post-apartheid constitution and South Africa is the only country in Africa where gay couples can be legally married.

Williams was an English theatre director born in Cornwall in 1906, who emigrated to Johannesburg in 1928 to become a teacher. He was a leading figure in the Springbok Legion, a South African movement of anti-fascist World War II veterans open to all races and genders. This was where he met ANC members such as Joe Slovo, Wolfie Kodesh, Jack Hodgson and Rusty Bernstein, all former servicemen. Williams joined the Congress of Democrats (the ANC's white wing) and the Communist Party, and was recruited into the ANC's armed wing, Umkhonto we Sizwe (MK).

Williams and Mandela spent a lot of time driving together and Mandela became very fond of the intelligent, soft-spoken man. But his role in Mandela's life was unknown outside a small group of MK insiders, even though Williams was well known in progressive social circles in Johannesburg. Sir Laurence Olivier is even said to have attended one of Williams's famous racially mixed parties.

His name came up again in 1995 when Albie Sachs, a judge on South Africa's Constitutional Court and former activist, paid tribute to Williams at a rally. As a result the South African author and gay rights activist Mark Gevisser began researching his life, which led to a film, *The Man Who Drove With Mandela*, directed by Greta Schiller and starring Corin Redgrave as Williams.

Williams was arrested with Mandela on 5 August 1962 and after his release returned to Britain. He died in 1979.

in the ANC who tipped him off about Mandela's movements, and this information was, in turn, relayed to the South African security police. In *Rogue State: a Guide to the World's Only Superpower* (2000), William Blum told how at a farewell party for Rickard in 1963, given by the infamous mercenary Colonel "Mad Mike" Hoare, Rickard had drunk too much and told those present the same story. Then in 1990 *The Atlanta Journal* reported that a retired, unnamed US intelligence officer claimed that a senior CIA officer, Paul Eckel, had told him within hours of Mandela's arrest: "We have turned Mandela over to the South African security branch. We gave them every detail, what he would be wearing, the time of day, just where he would be. They have picked him up. It is one of our greatest coups." A South African security police officer who had successfully infiltrated the Communist Party at the time, Gerard Ludi, confirmed in 1964 that he knew that the CIA had an agent inside the Natal ANC. The agency has always refused to comment on the issue.

Ahmed Kathrada, Mandela's friend and MK comrade, had an alternative view: he believed **British intelligence officers** could have been the informants. Two British officials were present when Mandela's plane from Dar es Salaam landed at Lobatse airport in Bechuanaland, and they could easily have had him followed and passed on information about him, Williams and the car they were travelling in. Other ANC activists suspected that **Bruno Mtolo** – a Durban trade unionist, communist insider and an MK saboteur – was either an agent for the security police or for a foreign intelligence agency, and may well have been the culprit. A heavy drinker, Mtolo was also present at Mandela's last meeting in Durban and later gave damning evidence against him in court.

A few days after Mandela's arrest, the Johannesburg *Sunday Times* ran the headline "Mandela was betrayed: Reds suspected". The report talked about a "fantastic story of intrigue and double-crossing", but didn't name the informant beyond saying he was believed to be a senior ANC figure and a communist "making a bid to control the underground ANC". In his 1981 book *Inside BOSS: South Africa's Secret Police*, Gordon Winter, a rogue member of the Bureau of State Security, claimed that the reward for information leading to Mandela's arrest had been claimed, but didn't reveal by whom.

Mandela has never liked to discuss who betrayed him, simply stating that it was part of history. But he did acknowledge that, in hindsight, he had been "imprudent" about his security. That would be putting it mildly. He consistently drove to distraction the small group tasked with his movements and security. His behaviour and utterances during his time on the run suggest that he was caught up in the romance of being a daring **revolutionary**, not unlike two of his heroes, Fidel Castro and Che Guevara, who had overthrown the Cuban government three years earlier. He wore the military fatigues he got in Ethiopia all the way from Addis Ababa to Lobatse to Liliesleaf, and again on the trip to Durban, with his handgun strapped to his belt. There were even whispers in ANC circles at the time that he actually wanted to be caught and use the court, his favourite public arena, to popularize his and the ANC's cause nationally and internationally.

When Mandela was charged, with Walter Sisulu, with inciting workers to strike illegally, he decided to represent himself "to enhance

The Old Fort Prison in Johannesburg. (© Roger de la Harpe/Corbis)

the symbolism of my role". He was also charged with leaving the country illegally. Once again, he recorded that the white policemen, prosecutors, magistrate and other officials treated him civilly and with dignity. While awaiting trial in the **Old Fort**, he was allowed food from outside and weekly visits from Winnie – the guards even turned their faces away when the two embraced.

Mandela's second in command at MK, Joe Slovo, acted as Mandela's legal adviser and immediately came up with a plan for Mandela to escape. It was a good plan: the policeman in charge of the courtroom cells (a friend of MK member Joe Modise) would let Mandela out during a court adjournment. But Mandela didn't want to escape. He feared that a failed escape could do the ANC great harm. He gave the document with the elaborate escape proposal – a specially made wig, clothes, getaway car and all – back to Slovo with the rest of his notes and papers and asked him to destroy them. Slovo thought the documents might later have significant historical value and kept them – he was correct, but unfortunately not in the way he thought.

On trial again

The trial started on 13 October 1962 in the **Old Synagogue** in Pretoria. It was political theatre such as South Africa had seldom seen before. Outside the courtroom a traditional *imbongi* (praise singer) danced and sang of Madiba and his clan. Despite a government ban on meetings or demonstrations about the arrests, a few hundred people did make it to court. Winnie arrived in a long, traditional Xhosa skirt and beaded headdress. Then Mandela emerged from the holding cell. No smart double-breasted suit this time. He was dressed in a leopard-skin *kaross* or cape with a bare shoulder with beads around his neck and arms, the traditional ceremonial dress of a **Xhosa chief**.

He caught everyone by surprise. After a stunned silence, the ANC supporters rose and shouted "Amandla! Ngawethu!" (Power to the people!). Mandela smiled and returned the salute with a clenched fist. His old flatmate Wolfie Kodesh said later: "It was amazing. He's this tall, big, athletic man ... and he was half naked. It was incredible, because as he came up, there was a complete hush. It was his tactic to look straight at the magistrate. Even the policemen, I honestly think they went pale, to see this huge man standing there in his national costume." The white magistrate, **J. van Heerden**, was so transfixed he "couldn't find his voice".

Realizing the impact and symbolism of Mandela's *kaross*, court officials tried to confiscate it and force him to wear a suit. Mandela was adamant: they had no jurisdiction over his clothes and he would fight them in the highest court over the issue. The officials relented, but forced him to wear Western clothes on the way from his prison cell to court and back. Mandela asked permission to address the court before he entered a plea. Typical of his approach, he first assured the magistrate that his words were not aimed at him personally because he didn't doubt van Heerden's "sense of fairness and justice". Mandela then asked the magistrate to recuse himself (ie stand

Mandela in Xhosa dress. (Apic/ Getty Images)

down on the grounds of conflict of interest), claiming that it was "improper and against the elementary principles of justice to entrust whites with cases involving the denial by them of basic human rights to the African people".

Mandela's petition was denied and the state called the first of sixty witnesses to prove that Mandela had engaged in mobilizing people to strike and that he had left the country without a passport. When magistrate van Heerden was seen driving in a car with a security policeman during a lunchbreak, Mandela again asked for van Heerden's recusal – but only after sending him a private note warning him of this move and assuring him, again, that it wasn't personal. Van Heerden, who referred to the accused throughout the proceedings as Mr Mandela, again denied his request.

After the state closed its case, Mandela surprised everyone by not calling a single witness. He simply stated that he was not guilty of any crime. Van Heerden: "Is that all you have to say?" Mandela: "Your Worship, with respect, if I had something to say I would have said it." The trial was adjourned to 7 November for Mandela to prepare his plea in mitigation of sentence. Just before the court resumed on 7 November, the young white prosecutor, P.J. Bosch, asked to meet with Mandela privately. Bosch took Mandela's hand and with tears welling up in his eyes told him how it pained him to be forced to ask the court for a prison sentence. Mandela's legal adviser and friend Bob Hepple was a witness to this incident.

Mandela speaks

And then Mandela took the stage. Not to make a plea in mitigation, but rather a powerful hour-long **political statement**. It was one that reverberated around the world. Not so much in South Africa, where newspaper editors were afraid of the repercussions if his statement were given too much publicity, but certainly in the rest of Africa and the Western world.

Mandela declared the laws of the apartheid government were "immoral, unjust and intolerable" and black people's consciences "dictate that we must protest against it, that we must oppose it and that we must attempt to alter it". The ANC had always sought peaceful solutions and on many occasions tried to engage the government, who decided "not to heed us, nor to talk to us, but rather to present us as wild, dangerous revolutionaries, intent on disorder and riot, incapable of being dealt with in any way save by mustering an overwhelming force against us and the implementation of every possible forcible means, legal and illegal, to suppress us". The apartheid regime, he continued,

> **"Whatever sentence Your Worship sees fit to impose upon me for the crime for which I have been convicted before this court, may it rest assured that when my sentence has been completed, I will still be moved, as men are always moved, by their consciences."**
>
> Nelson Mandela in his statement before sentencing, Pretoria 1962

"behaved in a way no civilised government should dare behave when faced with a peaceful, disciplined, sensible and democratic expression of the views of its own population".

Mandela accused the government of "setting the scene for violence" by employing violence in response to citizens' demands. He issued a grave warning that the dispute between the white government and black South Africans would finish up by being settled violently and by force. "Already there are indications in this country that people, my people, Africans, are turning to deliberate acts of violence and of force against the government in order to persuade the government, in the only language which this government shows, by its own behaviour, that it understands."

South Africa had never witnessed anything like this before; no black man had dissected and indicted the white minority government and the apartheid system so profoundly, reasonably and eloquently – or, indeed, publicly. He may have been an amateur when it came to underground military organization, but here in the Old Synagogue in Pretoria in 1962 he showed that he was a formidable and charismatic political leader of a stature never before witnessed in South Africa. Apartheid's supporters had every reason to be afraid of him.

Sentenced

It was almost an anticlimax when magistrate van Heerden sentenced him to three years in jail for incitement and two years for travelling outside the country without a valid passport. He had shown no remorse and there would be no possibility of parole. It was a **heavy sentence** for these crimes. Mandela turned to the public gallery and shouted with clenched fist held high: "Amandla!" The people, many in tears, responded by singing the hymn "Nkosi Sikelel' iAfrika" (God bless Africa), the anthem of the ANC and, later, of the whole country.

Mandela was allowed to say goodbye to Winnie in the cells below the court before he was taken away. There were no tears, no clinging to each other; he gave her advice – almost like a father figure – on how to conduct herself in his absence, and gave her a letter of love and encouragement written earlier. Winnie cherished this letter in her days without him, but the police later seized it in one of their raids on her house and it was never returned. The two had only been married for four years, of which less than half were spent together at home – the rest of the time he was either on the run or in detention. Although they did not know this on 7 November 1962, they were going to spend even less time together during the next 27 years.

This was also the beginning of a new life for Winnie Mandela as a public political figure: she was the Mandela not in jail, who still had a voice. After her husband's incarceration, she told the magazine *New Age*: "The greatest honour a people can pay a man behind bars is to keep the freedom flame burning, to continue the fight. My husband correctly said suffering in jail is nothing compared to suffering outside jail. Our people suffer inside and outside of the jails. But suffering is not enough. We must struggle."

Winnie was 26 years old when her husband went to jail. But at the time, she and Mandela – and the rest of the suddenly rather rudderless ANC – thought it was only going to be five years. There was a strange sense of optimism in the ANC and MK that having Mandela in jail would hasten "the revolution"; some even thought that the country would be free before 1967 when his time in jail would be up.

Walter Sisulu was also found guilty of incitement and received an even heavier sentence: six years in jail. But unlike Mandela, he lodged an appeal and was released on bail. He was put under house arrest but a few weeks later disappeared and went underground.

Convicted prisoner

Mandela was back in a cell in **Pretoria Central**, now as a convicted prisoner. He was given the standard prison outfit for black prisoners: short khaki pants, a tunic, a jersey and rubber sandals. Mandela refused to wear the shorts and also refused his first meal of cold maize porridge. The commander of the prison, **Colonel Jacobs**, offered him a compromise: he could have his own special meals and wear long trousers, but would be kept in solitary confinement with just thirty minutes per day for exercise. Mandela accepted, but after a few weeks decided that short pants and inedible food were preferable. Back with the other prisoners, he found himself sitting with his PAC counterpart, **Robert Sobukwe**. The two enjoyed each other's company, engaging in intellectual debate and even arguing about English literature.

Seven months later, in May 1963, Mandela was unexpectedly told to pack his meagre belongings and make ready to move. Chained to three other ANC prisoners, he was bundled into a closed prison van and driven through the night. When ordered out, the prisoners found themselves in the **Table Bay Docks** of Cape Town. According to some accounts, as the men walked down into the hold of a ferry, warders urinated on them from the quay, but Mandela has never referred to such an incident. The ferry then left for a twenty-minute trip across choppy waters before docking at an island in the bay about 12km from Cape Town. As the prisoners walked onto the quayside, they were met with shouts from prisoner warders: "Dis die Eiland! Hier gaan julle vrek!" (This is the island! Here you're going to die!). This was **Robben Island**, South Africa's Alcatraz, where most political prisoners after 1962 were kept.

Mandela stood his ground right from the start. When he contradicted a warder and the man threatened him, he coolly stated that if the warder touched him, he would take the man to court. After this the authorities treated him with reluctant respect. Mandela was in a large cell with the other ANC prisoners and in daytime they worked on the roads around the island. However, six weeks later, before he could adjust properly to life there, he was ordered to be returned to Pretoria. He only found out why when he arrived back at his old jail.

8 The Liliesleaf raid

"I ran for the toilet, grabbed my jacket and ran because I had notes in my pocket about where I was going to get the hand grenades made. I couldn't get to the toilet ... because the police had cut me off. They did say that I was running around like a headless chicken."

Denis Goldberg, recalling the Liliesleaf raid

The zealous revolutionaries in MK did not sit idle after Mandela had left South Africa for his trip in January 1962; the jailing of their commander-in-chief spurred them on to greater action. Sporadic acts of sabotage continued and more recruits were sent out of the country for military training abroad. In Port Elizabeth, **Govan Mbeki**, the head of a sabotage cell and a senior communist, emerged as a central figure. Alongside MK chief of staff **Joe Slovo** and a few others, Mbeki was one of the main planners of future violent onslaughts on the apartheid state. While under house arrest, following five months in jail in 1962, Mbeki decided to go underground and moved to MK's High Command Headquarters at **Liliesleaf farm** in Rivonia. Mbeki was an abrasive man and the most rigid ideologue of them all – he even tried to force the others at Liliesleaf into an ascetic routine which included no alcohol. He and Mandela never got on well, not even in later life.

Operation Mayibuye

Slovo, Mbeki and Arthur Goldreich started working on an ambitious plan of action and drew up a six page proposal for what they called **Operation Mayibuye**. "It can now be truly said," the document read, "that very little, if any, scope exists for the smashing of white supremacy other than by means of mass revolutionary action, the main content of which is armed resistance leading to victory by military means." The authors declared their belief that most people were convinced "that no mass struggle which is not backed up by armed resistance and military offensive can hope to make a real impact". They didn't think a general uprising of the people leading to a military solution was likely. "Rather, as in Cuba, the general uprising must be sparked off by organised and well-prepared **guerrilla operations** during the course of which the masses of the people will be drawn in and armed." The document said the large number of trained MK soldiers, "the guerrilla army", would return to South Africa by air and sea and would be joined by at least seven thousand recruits inside the country during the "initial onslaught".

> "We have no illusions about the difficulties which face us in launching and successfully prosecuting guerrilla operations leading to military victory. Nor do we assume that such a struggle will be over swiftly."
>
> Operation Mayibuye document

Denis Goldberg, a leader of the Communist Party and the Congress of Democrats, was in charge of the manufacturing of arms and ammunition at Travallyn, a farm near Krugersdorp, 40km west of Johannesburg. Goldberg didn't think small: he planned to make 48,000 landmines, 210 hand grenades and 1500 bomb timers, among other things. There were also plans to store a million aspirin tablets. The rifles, handguns and ammunition would have to

THE MYSTERY OF THE MISSING MAKAROV

Did Nelson Mandela, as he remembers it, bury the **Makarov pistol**, given him by his Ethiopian military instructor in 1962, in the gardens of Liliesleaf farm, or is he mistaken?

The farm in Rivonia, outside Johannesburg, is where Mandela stayed under the alias David Motsamayi while he was on the run from the police. In 2001 it was bought by the Liliesleaf Trust and turned into a museum. Back when the South African police raided the farm in 1963, Rivonia was a semi-rural area of smallholdings and dirt roads; today it is a completely built-up, wealthy suburb.

In 2006 Mandela told **Michael Wolpe**, head of the trust and son of one of Mandela co-defendants at the Rivonia Trial, that he had buried the pistol on the farm "about fifty paces from the kitchen". He later said he had buried it near an **oak tree**. Wolpe instructed archaeologists to search for the pistol, and large sections of the garden were dug up, and a neighbouring building even demolished. Metal detectors were used to scan the entire property. All to no avail. To make things even more confusing, it was established that there had never been any oak trees at the farm. Wolpe appealed through the media to anyone who might have found the pistol in the years before the trust bought Liliesleaf to come forward.

In April 2011 a neighbouring house on what was once Liliesleaf was put up for auction. Wolpe felt there was a possibility that the pistol was buried where the house was later built, but was not allowed to dig on the property. The Johannesburg *Sunday Times* reported in April 2011 that, because of its great historic and symbolic value, the estimated value of the pistol was now R22 million (about 3.5 million US dollars).

Many of Mandela's old comrades think he is mistaken, however, and that he may have confused different incidents. According to his own version of events he stuffed the pistol and his notebook in between the seats of the car when he was stopped by police and arrested outside Durban on 5 August 1962. This was also the version of **Cecil Williams**, the man who owned the car and who was driving with him at the time. The police took away the car, a black Austin Westminster with brown leather seats, and claimed never to have found either pistol or notebook. Williams never got the car back and left for England shortly afterwards.

"There's no pistol on Liliesleaf," says **Ronnie Kasrils**, a founder member of the ANC's armed wing and later a minister in Mandela's cabinet, "it's just a story."

come from outside the country. In hindsight, this was pure Walter Mitty stuff – even some of the insiders thought so. Bram Fischer later called it "an entirely unrealistic brainchild of some youthful and adventurous imagination. If ever there was a plan which a Marxist could not approve in the prevailing circumstances, this was such a one ... if any part of it at all could be put into operation, it could achieve nothing but disaster." Rusty Bernstein offered his own proposal of a more measured progression to armed conflict and of occasional raids from across the borders.

The proposal for Operation Mayibuye was formally put to members of MK's High Command in April 1963 and debated heatedly at several meetings at Liliesleaf. Slovo, Mbeki and some of those who had trained in China pushed the plan hard; others were very sceptical. "It was causing much debate and consternation among some of us" was Kathrada's verdict, and there are still different opinions as to whether Operation Mayibuye was official MK policy or not. In the first week of June, Slovo slipped out of the country in order to brief Oliver Tambo in London about Mayibuye and to make contacts in other African countries. He wouldn't return to South Africa for twenty-seven years.

Lax security

The fact that more than a dozen leaders of MK's High Command visited Liliesleaf undetected for months is an indication of how unsophisticated the **security police** of the 1960s were. All the people who arrived almost daily for meetings of either the Communist Party or MK (or both) were well known communists and no strangers to the police. These were Slovo, Kathrada, Sisulu, Mbeki, Denis Goldberg, Fischer, Bob Hepple, Harold Wolpe, Ruth First, Rusty Bernstein and Arthur Goldreich, the last of whom lived there. A number of MK recruits visited regularly. Bernstein and Kathrada were among those deeply concerned about the lack of security, Bernstein in particular "began to sense that, in the top MK echelons, there was a growing gung-ho spirit of recklessness… It was not shared by those of us who still lived and moved about in fear in the real world outside the fence."

The police were not even aware that there was such a place as MK Headquarters. They were concentrating their efforts on finding out where Walter Sisulu was hiding. On 19 June they detained his wife Albertina and his seventeen-year-old son Max, putting extreme pressure on them to betray his whereabouts. They knew for sure Walter hadn't left the country because on 26 June 1963 he had spoken during a broadcast of "Radio Liberation", via an illegal transmitter erected in a suburban back garden. "Sons and daughters of Africa", he had declared, "I speak to you from somewhere in South Africa. I have not left the country. I do not plan to leave. Many of our leaders of the African National Congress have gone underground. This is to keep our organisation in action, to preserve the leadership, to keep the freedom fight going."

Two days earlier the police had captured several **MK operatives** and put pressure on them to reveal Sisulu's hiding place. All these detainees had been frequent visitors to the Rivonia farm. The men at MK High Command knew this and finally realized that Liliesleaf was no longer a safe place. They decided to leave the farm after their last meeting on 6 July, but then agreed to another and, at Sisulu's insistence, scheduled their last meeting on the farm for 3pm on Thursday 11 July. It was not a good decision.

The raid

At 2pm on the day, a dentist cousin of Goldreich, who had been asked to improve Sisulu's disguise by making a false plate for his mouth, arrived at the farm. He seemed nervous and unduly curious and asked Kathrada if there was going to be "much bloodshed" in South Africa. The meeting itself, involving High

Command members Sisulu, Govan Mbeki, Raymond Mhlaba, Ahmed Kathrada, Rusty Bernstein and Denis Goldberg, with MK member Bob Hepple also in attendance, got underway at about 3.15pm. As it did so, a **delivery van** bearing the name of a well-known Johannesburg dry-cleaning company, Trade Steam Pressers, turned into the road that led to the Liliesleaf homestead. Two men in white dust coats were sitting in front and a rug screened the back of the van. A black guard employed by the Goldreichs told them to turn back. The driver said they were merely calling to see if they couldn't pick up new customers in the area. The men in the meeting saw the van approaching but ignored it; deliveries to the

A police photo of the living room at Liliesleaf shortly after the raid. Lieutenant van Wyck is on the far right, Warrant Officer Dirker is seated in the centre and Arthur Goldreich sits dejectedly on the far left. (Historic Papers, University of the Witwatersrand)

Goldreichs who were living on the farm were not unusual. Instead, according to Kathrada, the meeting remained focused "on the merits and demerits of the grand plans".

The farm guard insisted that the van must leave the property, and the driver reversed as if to turn around. Suddenly an Afrikaans voice shouted from behind the driver: "Slaan toe!" (pounce). It was the voice of Lieutenant **Willie van Wyk** of the South African Police. At which point ten policemen poured out, one with a police dog on a leash. Kathrada relates that the MK members were "electrified with shock".

Mbeki quickly stuffed the documents relating to Operation Mayibuye into an unlit coal stove. Mbeki, Kathrada and Sisulu then jumped through a window, but were confronted by policemen, one with a growling dog on a leash. According to his biographer and daughter-in-law, Elinor Sisulu, Sisulu asked the policeman as he was being handcuffed: "How are my wife and my son?" The policeman answered: "You ask about your wife and son now. You should have thought about them before you started all this." The police didn't recognize Kathrada, who had dyed his hair red and grown a big moustache to disguise himself as a Portuguese-speaker with the name Pedro Pereira. "Who is this white man?" one of the policeman asked. But as soon as Kathrada spoke, Lieutenant van Wyk and Warrant Officer **C.J. Dirker** recognized him. More policemen had appeared by this time. Arthur Goldreich, who was late for the meeting, now arrived back at the farm. When he saw the police cars and tried to turn around, he was stopped at gunpoint.

Kathrada wasn't the only person the police had difficulty recognizing: Sisulu had straightened hair and a Hitler moustache, Mbeki looked like a farm labourer with a boiler suit and balaclava, and the previously clean-shaven Goldreich had a full black beard and moustache. The police were totally surprised by their catch: eight men, six of them among the most wanted in South Africa; almost the entire High Command of MK. Willie van Wyk phoned his superiors to tell them: "We have hit the jackpot." It was the biggest single blow the security police had ever struck against the liberation movement. Only one big fish was missing: Joe Slovo. The biggest MK fish, Nelson Mandela, was already in jail. Acting on the evidence found at Rivonia, four other MK men were arrested within days: Harold Wolpe, Elias Motsoaledi and Andrew Mlangeni. Wolpe's brother-in-law and law partner, James Kantor, who had no links with MK, was also arrested.

Incriminating evidence

The Travallyn arms "factory" and the cottage where Kathrada had been hiding out were also raided. The Operation Mayibuye document was recovered from the stove, and dozens of other papers regarding recruitment, training, contacts with the Soviet Union and China, and bomb manufacturing were found. These included more than a hundred maps of **potential sabotage targets** such as government buildings, electricity pylons and railway lines. Most of these documents implicated Mandela; some were in his own handwriting. Diaries from his tour of Africa and his military training in Ethiopia, books on guerrilla warfare and notes and letters to Winnie were also discovered. This was despite the fact that he'd had repeated assurances from, among others, Joe Slovo and Rusty Bernstein that incriminating material had been destroyed.

It was the discovery of his link to Liliesleaf that prompted the police to order Mandela to be brought back to Pretoria from Robben Island shortly after the Rivonia raid. **John Vorster**, the Minister of Justice, said the "wealth of information that was captured in the Rivonia raid will considerably ease the task of the police in running to ground all internal subversive organisations". The head of the Security Branch, the notorious **Hendrik van den Bergh**, said the underground resistance was finally smashed. This was not far from the truth. Van den Bergh arrived at Liliesleaf later in the day. He told Goldreich that his men were true professionals. "The trouble with you, Goldreich, the trouble with all of you is that you are amateurs. You always have and you always will underestimate your enemy and that's why you're in shit." That wasn't far from the truth either.

The gloating security police said at the time that the Rivonia raid was the result of weeks of patient searching and reconnaissance. This was untrue. They were just lucky. In 1964 H.H.W. de Villiers, a judge of the Supreme Court, wrote in his book *Rivonia – Operation Mayibuye* that the policemen in the dry-cleaner's van were not even sure what Liliesleaf was. Discussing the moment the farm guard stopped the van, he writes: "This was the time for decision – whether to withdraw on the employee's peremptory instructions to leave because the master was not at home and tradesmen were not permitted to call there, or openly and immediately to test the police suspicion that there was more to Liliesleaf than met the eye." He added, "From the police point of view, this raid provided unexpected results".

James Kantor had heard that an MK man, detained on 24 June, had told the police that Sisulu was hiding out on a farm somewhere in Rivonia, and got paid R3000 for it. Teams of security policemen were driving around Rivonia for two weeks before they decided that the thatched cottage at Liliesleaf looked the most likely location. They didn't expect to find more than Sisulu's hideout. Another theory was that George Mellis, a young boy who lived on a neighbouring farm and often visited the Goldreich children, had told one of the police patrols that the people at Liliesleaf acted suspiciously.

The arrested men were held in **solitary confinement** with no access to family or lawyers, under the terms of the new General Law Amendment Act of 1963, the so-called **90-day Detention Act**. The black detainees were held in Pretoria Local prison and the whites in police cells at Marshall Square in Johannesburg. It was here that Harold Wolpe and Arthur Goldreich bribed Johannes Greef, a young warder with financial troubles, to help them escape.

Disguised as priests, the pair fled to Swaziland and from there flew to Bechuanaland. South African agents blew up the plane sent to fetch them from Francistown, but eventually they succeeded in flying out to Dar es Salaam.

After three months in confinement, the detainees were formally charged and were allowed, as prisoners awaiting trial, to be held in communal cells and receive visitors. The government decided not to stage the trial in the Johannesburg Supreme Court, as would have been normal practice, but to move it to the **Palace of Justice** in Pretoria. They were preparing for courtroom theatre of their own.

9 Rivonia trial

"We have no illusion about its outcome, whatever happens to us the history is on the side of the oppressed people. I am suggesting that you may expect anything. The state has a very strong case."

Walter Sisulu, in a letter to his son Max from prison, 1963

The political atmosphere in the country was highly charged after the **Rivonia arrests** and the government spent considerable energy whipping up "black communist terrorist" fears among its white supporters. The trial would be held without a jury, since the system had by then all but disappeared from the South African legal system. With the death penalty a possible outcome of the trial, the accused knew they had to get the best possible legal team together to defend them. But finding an attorney (solicitor) to take on the case was proving hard, with several lawyers suddenly finding themselves too busy to help.

Although he was about to emigrate to Australia, attorney **Joel Joffe** agreed to act for all the accused – except for James Kantor, who had organized his own counsel – and set about assembling a team of advocates (barristers). Top of Joffe's list was **Bram Fischer, QC**, the most prominent progressive advocate in South Africa. Joffe had no way of knowing that Fischer was, in fact, a senior Communist Party leader and deeply involved in the ANC's underground activities. While keen to assist his comrades, Fischer didn't want to be on the actual defence team as he knew there was a risk that he could be exposed as a co-

The Rivonia triallists. Top row (l to r): Nelson Mandela, Walter Sisulu, Govan Mbeki, Raymond Mhlaba. Bottom row (l to r): Elias Motsoaledi, Andrew Mlangeni, Ahmed Kathrada, Denis Goldberg. (UWCRIM Mayibuye/Link)

conspirator during the proceedings – he suspected that some of the documents found at Liliesleaf mentioned him or carried his signature. Joffe had secured the services of two young advocates, **George Bizos** and **Arthur Chaskalson**, who both insisted that Fischer be their team leader. After adding the bright advocate **Vernon Berrangé** to the team, Fischer finally agreed.

The security police were consistently uncooperative and did not even inform Joffe where his clients were held, nor that they were going to be charged on 7 October 1963. The following day the defence team met with ten of the eleven accused in an interview room in **Pretoria Local** prison. While discussions were taking place, a door opened and Nelson Mandela shuffled into the room wearing his khaki prison clothes and leg-irons. "It was a most extraordinary experience," Joffe remembers, "he came in and they all fell on him and hugged him. They were so pleased to see him." Most of his comrades hadn't seen him since his trial a year earlier, and some not since before his arrest in August 1962. Mandela was pale and hollow-cheeked with bags under his eyes; he'd only found out the previous day that he was going to be charged a second time. According to Joffe, Mandela immediately took command: "You could see the charisma and immense authority this man exuded."

The trial begins

On 9 October the men were driven in an armed convoy to the Supreme Court, housed in the imposing **Palace of Justice** building on Church Square in Pretoria. The square was full of symbols of Afrikaner nationalism: a huge statue of the Boer president, Paul Kruger, stood at its centre, in front of the Raadzaal, the old assembly building of the Transvaal Boer Republic parliament.

Mandela was the first to emerge from the cells below the court. He had lost so much weight and his face was so sallow that it took a few seconds for those in the public gallery to recognize him. But when he smiled and raised a clenched fist, they knew Mandela was back. He was still in his khaki prison uniform. "He was usually so elegant, such a snappy dresser, and they set out to humiliate him in his clothes," says co-accused Denis Goldberg, "but held himself so ramrod straight, so dignified." While they stood in the dock, Goldberg slipped him a small slab of chocolate that Mandela devoured on the spot.

THE JEWISH COMRADES

A striking feature of the first few years of **Umkhonto we Sizwe** (MK), the ANC's armed wing, was the prominent role played by South Africans from the country's tiny **Jewish community**. Many of them came from families that had been victims of the **Eastern European pogroms**, such as Joe Slovo, a lawyer born in Lithuania, who was MK's first Chief of Staff. Other prominent figures were the engineer Denis Goldberg, who worked as a weapons maker for MK; Latvian-born academic Ben Turok, who was jailed after being caught with an incendiary bomb; architect Rusty Bernstein, who helped to draft the Freedom Charter; the abstract painter Arthur Goldreich, who lived at Liliesleaf; script writer Ronnie Kasrils, a regional commander of MK; journalist Wolfie Kodesh, who organized Mandela's safe houses; the lawyers Harold Wolpe, named as a co-conspiritor at the Rivonia Trail, and Bob Hepple, who was arrested at Liliesleaf. Soon after the **Liliesleaf raid**, nearly all of the above left South Africa for the UK. The exceptions were Goldberg, who spent twenty-two years in jail, and Goldreich who moved to Israel.

Presiding over the court was the most senior judge in the province, **Quartus de Wet**. The state prosecutor was **Percy Yutar**, a small man with a high-pitched voice. Proud of his Jewish identity and highly ambitious, Yutar made his hatred of Jewish communists very clear. He later became the first Jewish attorney general of South Africa. Joffe thought him a "monster" and "an appalling little man", and he was referred to by the accused as the "Percy-cutor".

The indictment, which the defence hadn't seen before Yutar read it out, charged the accused not with treason, as was expected, but under the wide-ranging **Suppression of Communism Act** and the **Sabotage Act**. This way the onus of proof was less severe, and the Sabotage Act made provision for the death penalty. The indictment named 24 co-conspirators who had not been arrested, including Joe Slovo, Harold Wolpe, Michael Harmel, Jack Hodgson and Oliver Tambo, all in exile in Britain; Arthur Goldreich, in exile in Israel; and Moses Kotane, in exile in Tanzania. The court was adjourned for three weeks.

From the start of the trial, Mandela made himself part of the defence team. It was decided that the defence would not contest evidence known to be true but would concentrate on explaining the actions and motivations of the accused to the rest of the country. Mandela was planning a show trial of his own, using the court as a platform from which the ANC could state its case unhindered to a national and international audience.

Goldberg remembers Mandela lecturing him on strategy: "Denis, when you talk Marxism you must talk about South Africa. Don't come with all the theories of feudalism and the development of classes in Europe, because our people don't understand these things, it is not part of our discipline."

On 29 October the men were back in court, Mandela already looking healthier from the food brought from outside prison. This time the gallery was packed with friends and family of the accused. Mandela raised his clenched fist and shouted a powerful "Amandla!" and got the customary "Ngawethu!" back. Neither Bob Hepple nor James Kantor went along with this routine, making the point that they were in a different position from their co-defendants.

Fischer then proceeded to shred Yutar's indictment to pieces. Mandela was charged with acts of sabotage that took place while he was safely in jail, he told Mr Justice de Wet, and the other acts of sabotage mentioned took place before the act came into power. When the judge asked Hepple, the only one who had no counsel representing him, what his reaction to the indictment was, an excited Yutar jumped up and triumphantly announced that Hepple was going to be his first witness and that the charges against him were thus withdrawn.

The public gallery was shocked and thought it was a major victory for the state, but the accused knew that it was going to happen. Hepple had already revealed that he wasn't prepared to hang for **Operation Mayibuye**, which he'd had little to do with and had always opposed as an insane plan. A few days earlier he had told Mandela that the state had offered him indemnity in exchange for his testimony. Yutar had apparently pleaded with Hepple, who was from a Jewish background, to turn against the accused and "save the Jews of South Africa". Mandela's response was that he would be "finished" if he did that, even though he knew Hepple didn't really belong among the accused. When Hepple mentioned the alternative idea of fleeing the country, Mandela agreed that this would be a better outcome, and a little later Hepple did manage to escape over the border. Arriving in **Dar es Salaam**, he told the media that he never intended to testify against the others, and, in fact, supported their cause. He also talked about the security police's methods during his detention: on one occasion they had made him stand on the same spot for three days, and on another a police officer had played Russian roulette with him.

Back in the Supreme Court an irritated Mr Justice de Wet rejected Yutar's indictment, which meant that there were no charges to answer. But the moment the judge disappeared from the court, the notorious Captain Theunis Swanepoel rushed to the dock and, thumping each of the accused on the shoulder, declared: "I arrest you on a charge of sabotage." The men were then taken back down to the cells and from there returned to jail.

The main charge

The Rivonia Trial proper started on 3 December 1963. Mandela was **Accused Number One** and had to enter his plea first. His words sent a ripple of whispers through the court: "The government should be in the dock, not me. I plead not guilty."

Accused Number Two was **Walter Sisulu**: "It is the government which is guilty, not me." The judge sternly warned he wasn't going to tolerate political speeches, only a plea of guilty or not guilty. Sisulu was unfazed: "It is the government which is responsible for what is happening in the country. I plead not guilty." This was ech-oed by the other accused, with Kantor the only exception, saying, "I am not guilty, My Lord."

Yutar's trump card was the document proposing Operation Mayibuye. The accused had planned to immerse South Africa in chaos and turmoil and to deploy thousands of trained guerrillas who would be joined by even more locals, he said. "Their combined opera-tions were planned to lead to confusion, violent insurrection and rebellion, followed at the appropriate juncture by armed invasion of the country by military units of foreign powers. In the midst of the resulting chaos, turmoil and disorder it was planned by the accused to set up a revolutionary government to take over the administration and control of this country."

Fischer and his colleagues were shaken. If the prosecution could prove all this, surely the main conspirators would face the **death penalty**. Over the next months, Yutar presented hundreds of documents, notes, diaries, maps and books found at Liliesleaf and Travallyn. Dozens of these implicated Mandela, who had absolutely no part in the planning of Operation Mayibuye, with many in his own handwriting or carrying his signature. It included his notes on his own and others' military training – and the notes on his planned escape during his previous trial, which he had given to Slovo with the request that they be destroyed.

The careless handling of Mandela's papers has always been a sensi-tive issue with the MK commanders and ANC leaders and there has been a lot of whispering over the decades about who was responsible. Mandela repeatedly asked his colleagues whether his documents had been destroyed, and they assured him that they had. Just before he was sentenced in 1962, he specifically asked Walter Sisulu to make sure this had been done.

It is known that Slovo decided not to destroy the escape notes because they could have future historical significance. It is also known that Arthur Goldreich had discovered a bunch of Mandela's papers at Liliesleaf and agreed with Ruth First, Slovo's wife and herself a senior communist, that these should not be destroyed but saved for posterity. The police found all of these. Other comrades were equally careless, and had all Mandela's papers been destroyed as requested, the state would have had a very weak case against him. Sisulu said later: "Nelson felt that the fact that he was linked to the whole business was because we were responsible for not taking appropriate steps."

Yutar called a total of 173 witnesses, starting with the labourers and domestic workers at Liliesleaf. His star witness was Mr X, **Bruno Mtolo**, a member of MK's Natal command who had planted several bombs on behalf of MK. Mtolo had met Mandela in Durban just before the latter's arrest, and he had been to Liliesleaf for meetings with Mbeki, Kathrada and Sisulu. He turned against his comrades immediately after his arrest, claiming to be disillusioned with MK's leadership because they were living in luxury while ordinary members didn't even get paid. Mtolo clearly relished his star role in court and boasted about his eloquence and good memory. "Dr Yutar said that in all his years of practice he had never come across any person, not even a European, with a memory like mine," he said later. After the trial, Mtolo wrote his autobiography, *The Road to the Left*. In it he gave a detailed account of the first five years of MK, painting its leadership as arrogant, self-serving, corrupt and pawns of white communists, but not including Mandela in his hatchet job. Mtolo singled out Walter Sisulu for much of his scorn, calling him a power-drunk fat cat and making pejorative remarks about his light complexion.

The other witness who inflicted serious damage to the defendants' case was **Patrick Mthembu**, an MK commander and regional ANC leader who was trained in China. He blamed much of his own MK activities on Elias Motsoaledi, but also implicated most of the accused with testimony about his personal contact with them and about the MK sabotage campaign.

Winnie Mandela with fist clenched leaving the Palace of Justice at the time of the Rivonia Trial. (OFF/AFP/Getty Images)

The state's last witness was Warrant Officer **Carl Dirker**, an old acquaintance of several of the accused. To make the state's case stronger, Dirker embellished the facts by stating, for example, that the Operation Mayibuye document was on the table at Liliesleaf when the police arrived, thus implying that it had just been discussed and that all those arrested were members of MK's High Command. Vernon Berrangé's brilliant cross-examination destroyed much of this hardened policeman's evidence; Dirker fell into virtually every trap the advocate set for him. He admitted that a judge in a previous case had labelled him a "consistently evasive" witness, and at one point even burst into tears.

By the end of the state's case, it was abundantly clear that Mandela, Sisulu and Mbeki were completely implicated, while the case against the others, especially Bernstein, was much weaker. There was no evidence that Kantor was involved in anything illegal and he was later found not guilty and released.

Mandela insisted, and his co-accused agreed, that he should start the defence case by making a statement from the dock rather than giving evidence, in which case he would be subjected to cross-examination. Such a statement carried much less legal weight than ordinary testimony and would weaken his own case, but Mandela insisted that the sentence he was facing was not as important as explaining the ANC's position to South Africa and the world: "I felt we were likely to hang no matter what we said, so we might as well say what we truly believed," Mandela wrote. He spent weeks preparing his speech and resisted all efforts by Bram Fischer to soften some of the statements. When Fischer took the speech to another senior advocate he was advised that if Mandela were to read it out in court, he would be signing his own death penalty.

The case for the defence started on 20 April 1964. Fischer stated that some concessions would be made, but that it would be denied that MK was a formal structure of the ANC; that the ANC was a tool of the Communist Party; that MK ever officially adopted Operation Mayibuye; and that there were ever any plans to involve foreign forces.

Mandela's defence speech

It was then time for Mandela to make his most famous speech, and his last public utterance for 26 years. He began by admitting that he was a founder and leader of MK and had planned the sabotage campaign. "I did not plan it in a spirit of recklessness, nor because I have any love of violence. I planned it as a result of a calm and sober assessment of the political situation that had arisen after many years of tyranny, exploitation and oppression of my people by whites." He went on to say that the ruthless application of apartheid laws had made violence by black South Africans inevitable and "unless responsible leadership was given to canalise and control the feelings of our people, there would be outbreaks of terrorism which would produce an intensity of bitterness and hostility between the various races of this country".

Violence was necessary because without it black people would not succeed in their struggle against apartheid, because all **non-violent strategies** had failed. "But," Mandela explained to the hushed court-room, "the violence which we chose to adopt was not terrorism. We who formed Umkhonto were all members of the African National Congress and had behind us the ANC tradition of non-violence and negotiation as a means of solving political disputes. We believed that South Africa belonged to all the people who lived in it, and not to one group, be it black or white. We did not want an interracial war and tried to avoid it to the last minute."

To the prosecution's contention that the ANC was merely an instrument of the South African Communist Party, Mandela responded that there had indeed been close cooperation between the two parties – "but cooperation is merely proof of a common goal, in this case the removal of white supremacy, and is not proof of a complete community of interests". He reminded the court that white people could not become members of the ANC itself, while the Communist Party was open to all. The ANC's goal was to gain **full political rights** for all and harmonize the different classes, while the communists emphasized class distinctions, sought the removal of capitalism and the establishment of a workers' government. He was an "African patriot" influenced by aspects of Marxism, Mandela said, but not a communist and his views differed fundamentally from some aspects of Marxist ideology.

Mandela went on to explain what the ANC and the black majority really wanted: a just share in the whole of the country, security and a stake in society. "Above all, we want equal political rights, because without them our disabilities will be permanent. I know this sounds revolutionary to the whites in this country, because the majority of voters will be Africans. This makes the white man fear democracy. But this cannot be allowed to stand in the way of the only solution which will guarantee racial harmony and freedom for all. It is not true that the enfranchisement of all will result in racial domination."

> "Political division based on colour is entirely artificial and, when it disappears, so will the domination of one colour group by another. The ANC has spent half a century fighting against racialism. When it triumphs it will not change that policy."
>
> Nelson Mandela in his statement at the Rivonia Trial

Mandela came to the end of his statement after almost five hours. "This then is what the ANC is fighting," he concluded. "It is a struggle of the African people, inspired by their own suffering and their own experience. It is a struggle for the right to live." He then put down his prepared statement, paused, looked straight at the judge, and said the words which would be recalled for decades afterwards: "During my lifetime I have dedicated myself to this struggle of the African people. I have fought against white domination, and I have fought against black domination. I have cherished the ideal of a democratic and free society in which all persons live together in harmony and with equal opportunities. It is an ideal which I hope to live for and to achieve. But if it needs be, it is an ideal for which I am prepared to die."

> "At the beginning of June 1961 ... I, and some colleagues, came to the conclusion that as violence in this country was inevitable, it would be unrealistic and wrong ... to continue preaching peace and non-violence at a time when the Government met our peaceful demands with force."
>
> Nelson Mandela in his statement at the Rivonia Trial

After he stopped speaking, there was a stunned silence in court, some say up to a minute. "There was this intense pause," recalls Joffe. "As he sat down, the court was very quiet and then a sort of sigh went up from all the black people listening." **Albertina Sisulu**, who was seated in the public gallery, recalls: "By the time he had reached the end of his address we were moved beyond words. And the women! The women were all in tears. When he said 'I am prepared to die', I did not realize that tears were pouring down my face."

It was a political speech that stands among the most powerful in modern history and it was to receive worldwide publicity.

The case continues

Sisulu was the first of the defence witnesses. Led by Fischer, he explained that the proposal for Operation Mayibuye was discussed by the MK leaders, but because there were strong differences of opinion, there was never a decision to launch into **guerrilla war-**

fare. His own opinion was that it was not a feasible option at the time. Unable to cross-examine Mandela, Yutar took all his frustrations out on Sisulu, who, he believed, would be an easy target because of his relative lack of education. Hour after hour Yutar tried to trap and trick Sisulu, but he remained unfazed. Joffe called Sisulu's performance "a triumph" and felt that the whole court was impressed by his "tremendous sincerity, calm, conviction and certainty". Kathrada, Mhlaba, Bernstein, Mbeki and Goldberg gave testimony after him, and Mlangeni and Motsoaledi made short statements.

A month after the defence launched its counter-offensive it was time for the **legal arguments**. Yutar launched a highly theatrical political attack on the defendants, accusing them of "amazing deceit". Referring to the relatively small number of card-carrying ANC members, he said, "Although they represented scarcely more than one percent of the African population, they took it upon themselves to tell the world that the Africans in South Africa are suppressed, oppressed and depressed." Fischer calmly dealt with the problem areas in the defence case, reiterating that MK was not part and parcel of the ANC; that neither organizations was a front for the Communist Party; and that Operation Mayibuye was not officially adopted by the MK High Command nor dates set for the launch of guerrilla warfare.

Two days earlier, the **United Nations Security Council** had demanded that the apartheid government release the accused and set all political prisoners free. Demonstrations in support of Mandela and his colleagues took place in Europe and the United States, and a vigil was held at St Paul's Cathedral in London. Nelson Mandela was being hailed as one of the greatest freedom fighters of the century.

The verdict

When the verdict was announced, Justice de Wet found all the accused, except one, guilty as charged. The exception was Rusty Bernstein who, nonetheless, was immediately re-arrested. Back in jail, the condemned men were preoccupied by one topic only: the likelihood that they would be sentenced to death. Considering the mood in the country and the heavy sentences meted out for lesser crimes, it was a very real possibility. The men's lawyers even briefed them on how the death penalty would be read out by the judge, and Mandela prepared a statement for such an eventuality – he was prepared to die and knew his death would be an inspiration to South Africans. Mandela, Sisulu and Mbeki decided not to appeal, even if they were given the death penalty. "Our message was that no sacrifice was too great in the struggle for freedom," Mandela said.

On 12 June the prisoners saw a great crowd assembled in Church Square as they arrived from prison. Fischer and his team offered just two witnesses in mitigation: **Alan Paton**, leader of the Liberal Party and author of the novel *Cry the Beloved Country*, and **Harold Hansen**, a senior Johannesburg advocate. Paton spoke of the men's courage and integrity and added that clemency would be in the interest of the whole country. Hansen told the judge he should remember that his own Afrikaner people had resorted to violence, rebellion and treason in their fight against British imperialism.

Sentencing

When the moment of truth arrived, the judge's first words were alarming: he wasn't convinced that they'd had such altruistic motives as they'd pretended, he said, because "people who organize a revolution usually take over the government and personal ambition cannot be excluded as a motive." The crime of which they had been convicted was essentially the crime of **high treason**, he added, but the

The defiant Rivonia triallists are driven away to begin their life sentences, 16 June 1964. (OFF/AFP/Getty Images)

state had decided not to level this charge. And then came the words that brought huge relief: "Bearing this in mind and giving the matter very serious consideration, I have decided not to impose the supreme penalty which in a case like this would usually be the proper penalty for the crime, but consistent with my duty that is the only leniency I can show. The sentence in the case of all the accused will be one of life imprisonment."

At this point Mandela turned to the gallery and flashed a huge smile at Winnie and his mother, who had attended the hearing from the beginning. When the sentence was relayed to the crowd outside, the whole Church Square reverberated with the singing of

"Nkosi Sikelel' iAfrika" and a lot of cheering and ululating. The next day *The New York Times* called Mandela and his colleagues "The George Washingtons and Ben Franklins of South Africa", while *The Times* described the South African government as the guilty party.

WHERE ARE THEY NOW?

Apart from the eight men sentenced to life imprisonment, the **Rivonia Trial** had a profound effect on the lives of the others involved in it.

The lead counsel for the accused, **Bram Fischer**, continued with his underground activities after the trial and tried to revive the High Command of MK. He was arrested in September 1964 and charged with being a member of the banned Communist Party. After skipping bail he went underground, but was re-arrested in November 1965 and sentenced to life imprisonment. After contracting cancer, he was finally released on compassionate grounds in April 1975 and died a few weeks later.

Prosecutor **Percy Yutar**'s dream of becoming South Africa's first Jewish attorney general came true in 1968, but his role in the Rivonia Trial became a source of great embarrassment after Mandela's release in 1990. In a reconciliatory gesture, Mandela later invited Yutar to lunch at the presidential residence in Pretoria. Yutar died in 2002.

After his re-arrest, **Rusty Bernstein** fled to London with his wife Hilda where he practiced as an architect. He returned to South Africa in 1994 to help with the ANC's election campaign, and at regular intervals after that. He died at his home in England in 2002. **Bob Hepple** also went into exile in England, where he eventually became a distinguished professor at Cambridge and an author of several seminal legal works. He was knighted in 2004.

Defence attorney **Joel Joffe** settled in London where he founded an insurance company and served as chairperson of Oxfam. He was awarded a CBE in 1999 and a year later became a life peer as Baron Joffe of Liddington. Defence counsel **Arthur Chaskalson** became the first President of the Constitutional Court of a democratic South Africa in 1994 and Chief Justice six years later. In 2001 he was appointed by the UN as a judge at the International Criminal Tribunal for the former Yugoslavia.

Former MK commander turned state witness **Patrick Mthembu** was assassinated not long after the trial, probably by members of MK.

On 13 July 1964 Nelson Mandela, Walter Sisulu, Govan Mbeki, Elias Motsoaledi, Andrew Mlangeni, Raymond Mhlaba and Ahmed Kathrada were flown by military aircraft to Robben Island. Denis Goldberg went to Pretoria Central Prison, since apartheid law forbade the holding of black and white prisoners within the same institution. The convicted men were now revered heroes and symbols of the resistance against apartheid, but their imprisonment was a serious setback for the struggle and devastated the ANC. After a while, the sabotage campaign simply petered out. As for the attitudes of most white South Africans, these now hardened while the apartheid government's stance failed to soften even slightly.

10 Robben Island

"A tiny outcrop of limestone, bleak, windswept and caught in the wash of the cold Benguela current, whose history counts the years of our people's bondage. My new home."

Nelson Mandela, from his unpublished memoirs

Robben Island, a kidney-shaped piece of land about 5 kilometres square, is the summit of an ancient mountain in the middle of Table Bay. It was once home to thousands of Cape fur seals ("robben" is Dutch for seals) and has been used as a prison for more than three centuries. From the mid-nineteenth century, it was also a leper colony, then in 1963 the apartheid government turned the island into a jail for those they regarded as political lepers.

In the distance can be seen the inviting sight of **Cape Town** with Table Mountain looming up behind it. But in Robben Island's long history as a penal settlement, only a few prisoners have managed to escape by boat (see p.152); none by swimming the ten kilometres of icy, rough seas.

Winters are wet and severe on the island, and that of 1964, as the seven Rivonia convicted men arrived, was particularly harsh. The jail and the prison regime had changed since Mandela left to go on trial: the coloured warders had been replaced by whites, apparently because the former were "too soft" and more susceptible to political influence, and a new cell block had been erected for political prisoners. To Mandela, Robben Island had now become "the harshest, most iron-fisted outpost in the South African penal system".

Prison life

Shortly after the seven arrived on the island, the prison commander advised the head of prisons that it was "extremely undesirable" that the political prisoners should come into contact with the ordinary convicts "as they will definitely continue with their undermining activities which will cause endless trouble". The seven were housed in single cells of about seven square feet surrounding a concrete courtyard. Their section was called *khulukuthu*, prison terminology for isolation cells, but its official designation was **B Section**.

Each prisoner's cell was marked by his name and prison number. Mandela's was **466/64**, meaning he was the 466th prisoner to arrive in 1964. Although the government viewed the political prisoners as a dangerous threat to the state, the **Rivonia Seven** were treated very differently from the other convicts – an unstated recognition that they weren't really criminals. Mandela, in particular, was treated with respect. Although there were many instances of humiliation and rough treatment, the only serious incident that took place at this time involved Johnson Mlambo, a PAC prisoner, who – according to his testimony before the Truth and Reconciliation

> "We're thankful that winter is over. We started working a few days ago, mending clothes and sewing buttons; don't know for how long."
>
> Ahmed Kathrada, letter from Robben Island, 30 August 1964

View of Robben Island with Cape Town and Table Mountain in the background. (Charles O'Rear/Corbis)

Commission – was buried up to his neck in the sand with warders threatening to urinate on his face.

The regular torture on Robben Island, especially in the early years, was the **isolation** in such grim surroundings; the poor food; the rigid, monotonous routine; the verbal abuse from some warders; and the restrictions on communication with loved ones. Prisoners had to sleep on the floor on a sisal mat covered with soft felt. The cells were completely bare but for a bottle of water and a bucket. Mandela complained that the cells were damp, but the commanding officer simply replied that their bodies would absorb the moisture.

The prisoners were woken at 5.30am to go to the bathroom, after which a breakfast of cold maize meal porridge was served at 6am. They were then taken to the courtyard for the task of **crushing stones** with hammers. This continued until noon and a lunch of boiled maize and a drink, *phuzamandla*, made from maize flour and yeast.

THE ISLAND

For 150 years – between **Bartolomeu Dias**'s rounding of the Cape of Good Hope in 1488 and the first permanent settlement at the Cape – Robben Island was used by passing sailors as a source of fresh water and meat, and as a communications post.

Shortly after the Dutch settlement of 1652, the island became a prison for "undesirable" political elements: rebellious slaves, Khoisan who resisted colonial settlement, and indigenous leaders exiled from other Dutch colonies. A shrine or *karamat* built over the grave of **Sayed Abdurhman Motura**, a Muslim imam who died in 1754, is still preserved on the island.

When the British took over as colonial power, they continued to use the island as a place of banishment, mainly for Xhosa leaders who resisted the colonial expansion into the Eastern Cape (later known as Transkei). One such leader – revered by Mandela and his colleagues – was **Makhanda** (also spelled Makana), a Xhosa philosopher, spiritual leader and military general who had led a force of some 10,000 warriors in an unsuccessful assault on the British garrison at Grahamstown on 22 April 1819.

The details of his escape from the island are shrouded in myth, but it seems that in late 1819 (or early 1820) he was one of thirty prisoners who managed to seize three small whaling boats and head for the mainland. Close to the shore, Makhanda's boat capsized and he was drowned with several others in the surf at Bloubergstrand.

According to some of the escapees, Makhanda was clinging to the rocks, shouting encouragement to the others. A white missionary reported that his body was washed up on the shore, but some Xhosa sources claim he made it alive to the beach and was shot by British soldiers who then threw his body into the sea.

In the mid-nineteenth century the island began to be used as a colony for lepers and mentally disturbed patients, but this ended in the 1930s when the **South African Defence Force** occupied the island as a strategic base for the defence of Cape Town. The cannon batteries built during World War II have recently been restored.

In 1961 the apartheid government started sending common law prisoners to the island and from 1963 it became the primary prison for political prisoners. After South Africa became a democracy in 1994 the island was declared a museum and now receives many visitors daily, Mandela's cell being the main attraction. The island was declared a **UNESCO World Heritage Site** in 1999.

At 4pm they were allowed to wash, with their one **cold shower** of the week taking place on Wednesdays. Supper was at 4.30pm: more porridge, one vegetable and a scrap of meat every second day. At 6pm they were back in their cells and ordered to sleep by 8pm, though the lights were never switched off. The next morning the routine started all over again. Weekends were worse: the prisoners were locked in their cells all the time with short exercise periods in the morning and afternoon. In the early years, they had no radios or reading matter; they simply had to sit there with their own thoughts.

On the island apartheid was taken to extremes. Coloured and Indian prisoners got slightly better food and were allowed underwear, long trousers and socks, while black prisoners were forced to wear short pants. In traditional black culture, shorts were viewed as only appropriate for young boys. After a few days back on the island, Mandela lodged a formal complaint and was given trousers, but when he refused to wear them unless his fellow prisoners also got them, they were taken away.

Dealing with the routine

Mandela and Sisulu established a **pragmatic strategy** to deal with the prison authorities. There would be no unnecessary provocation of warders; fair and respectful treatment was rewarded by cooperation. The prisoners had to maintain the moral high ground at all times. But there would also be no compromise on assaults, verbal abuse or extreme conditions. Such instances would be formally protested against, mostly by Mandela, who was the undisputed leader of the B Section. The aim of this strategy was to make life in jail as tolerable as possible while continuing to campaign for better conditions.

Mandela, Sisulu and other political prisoners later wrote or gave interviews about their lives on the island. The same incidents are frequently recalled, most of them seemingly minor, others more serious. What is striking about these accounts is the huge number of days that are unaccounted for, simply because nothing – save the monotonous daily routine – occurred.

The seven were not the only political prisoners in Section B. There were thirteen others, including PAC member Zephania Mothopeng, the Maoist revolutionary Neville Alexander, Eddie Daniels of the African Resistance Movement, and MK leaders **Mac Maharaj** and **Wilton Mkwayi**, who were arrested after the Rivonia swoop. At times common law criminals were also put in Section B in order to spy on the politicos and, it seemed, to provoke them. An unknown number of other political prisoners had arrived on the island in the months before the Rivonia Seven got there and some of these also later joined B Section.

About a month after the Mandela group's arrival the prisoners were unexpectedly told to put away their hammers and were given needles and thread to mend old prison uniforms. The reason for the change became apparent the next day when a reporter and photographer from the British newspaper *The Daily Telegraph* arrived. Mandela knew the conservative political stance of the paper but reluctantly gave the reporter an interview to explain the prison conditions. The photograph the paper published, of Mandela and Sisulu in the court-yard with heaps of prison jerseys lying in the background, was the first of Mandela on Robben Island

The lime quarry

Early in 1965 the B Section prisoners were taken to **quarries** on the island to dig out the lime – their daily activity for a long time to come. During the first months they were made to work hard, but they still preferred it to their courtyard work because it got them out of the prison and they enjoyed the daily walk to and from the quarries. However, the harsh sun on the bright white lime permanently dam-aged Mandela's eyes, since initially prisoners were not allowed to wear sunglasses. Older men, like Sisulu (who was 52 in 1964), could ask for exemption from working in the quarry, but nobody did: "Going to work was an advantage, not a disadvantage," Sisulu said. "It enabled you to communicate with your fellow prisoners."

On the first day of walking to the quarry, the warder in charge ordered them to go faster. The more he shouted, the slower Mandela walked, followed by the rest of the party. In the end he had to beg them to pick up the pace. But this kind of obstinacy did not always have positive results. Frustrated by the lack of reaction to complaints, Mandela approached a senior officer of the prisons department, **Brigadier Aucamp**, who was on an inspection of the island. Realizing that Aucamp was the jail commander's superior, Mandela walked towards him – completely against regulations. The warders sharply ordered him to move back, but he refused, addressing the brigadier

A posed photograph, taken for The Daily Telegraph showing prisoners breaking stones in the front row and sewing mail bags in the second. (UWCRIM Mayibuye/The Telegraph/Link)

directly. Aucamp wouldn't even hear him out, and Mandela was given four days in **solitary confinement**. He later acknowledged that his approach was a mistake, because "the best way to effect change on Robben Island was to attempt to influence officials privately rather than publicly."

Within months the conditions at the lime quarry were relaxed and it became a place where political discussions were allowed to take place. Following Prime Minister Hendrik Verwoerd's assassination on 6 September 1966, this more tolerant regime ended with the arrival at the quarry of warden **van Rensburg**, a cruel and racist man with a swastika tattooed on his forearm. He made the men work extremely hard and insulted them at every possible occasion.

Then one day in 1967 the prisoners had an argument about whether there were once tigers in Africa. Some indigenous languages had a word for tiger, but these could simply have been wrongly translated and actually refer to leopards. As the argument got louder, van Rensburg, a badly educated Afrikaner, shouted at them: "You talk too many and you work too few!" The men couldn't stop themselves from laughing at his bad grammar, and van Rensburg felt so humiliated that he had Mandela and another prisoner handcuffed and thrown into solitary confinement. All conversation was henceforth banned at the quarry.

The regime eases up

Despite this incident, the prison regime was gradually relaxing over the years as a result of the prisoners' unrelenting efforts, but also because of the agitation of outsiders like the **International Red Cross**, whose representatives visited the island from time to time. In 1967 a prisoner who had just been released and gone into exile, Denis Brutus, appeared before the UN Special Committee on Apartheid and gave testimony about the conditions on the island.

ESCAPE FROM THE ISLAND

"We are revolutionaries. It is our duty to try and escape the clutches of the enemy," Nelson Mandela told fellow prisoner **Eddie Daniels**. According to Daniels, Mandela was obsessed with escaping from the moment of his arrest, so Daniels took him at his word and devised an elaborate escape plan for him.

Due for release in November 1979, Daniels planned the escape for New Year's Day 1981 so that he could assist from the outside. A trusted helicopter pilot would be recruited to fly with him to the island, and at exactly 9.15am a winch and cable attached to a large basket would be lowered above the courtyard of B Section. If contacted by radio, the pilot would say they were well-wishers bringing presents to the warders. The flight was unlikely to cause much concern since helicopters regularly flew over the island.

Mandela would be in the yard when the basket was lowered and other prisoners would block the corridors to prevent the warders from getting outside. The helicopter would fly Mandela to the grounds of a **foreign embassy** in Cape Town, a flight of just a few minutes and thus too short for attack aircraft to be scrambled. At the embassy they would ask for political asylum.

Mandela and Sisulu liked the plan and decided Sisulu should stay behind to act as leader of the prisoners. Daniels smuggled the detailed plan to Lusaka for the ANC's approval, but he never heard from them. He was later told the leadership was discussing the idea when they were warned of a South African Defence Force raid and destroyed all documents as a precaution.

Another escape plan, devised by Mac Maharaj, was for Mandela to ask for a dentist's appointment in Cape Town and once in the dentist's chair to demand that the warders respect his privacy. He could then escape into the street where a car would pick him up. Mandela, **Maharaj** and **Wilton Mkwayi** did exactly that, but as they stood in the dentist's waiting room, they noticed that there was not a soul to be seen in the usually busy street. The police had got wind of the plan and were setting them up. The three had their teeth seen to and quietly returned to the island."

Mandela gives credit to **Helen Suzman**, at that stage the only member of the Progressive Party in South Africa's white parliament, for a lot of the changes in the way the political prisoners were treated. Described as a "liberal bulldog" by a government minister, Suzman wouldn't take no for an answer to her requests to visit the island. She had heard accounts of the conditions from lawyers who had visited their clients, and was finally allowed there in 1967. This was shortly after the warder van Rensburg had laid charges against Mandela and others because of the lime quarry incident.

Suzman met Mandela, who was designated by the others to speak on their behalf, at his cell. Her gave her a full briefing on the poor food, the need for the prisoners to study and the ban on newspapers and other reading matter. He then specifically complained about van Rensburg. Suzman went back to Cape Town and reported her findings to the Minister of Justice. Van Rensburg was moved off the island within days.

Major changes were made during and after 1967. A new hospital was built; the number of visitors and letters allowed were substantially increased; all prisoners were given long trousers; most prisoners wanting to study were allowed to do so; sports on Saturday mornings were introduced (soccer, rugby, boxing and table tennis); the single-cell prisoners could play chess, bridge, draughts and Scrabble; and Sunday services were organized with ministers and priests coming from the mainland.

The need for news

But the political prisoners had an even more pressing need: to be informed of events in South Africa and the rest of the world. The only information on what was happening in the country and inside the ANC was from the occasional new prisoner. The men desperately wanted access to **newspapers**. Not being able to read the newspapers was "a punishment I cannot describe", said Sisulu. But clearly the apartheid government viewed the prisoners' isolation from the world as part of their punishment and a way of undermining their political resolve.

Three anecdotes illustrate the extent of the men's yearning for news. On one occasion Eddie Daniels stole a newspaper from a visiting priest's bag while he was praying. On another occasion Mac Maharaj blackmailed a warder who had asked him to write an essay for a competition: a newspaper every day or he would report the warder to his commander. The warder supplied Maharaj with a newspaper every day until he was transferred six months later. Mandela tells the story that the warders who oversaw them at the quarry often had their lunch wrapped in newspaper. When they threw the wrapping away in the rubbish bin, there was a scramble by prisoners to rescue it to see if there was something on those pages that could give them a glimpse of what was going on in the country. Prisoners were later allowed to subscribe to *Reader's Digest* and other non-political magazines.

A brief set-back

The arrival of a new head of prison in 1970, **Colonel Piet Badenhorst**, led to a sharp deterioration in conditions. Badenhorst was an abusive, foul-mouthed character who believed prisoners should be terrorized to keep them in their place. During a visit to the lime quarry, he shocked prisoners and warders alike by cursing Mandela and telling him to "pull your finger out your arse". Badenhorst downgraded the political prisoners' classification, which determined their privileges, and suspended all legal procedures on the island. When some prisoners launched a hunger strike, he had them **beaten by warders** and even forced the dignified Sisulu to stand naked in his cell while it was being searched.

But when the **Commissioner of Prisons** and three judges of the Supreme Court paid an inspection visit to the island some months later, Mandela addressed them frankly and forcefully about Badenhorst's behaviour – in Badenhorst's presence. Badenhorst was so outraged that he threatened Mandela right there and then, which gave Mandela the opportunity to say to the judges, "You can see for yourself the type of man we are dealing with as commanding officer." Badenhorst was removed from his position three months later, and conditions on the island improved drastically.

Continuing the struggle

Mandela and his comrades were adamant that Robben Island should also be used as "a site of struggle" by the ANC. The first step in this strategy demanded an elected leadership structure, the second the provision for **intellectual debates** and **political education**.

The ANC High Organ was established with the four most senior ANC leaders as members: Mandela, Sisulu, Govan Mbeki and Raymond Mhlaba, with Mandela as leader. They were sensitive to criticism of Xhosa-speakers being dominant, so they co-opted a fifth member on a rotational basis – Ahmed Kathrada was one of those.

The High Organ was not always united. In the beginning, Mandela and Sisulu had long arguments with Mbeki and Mhlaba on the old question of Operation Mayibuye and how guerrilla warfare could be successful in South Africa. Mandela's opinion was that MK could never operate from bases inside the country and had to follow the example of the liberation movements in Angola and Mozambique, who fought from bases in neighbouring countries.

Mandela and Mbeki didn't get along well, with Mbeki even questioning Mandela's leadership status on the island. He sharply criticized Mandela's contact with Chief Mangosuthu Buthelezi, leader of the KwaZulu Bantustan and a former Fort Hare student and ANC Youth League member. The two also differed sharply on whether the ANC and the Communist Party were distinct organizations and on interpretation of the Freedom Charter's clauses on the economy. Mbeki insisted that the ANC had to strive for a people's democracy, with the Communist Party, rather than the ANC, leading the people during the final stages of socialism. Mandela believed the Freedom Charter was not a blueprint for socialism and he advocated a bourgeois socialism with the ANC as the leader of all the anti-apartheid forces.

Mandela's more pragmatic approach was undermined with the arrival on the island of prisoners from the **Black Consciousness**

Movement, who excluded all cooperation with white South Africans (including communists), and of a new generation of younger men radicalized by the township uprisings started by the Soweto revolt of June 1976. These young radicals viewed Mandela and the old guard as "soft" and "too moderate" and rallied around another hardline ANC communist (some called him a Stalinist), **Harry Gwala**, who also preached a violent seizure of power in South Africa.

Mandela went out of his way to listen to the newcomers and not to antagonize them, but still stuck to his guns. Twenty years later Kathrada wrote in a newspaper article that Mandela's wisdom, foresight and cool head were indispensible during this time because he always "brought the polemics down to earth". Mandela, said Kathrada, reminded everyone that it was never envisaged that MK could achieve a victory over the apartheid army and that "MK's

A Daily Telegraph photo of 1964 showing Mandela (left) and Walter Sisulu in the prison yard. (BAHA/Africa Media Online)

primary aim was to engage in armed struggle alongside the political struggle and mass mobilization; that the two together would force the enemy to the negotiation table." Mandela gradually won over most of the young Turks.

Despite the prison's best efforts, the **High Organ** occasionally succeeded in getting notes and messages out to the ANC leadership in exile in Zambia and to receive messages back. Winnie Mandela and barrister George Bizos did much of the smuggling during their visits to the island. When it was proposed that the ANC admitted Indians, coloureds and whites as members at their conference in Tanzania in 1969, the Lusaka leadership consulted the High Organ first. When Mandela got news of the abuse of power by commanders of ANC military camps in Zambia and the appalling conditions recruits were living under, a letter was smuggled out to Oliver Tambo demanding changes. But when some in the exiled leadership wanted to make him ANC president in Tambo's place, in what was a failed palace revolution, Mandela firmly declined.

In 1974 Mandela was asked by some of his friends in B Section to write his **memoirs** so they could be published overseas and strengthen the ANC's case. Mandela eventually produced some 500 pages, condensed by fellow prisoner Isu Chiba into tiny script. Mac Maharaj then smuggled the manuscript from the island on his release in December 1976, taking it with him when he left the country six months later and giving it to the ANC leadership in Lusaka. It was never published. According to the most credible version of the story, some MK commanders in exile didn't like Mandela's views on how the armed struggle had developed. When the prison staff discovered the original manuscript, buried in the prison courtyard, Mandela and Sisulu were forbidden from external studies for four years as punishment. The manuscript was retrieved from the prison authorities after 1990 and formed the basis of Mandela's 1994 autobiography, *Long Walk to Freedom*.

Self-improvement

Most of the political prisoners enrolled on correspondence courses at the **University of South Africa**, or other educational institutions, and many had gained multiple degrees by the time they were released. Studying became a popular way of escaping the boredom and depression of life in jail. "At night, our cell block seemed more like a study hall than a prison," Mandela writes in his autobiography. But the "University of Robben Island" (also called the Makana University, after the nineteenth-century Xhosa chief) was about more than just obtaining degrees. Under the leadership of the High Organ, **regular lectures** were organized and discussion groups formed, often leading to intense debates. "Syllabus A" was a course in ANC history, taught by Walter Sisulu, a man with a great memory, a love of history and a

THE DAY THE YOUTH REVOLTED

Government repression was severe during the 1970s and there was virtually no ANC presence inside the country. But the youth of South Africa were angry and frustrated and in 1976 organized a march for the **16 June** to protest the inferior system of Bantu education and the use of Afrikaans as the language of instruction in black schools.

The police confronted the fifteen thousand marchers in Soweto and ordered them to disperse. When they refused, police dogs were set on the pupils and teargas fired. The pupils started throwing stones at the police, some of whom responded by firing live ammunition into the crowd. This unleashed a fury among the young people and running battles with the police continued until after dark. Officially twenty-three people were killed, but the real figure was estimated to be closer to two hundred.

The Soweto Uprising, as it was later known as, quickly spread to nearby townships and eventually throughout the whole country, lasting for months. Hundreds left South Africa to join the ANC for military training in Zambia and Angola, and many were detained and sent to Robben Island.

This day in June 1976 proved to be a turning point in South Africa's history and peace never really returned to the country until after 1990.

gift for communicating. His lectures were even popular among prisoners from other political persuasions. Mandela's course on political economy formed part of "Syllabus B". Most of the lectures were held and discussed at the lime quarry.

By the mid-1970s the prison regulations had become so relaxed that more **sports facilities** had been built and Mandela was allowed to start a **vegetable garden** – he harvested a thousand tomatoes at the end of one season. In 1977 the practice of making the political prisoners do hard labour was stopped. Mandela and fellow prisoners were also now allowed to receive regular visits and write and receive letters every week, where initially he was allowed only one letter from an immediate family member every six months.

Mandela's authority

During all his years in prison, Mandela was treated differently from the other political prisoners, and almost always with respect. He was allowed more visitors and was recognized as the most important personality on the island, sometimes to his own embarrassment. This was partly a result of his charismatic leadership qualities and his proud and dignified demeanour, but there may well have been a sense on the part of his jailers that he could one day be their leader too. Those warders and officers who got to know him, knew very well he was not the dangerous communist terrorist that government propaganda suggested. This was confirmed by at least two of the warders who became close to Mandela, **Christo Brand** and **James Gregory**.

Billy Nair, also imprisoned in 1964, says about Mandela's relationship with the warders: "Madiba was very good with them. A new chap would be posted to Robben Island, he's anxious to meet him, he's heard about Mandela, terrible, dangerous. The first time he comes, he's taken to Madiba's cell. Sits down and Madiba accommodates him, opens a packet of biscuits and makes tea for him. The warder confesses, 'but we were told you are a terrorist!' Madiba says, 'no, no'. And the warder – not only one, dozens of them – got a different picture."

Mandela's lawyer, George Bizos, remembers the first time he went to see his client on the island in August 1964. Mandela was driven to the consultation room on the back of a pick-up truck with eight guards. They embraced and then Mandela said, "George, you know this place has already made me forget my man-

> "Madiba was a very striking, commanding personality, but he was also a very nice person, very polite, very courteous... Although we were made to wear short pants and sandals, somehow his demeanour was never reduced by that. His whole person was chief-like: he walked with a certain gait, in a very dignified way."
>
> Fikile Bam, lawyer and Robben Island prisoner

ners. I haven't introduced you to my guard of honour." Mandela then introduced him to each warder by name.

Missing family

But while everyone on the island knew Mandela the political leader, few ever had a glimpse of his private life and the trauma he had to endure. He had a wife who was constantly being harassed by the security police and he had four children who had to grow up without a father.

Mandela's mother visited him in jail in 1968, accompanied by his sister Mabel and two of his children with Evelyn: **Makgatho** and **Makaziwe**. His other son, **Thembi**, lived in Cape Town but resented the break-up with his mother and refused to have any contact with his father. Mandela knew he would not see his mother again, and she died of a heart attack a few weeks later. He was refused permission to attend her funeral.

Less than a year later, in July 1969, warder Gregory brought Mandela the news that Thembi had died in a car crash. The otherwise controlled Mandela was rocked to his core – "paralysed", he recorded afterwards. He had last seen his son five years earlier at the Rivonia Trial. Gregory says Mandela simply said "Thank, you, Mr Gregory", and walked away, but he could see in Mandela's eyes "the sternness I was to recognise when he struggled to maintain self-control". Mandela went to his cell and did not come out for dinner. According to the warder on duty, he did not sleep or eat; he just stood in one spot gazing out the window. When Sisulu heard the news, he went to Mandela and held his hand for a long time. The next morning Mandela asked for permission to attend his son's funeral, but it was again refused.

His agony lasted for weeks as he tried to deal with the pain and guilt and fought to control his emotions. In his book *Goodbye Bafana: Nelson Mandela, My Prisoner, My Friend* (1995), James Gregory wrote: "There was the hard set face, a coldness that was different from the friendly smile he would normally give. He was also cutting himself off from other ANC people. I noticed that when they were in the yard Nelson did not walk to be with them in the usual manner."

Winnie's ordeal

Mandela was already deeply distressed about what was happening to his wife Winnie and their daughters Zindzi and Zenani. Winnie had become involved in **underground activity** herself, but the security police had informers close to her and she was arrested at the Mandela home in May 1969 and detained under the Terrorism Act. What followed during the next 500 days would change her forever.

Held in a tiny cell in Pretoria Central Prison, Winnie was subjected to severe **mental torture**: she was given the names of men who had supposedly confessed to having sex with her; she was told her closest friends had betrayed her; she was deprived of proper sleep. The chief interrogator was **Theunis Swanepoel**, the same security police officer who had harassed Mandela and colleagues during the Rivonia Trial. After six days she signed a confession, but her solitary confinement continued. In July 1969 Swanepoel walked into her cell and coolly told her that her stepson Thembi was dead.

After six months in detention Winnie was formally charged, but when it became clear that the police had tortured some of the state witnesses, the charges were withdrawn. They were soon reinstated, however, and her detention continued. She was eventually acquitted and released having spent 491 days in detention. Two weeks later she was served with an order that amounted to **house arrest**. The experience changed Winnie Mandela forever. She reflected on this time many years later and said it was "what brutalised me so much that I knew what it is to hate".

The authorities made sure that Mandela knew about his wife's incarceration. He said years later that the knowledge that she was in jail and their children were without parents was more difficult to deal with than anything else.

Winnie was given special permission to visit Mandela in prison in November 1970. They had only thirty minutes together and were not allowed to touch, but he noticed the changes in her and worried even more. Still, his love for Winnie and his children, and his memories of their time together, were a help to him while in prison. In a letter he sent Winnie on 2 April 1969, he referred to a family photograph she had sent him: "the picture has aroused all the tender feelings in me and softened the grimness that is all around. It has sharpened my longing for you and our sweet and peaceful home." Two months later he wrote to her: "Since the dawn of history, mankind has honoured and respected brave and honest people, men and women like you darling – an ordinary girl who hails from a country village hardly shown on most maps…"

In June 1970 he wrote to **Zindzi** and **Zenani** that, though he wasn't sure whether they were receiving his letters, "the mere fact of writing down my thoughts and expressing my feelings gives me a measure of pleasure and satisfaction."

Prison transfer

On 31 March 1982 Mandela was told out of the blue that he was going to be **transferred** to a prison on the mainland. That evening he was taken with Walter Sisulu, Raymond Mhlaba and Andrew Mlangeni to **Pollsmoor Prison** in Cape Town. The motive behind this move by the authorities has never been explained, but it was at least partly in response to a new national and international "Free Mandela" campaign that was spreading like wildfire, having been started in 1980 by **Percy Qoboza**, the editor of a black South African newspaper. Another theory was that the government wanted to undermine both the unity of the political prisoners on the island and Mandela's leadership.

But the much-improved conditions at Pollsmoor suggested the government was already suspecting they would soon have to start talking to Mandela about his release. The food was much better; the men had much more space; there was access to newspapers, radio and television; and they were allowed to buy tinned food. Mandela was even given aan additional room to read and write in. Warder James Gregory, who was transferred with them, handpicked the other warders to make sure the prisoners would be treated with respect. Mandela was allowed his first contact visit with Winnie, an emotional moment for them both. Significantly, the hard-line Govan Mbeki, fellow member of the High Organ, was not transferred with them.

Mandela and his friends in Pollsmoor would soon find out that the political landscape in South Africa was rapidly changing, and just how this was about to affect them.

11 Release and rebirth

"I stand here before you not as a prophet but as a humble servant of you, the people. Your tireless and heroic sacrifices have made it possible for me to be here today. I therefore place the remaining years of my life in your hands."

Nelson Mandela, following his release, 11 February 1990

When undemocratic regimes initiate reform, it often leads to an upsurge in resistance, which in turn results in an increase in repression. This was exactly what happened in South Africa from the late 1970s onwards, and Nelson Mandela was a central figure in the unfolding events.

Until the mid-1970s, the white minority government in South Africa felt comfortable because it was surrounded by other states ruled by white minorities: **Namibia**, which was run as a South African colony; **Rhodesia** (later Zimbabwe), where whites under Ian Smith had announced a unilateral declaration of independence (UDI) in 1965; and **Mozambique** and **Angola**, which were under Portuguese colonial rule.

But, following the revolution in Portugal in 1974, the Portuguese withdrew from their colonies and Angola and Mozambique became independent under the leadership of their liberation movements.

In 1978 the **Security Council** of the United Nations adopted a resolution demanding Namibia's independence, and the pressure for South Africa to withdraw from its colony increased. The long and bloody war of liberation in Zimbabwe escalated during this time, eventually leading to independence under Robert Mugabe's Zimbabwe African National Union in 1980. South Africa had become a beleaguered white island in a sea of black nationalism.

Attempts at reform

Prime Minister John Vorster was feeling the pinch. His response was to pursue, as forcefully as ever, the apartheid ideology while initiating a policy of **détente** with other African states. Between 1970 and 1975 he met with the heads of state of Malawi, Ivory Coast, Zaire (now the Democratic Republic of Congo), Gabon and Liberia.

Following a government scandal in 1978, Vorster was replaced by **P.W. Botha** who soon declared that white South Africans had to "adapt or die". He started relaxing some apartheid laws by legalizing black trade unions and scrapping job discrimination, and in 1981 replaced the whites-only Senate with an advisory **President's Council** consisting of whites, Indian South Africans and coloureds. Soon after, he announced that Indians and coloureds would have their own elected assemblies and that these would form the parliament with the white assembly, which would continue to have the final say over legislation.

Black exclusion

The continued blatant exclusion of black South Africans from political participation triggered massive resistance and led to the formation of the **United Democratic Front** (UDF) in 1983. This

P.W. Botha (centre) visiting the black township of Soweto in 1979, a year after he became Prime Minister. Though he implemented a few reforms, Botha was no less repressive than his predecessors. (Selwyn Tait/Sygma/Corbis)

was a broad-based mass movement of religious groups, civic and professional associations and trade unions which, like the ANC, pledged allegiance to the Freedom Charter of 1955. It threatened to make South Africa "ungovernable" and between 1984 and 1988 there were daily violent confrontations between UDF supporters and the police, with thousands of people detained without trial. The Botha government unleashed clandestine units such as the **police death squad** based at Vlakplaas outside Pretoria and the military dirty tricks team, the cynically named **Civil Cooperation Bureau** (CCB).

In 1985 all major international banks decided to stop rolling over loans to South African borrowers, a move that led to the devaluation of the currency (the rand) and a flight of capital from the country. The following year the US, the Commonwealth and the European Community imposed stiff political, economic and financial **sanctions** on the country. Apartheid South Africa was completely isolated and faced the worst financial and economic crisis of its existence. Internally the country was on the brink of a bloody civil war.

MUGGER OF THE NATION

When **Winnie Mandela** ended her exile in the village of Brandfort in 1984 and returned to Soweto, she quickly became a huge embarrassment to her husband and a headache to the leaders of the internal resistance movement, the United Democratic Front (UDF). She took to wearing a khaki military uniform, complete with boots and beret, was alleged to have had several affairs with younger men, and was prone to making reckless statements.

The brutal "necklacing" of suspected collaborators and spies started during this time: a car tyre was put over the victim's head, filled with petrol and set alight. On 13 April 1985 Winnie stood on stage in a township west of Johannesburg and encouraged this gruesome practice: "We have no guns. We have only stones, boxes of matches and petrol. Together, hand in hand, with our boxes of matches and our necklaces we shall liberate this country."

By 1987 she had surrounded herself with a gang of young men who she called the **Mandela United Football Club**. Only they didn't play football. These were her "bodyguards" and "companions" and they ran wild, terrorizing the residents of Soweto and getting involved in turf wars with other gangs. In July 1988 residents who were fed up with the gang's activities burned down Winnie's house. Nelson Mandela ordered her to disband the club, but she refused, saying they were "rescued street children". That year the club accused a boy named **Lolo Sono** of being a spy. He was last seen badly beaten and bruised in Winnie's minibus. Shortly afterwards a fourteen-year-old child activist, **Stompie Seipei**, was also accused of working with the police. He was abducted and brutally beaten in Winnie's home, with her watching. The club's "coach", Jerry Richardson, later admitted that he had slit Stompie's throat on Winnie's orders and was sent to jail for life. Winnie was later convicted of his kidnapping and given a jail sentence, changed to a heavy fine on appeal.

The harassment of Winnie Mandela

The key to cutting this Gordian knot was Prisoner 466/64. But to understand how Nelson Mandela became involved in resolving the crisis of the mid-1980s, one has to go back to 1977. In May of that year the police removed Winnie Mandela from her home in Orlando and took her to a small town, **Brandfort**, in the Free State province about 400km south of Johannesburg. Winnie had

In order to monitor Winnie, the **Mandela Crisis Committee** was formed and reported on her wayward behaviour to Mandela. But she always assured her husband the reports were lies and that the media were making up stories about her. In his autobiography, Mandela wrote: "Perhaps I was blinded to certain things because of the pain I felt for not being able to fulfill my role as husband to my wife and a father to my children." Still, he was so angry with her that he once refused to see her when she arrived to see him in jail.

The day after Stompie's body was found and identified, the UDF leadership took the unprecedented step of publicly distancing themselves from Winnie, "We are outraged at Mrs Mandela's complicity in the recent abduction and assault of Stompie… We are not prepared to remain silent where those who are violating human rights claim to be doing so in the name of the struggle against apartheid." A newspaper columnist wrote that she had moved from Mother of the Nation to Mugger of the Nation.

In 1997 the **Truth and Reconciliation Commission** (TRC) held a special hearing on Winnie, at which she defiantly denied all allegations and refused to ask the victims' families for forgiveness. The TRC nevertheless found that she was "politically and morally accountable for the gross violations of human rights committed by the Mandela Football Club." The TRC chairman, **Desmond Tutu**, practically forced her to hug Stompie's mother and to admit that "something had gone horribly wrong".

At the time of Mandela's release, Winnie was having a public affair with a young lawyer, **Dali Mpofu**, who moved in with her in 1989. The first night Mandela spent back in his Orlando home in February 1990, Winnie left and only returned before daybreak. In 1992 Mandela announced their separation at a press conference. They were divorced four years later.

been involved with the revolt by young people in Soweto, and the minister of Justice, Jimmy Kruger, wanted her out of the way. She was now restricted to one of the most desolate places in the country, forced to live in a miserable little house with no running water in a township of mostly illiterate people who spoke only Sesotho and Afrikaans. In addition her friends were banned from visiting her. Winnie – by now called the "Mother of the Nation" by the black press – was continually harassed by the police and treated with hostility by the white residents. If her long detention changed her, her seven-year Brandfort experience drove her over the edge and she began to drink heavily.

Winnie needed a lawyer, so she went to the only one in town, **Piet de Waal**, a respected member of the town's conservative Afrikaner community. De Waal's wife, Adele, immediately liked and admired Winnie and she became a regular visitor to the couple's home – it was the only place where she could have a hot bath. Piet de Waal just happened to have been a student friend and tennis partner of **Kobie Coetsee**, who suceeded Jimmy Kruger as Justice Minister in 1980. In letters to Coetsee, de Waal urged him to lift Winnie's banning orders and allow her to return to her home. He also made a case for the release of Mandela as a first step in defusing the alarming conflict in the country. The seed was planted. "You could say that's where the whole process started," Coetsee later remarked.

Reassessing Mandela

Coetsee had the good sense to suspect that not all he had heard about Mandela was necessarily true, and started wondering what this famous prisoner was like as a human being and a political thinker. He commissioned a report on Mandela and in early 1981 received a remarkably true and insightful assessment. "There exists no doubt that Mandela commands all the qualities to be the Number One black leader in South Africa," the report declared. "His period in prison has caused his psycho-political posture to increase rather than decrease and with this he has now acquired the characteristic prison charisma of the contemporary liberation leader."

According to the report, Mandela was "exceptionally motivated" with an "unflinching belief in his cause and in the eventual triumph of African nationalism". He was a practical and pragmatic thinker with strong self-belief, jovial, tactful and showed "no visible signs of bitterness towards whites, although this may be a fine game of bluff on his part". He had an "unbelievable" memory and thought that "self-discipline, and continually taking the initiative, to be prerequisites for success".

South Africa was pretty isolated in the international community by the mid-1980s, although US President Ronald Reagan and British Prime Minister Margaret Thatcher kept the doors of communication open. By 1984 these two "friends" had also started putting pressure on the Botha administration for radical reform and the release of Mandela as a starting point for negotiations with the black majority. Returning from a meeting with Thatcher in 1984, at which she again asked for Mandela to be released, Botha told Coetsee that "we [the government] had painted ourselves into a corner". How were they going to get out of it?

In January 1985, Botha revealed that Mandela was now on the agenda. In a parliamentary speech he offered to release him "on condition that Mr Mandela gives a full commitment that he will not make himself guilty of planning, instigating or committing acts of violence for the furtherance of political objectives". The offer was clearly made in the knowledge that Mandela would never abandon the armed struggle unilaterally. Indeed, the escalation of violence against the state was still an integral part of the ANC's stategy, and had Mandela gone against it his party would have rejected him. But the offer did allow Botha to say (with the ears of Washington and London in mind) that it was "… not the South African government which now stands in the way of Mr Mandela's freedom. It is himself."

Mandela used Botha's move to score his own point. His daughter Zindzi dramatically read his response to Botha's speech at a UDF mass rally in Soweto on 10 February 1985. These were Mandela's first public words in 24 years. "I am surprised at the conditions that the government wants to impose on me. I am not a violent man," he said. He gave a rundown of the times the ANC had pleaded with the government to meet for talks and said it was only when all other forms of resistance were exhausted that they turned to armed struggle. Mandela said he loved his own freedom dearly, "but I cannot sell my birthright, nor am I prepared to sell the birthright of my people to be free." What would his freedom mean, he asked, if the ANC remained an illegal organization? "What freedom am I being offered when I may be arrested on a pass offence? What freedom am I being offered to live my life as a family with my dear wife who remains in banishment in Brandfort?" Mandela's speech concluded under thunderous applause: "Only free men can negotiate. Prisoners cannot enter into contracts. I cannot and will not give any undertaking at a time when I and you, the people, are not free."

> "Let Botha show that he is different… Let him renounce violence. Let him say he will dismantle apartheid. Let him unban the people's organisation, the ANC. Let him free all who have been imprisoned, banished or exiled for their opposition to apartheid."
>
> Nelson Mandela, from a speech read out by his daughter, 1985

In a typical Mandela move, he followed his harsh criticism of the government with a polite letter to Coetsee, who was now also the minister responsible for prisons, requesting a private meeting. He did not tell any of his fellow prisoners about the letter. Coetsee did not reply, explaining much later that he wanted to meet with Mandela, but not "behind bars".

Another consideration now kept Mandela's continued incarceration high on the government's agenda: he was suffering from an **enlarged prostate** and in November 1985 was admitted to the Volkshospitaal in Cape Town, a high-status, whites-only government hospital. Mandela's health focused the minds of Botha's security advisers. **Mike Louw**, the deputy head of the National Intelligence Service (NI), later recalled in an interview that he and his colleagues told the government that there would be "hell to pay" if Mandela were to die in prison. "Nobody in the world would believe us if we said we treated him humanely. People will simply believe we killed him in an apartheid jail ... We told them [the government] that we had to find a way to release him, and find it quickly."

But it took another coincidence to get things moving. On the day before Mandela's operation, Kobie Coetsee and Winnie Mandela were on the same Johannesburg to Cape Town flight – she to visit her husband in hospital. Coetsee recognized her and assured her that Mandela would get the best medical care available. During the flight, Winnie went and sat next to Coetsee in business class. It is not known what was said, but it was after this conversation that he decided to visit Mandela.

Mandela was his affable self when the minister walked into his private hospital room. "I'm sorry we have not met before," he said with a smile – a probable dig at Coetsee's failure to respond to his earlier letter. Both men were polite with each other and Coetsee dropped a strong hint that matters were really beginning to progress. He told Mandela he was looking at ways of putting him "in a situation between prison and freedom". The wheel had been set in motion, but it was a wheel that was to turn very, very slowly.

The first step of Coetsee's plan was to give Mandela his own spacious quarters at **Pollsmoor**, separate from Walter Sisulu, Raymond Mahlaba, Ahmed Kathrada and Andrew Mlangeni, his cellmates prior to his hospital visit. They were angered by this, but Mandela pacified them by suggesting that it would make future contact with the government easier. This was the beginning of Mandela's personal strategy of dealing with the government on his own, only informing his ANC colleagues later. He did send his lawyer, George Bizos, to Lusaka to inform Oliver Tambo of developments, and early in 1986 Mandela was given the green light to proceed with "talks about talks".

Shifting attitudes

Around this time, a school of thought emerged in the ruling establishment that a political settlement with the black majority was the only way out of the **national crisis**, and that Mandela and the ANC were the uncontested political leaders of black South Africans. **Roelf Meyer**, a young deputy minister of Law and Order (as the police ministry was renamed) and later a key government negotiator, was part of an influential group in the ruling National Party that was lobbying for a new strategy of negotiation and the phasing out of apartheid measures. The head of the National Intelligence Service, **Dr Niel Barnard**, claims he personally told P.W. Botha on more than one occasion in mid-1985 and early 1986 that a negotiated settlement with the majority was the only option and that Mandela was the key. Botha listened, says Barnard, but he was reluctant, because he came from a military tradition (he was minister of Defence for many years) and the military were against talks "with the terrorists".

The idea that apartheid had to be abandoned for a system that accommodated the black majority was also being hotly debated by the **Afrikaner intelligentsia** during the mid-1980s. This included

INCOGNITO

At Christmas 1986, **Colonel Gawie Marx**, the deputy chief of Pollsmoor prison, gave Nelson Mandela a present – a sightseeing tour of Cape Town, a city he had only had a few glimpses of in the last 24 years. The story goes that when Mandela tried to get into Marx's car, he couldn't open the door. The last car he had been in was the old Austin at the time of his arrest in 1962, when doors had a handle protruding from the outside instead of flush with the bodywork. At one point during their travels Marx stopped at a café to buy a soft drink and left Mandela alone with the keys still in the ignition. "I had a vision of opening the door, jumping out, and then running and running until I was out of sight," remembers Mandela, who became very agitated. He was relieved when Marx came back.

Mandela says of this first trip, "I felt like a curious tourist in a strange and remarkable land." In the months after that, **Warrant Officer James Gregory** took Mandela on many trips around the Cape. They strolled on the beach, had lunch in restaurants and even walked among people on the streets. Because Mandela had not been seen in public for so long and newspapers were forbidden to publish photographs of him after he was jailed, nobody recognized him.

the Afrikaans churches; the business community (who were suffering from the declining economy); academics at Afrikaans universities; and the powerful Afrikaner Broederbond (brotherhood), a secret males-only society to which most National Party politicians and Afrikaner professionals belonged. The head of the Broederbond, Professor Pieter de Lange, secretly met with **Thabo Mbeki**, the son of Govan and the ANC's "super-diplomat", at a conference in New York in 1986 and told him over lunch that the Pretoria government was preparing for fundamental change and eventually a proper democracy. De Lange reported back to Botha and shortly afterwards the Broederbond drew up a working document. This proposed black participation in drawing up a new constitution, which in turn would mean a black president and a government with a majority of black members. At the time this was radical stuff.

The same year also saw the resignation from parliament of **Frederik van Zyl Slabbert**, the leader of the Progressive Federal Party (the official opposition), because he now regarded the white parliament as an irrelevant body. His resignation and the announcement that he was going to pursue efforts to bring about negotiations with the black majority shocked the Afrikaner establishment. The following year van Zyl Slabbert and the poet **Breyten Breytenbach**, who had been jailed for his anti-apartheid activities, led a group of sixty Afrikaner intellectuals to a meeting with the exiled ANC leadership in Dakar, the capital of Senegal. It was an event of huge symbolism that went a long way to undoing the demonization of the ANC in the eyes of whites, and put the concept of negotiations with the black majority firmly on the public agenda.

Back at Pollsmoor, Mandela was becoming impatient with the slow progress and asked for a meeting with Kobie Coetsee. They ended up having three long meetings at Coetsee's official residence, all in the highest secrecy. After the first, Coetsee asked the commander at Pollsmoor prison to take Mandela on trips outside, into the Western Cape, so he could see how the country had changed during his time in jail. Warder James Gregory, who by now had developed a deep admiration for Mandela, drove him all over the Cape Peninsula, the West Coast and further inland.

Talks begin

In April 1986, P.W. Botha asked National Intelligence Chief Niel Barnard to head a small committee and start **formal talks** with Mandela. Sisulu and Kathrada were very apprehensive about this, as was Oliver Tambo when rumours of the plan reached him. Mandela assured them that he was still only "talking about talks". Barnard claims that the first meeting occurred on Thursday, 28 April 1988;

according to Mandela it was a week later. It took place in the office of the Pollsmoor Commander, Fred Munro, and was attended by the Commissioner of Prisons, Johan Willemse, the Director General of Prisons, Fanie van der Merwe, as well as Barnard and Mandela. Barnard's deputy, Mike Louw, would also be present at all future meetings.

Barnard recalls: "Mr Mandela walked in, wearing gumboots and a blue uniform. His clothes did nothing whatsoever to diminish his dignity and obvious stature; it stared us in the face. He had been in jail for almost a quarter of a century. I knew we had to get him out of the prison environment and get him to know life and the ways of life outside jail."

Barnard wanted to know how Mandela saw a future political settlement – "would he want to chase the whites into the sea, that kind of thing" – and about his views on violence and communism. During that meeting and the ensuing 46 that took place over the following eighteen months, Mandela convinced the government representatives that it would be counter-productive to demand that he denounce the armed struggle and the Communist Party because that would make it impossible for him to lead the ANC into fully fledged negotiations for a **new constitution**.

Only those present, along with Botha and Coetsee, knew about the talks with Mandela. Botha only told his own government ministers in July 1989, more than three years later. Barnard advised Botha to keep it from his colleagues "because politicians are genetically unable to keep secrets" and news of the talks would have forced both the National Party and the ANC into public posturing, making the talks more difficult.

Barnard was the driving force behind the negotiations initiative – a very unlikely one, because he was a staunch Afrikaner nationalist and widely viewed as a hawk in the government. But Botha trusted him unreservedly, and Barnard's intelligence background told him that merely "reforming" apartheid would only deepen the crisis. Apart from his meetings with Mandela, Barnard also sent a respected Afrikaner academic, **Professor Willie Esterhuyse**, to make contact with Thabo Mbeki in London and followed it up with three secret meetings in Europe between senior NI officials, Mbeki and his ANC colleague **Jacob Zuma**.

When Mandela turned seventy on 18 July 1988, it was celebrated with a huge **rock concert** at London's Wembley Stadium, featuring stars including Stevie Wonder, Harry Belafonte and Roberta Flack. The concert was attended by seventy-two thousand people and the TV broadcast watched by some two hundred million viewers in sixty countries. Calls for his release increased dramatically inside and outside the country.

But Mandela's health was deteriorating. He had developed a cough and had little energy. A few weeks after his birthday he was examined at a top teaching hospital where doctors found fluid on his lung and diagnosed early signs of **tuberculosis**. The South African government was deeply worried and saw to it that he got the best treatment available in the country. He spent six weeks at the hospital and recovered completely.

Instead of returning to Pollsmoor, Mandela was moved, on Coetsee's orders, to a comfortable house in the grounds of **Victor Verster Prison** outside Paarl (some 50km from Cape Town). There he had his own cook and cleaner (Warrant Officer Jack Swart), a stocked bar, a TV, radio and swimming pool. He was allowed to send an employee to the shops for whatever he wanted to buy, could subscribe to any newspapers and had no restrictions on visitors. Many came to see him, including the leaders of the internal resistance movement, the United Democratic Front.

Mandela had been putting pressure on Barnard to organize a meeting with P.W. Botha. But this was put on hold when Botha had a stroke on 18 January 1989. He resigned as leader of the National

Celebrating Mandela's 70th birthday at Wembley Stadium, London.
Another concert was held at the same venue two years later to mark his
release from prison. (Ebet Roberts/Redferns)

Party a month later to be replaced by F.W. de Klerk, but remained as president until August of that year.

In anticipation of his meeting with Botha, Mandela prepared a **ten-page document** stating that the time had arrived for proper negotiations to reconcile the demands of black South Africans and white fears of black domination. The meeting took place in great secrecy at the president's residence in Cape Town on 5 July 1989. Mandela was dressed in a new suit, but was unable to knot his necktie or tie his shoelaces properly, having not done so for 25 years. A prison service major looked after his tie before he left, but it was only as they were waiting for Botha that Barnard saw his shoelaces were tied very clumsily, so the head of the feared National Intelligence Service got on one knee in front of Prisoner 466/64 and retied them.

The crusty old white president, known by his own supporters as the Big Crocodile, outdid himself, smiling and pouring tea for Mandela. According to Barnard, the two exchanged remarks about their health "as older men tend to do" and talked mainly about Afrikaner history, with Mandela referring to the 1914 Rebellion, when Afrikaners rose up against the government. The only current political reference came when Mandela asked Botha to release Walter Sisulu and others from prison, to which Botha gave a non-committal reply. But it appeared as if Botha's stroke had also killed his enthusiasm for bold political moves and he resigned the predidency in a huff a month after his meeting with Mandela, following an unpleasant confrontation with his cabinet, most of whom felt the need for a rapid progression of the **politics of negotiation**.

F.W. de Klerk, a conservative Afrikaner from a long line of National Party politicians, was inaugurated as South Africa's president on 20 August 1989. He was deeply moved by his pastor Reverend Pieter Bingle's statement at the ceremony that de Klerk was called by God to act fearlessly and to "find new ways where roads had entered culs de sac".

De Klerk was immediately briefed on the extent of the talks with Mandela and the ANC, of which he knew very little. He was enough of a pragmatist to realize that there was no going back. But he was confronted with four other realities: South Africa's occupation of Namibia was about to end, with independence day scheduled for March 1990; the Soviet Union and the entire Eastern Bloc were crumbling (thus removing the "communist danger" his party had feared so much); Britain, the United States and Germany continued to press hard for the release of Mandela and the ending of apartheid; and the internal resistance showed no signs of abating.

The ANC's leadership in exile, nervous about fast-moving events in which they had no part and suspicious of the apartheid government's true intentions, made its own move in the negotiations dance a day after de Klerk's inauguration. In what became known as the **Harare Declaration**, the ANC said it believed "a conjuncture of circumstances exists which, if there is a demonstrable readiness on the part of the Pretoria regime to engage in negotiations genuinely and seriously, could create the possibility to end apartheid through negotiations". But to make sure this happened, the ANC also announced they would intensify the armed struggle and continue calling for the international isolation of South Africa.

Only two months after taking office, de Klerk sanctioned the release from prison on 15 October of Walter Sisulu, Ahmed Kathrada, Andrew Mlangeni, Elias Motsoaledi, Ray Mhlaba and two other political prisoners. This was to prepare the ground for the release of Mandela and to "test the waters". On 4 December de Klerk flew his cabinet and senior officials to a two-day meeting at a secluded game reserve where, after some debate, it was agreed that the ANC and other political organizations had to be legalized and all political prisoners released as a prelude to political negotiations.

A week later, on 13 December, de Klerk met Mandela in Cape Town. They both knew that it was their responsibility to complete the processes that had been started – they both also knew that Mandela was likely to replace de Klerk as president of the country. It was a businesslike meeting with no tea or small talk, the two politicians sizing each other up. Mandela found de Klerk to be a "man of integrity" and de Klerk said he knew Mandela was someone he "could do business with".

The big moment was to be de Klerk's speech at the opening of parliament on 1 February 1990. Mike Louw, by now a central figure in the unfolding drama, provided the framework of the speech. De Klerk also consulted his senior colleagues, with the Minister of Defence, Magnus Malan, arguing vociferously that the Communist Party couldn't possibly be legalized. But as de Klerk went to the podium, no one knew exactly what he was going to say. The speech only lasted thirty minutes, but it changed South Africa forever. The ANC, the Communist Party, the PAC and other organizations were legalized. Political prisoners would be released. Negotiations for a political settlement would begin soon. And Nelson Mandela would be a **free man** in the coming few days with no preconditions. The country, the ANC leadership in exile and people interested in South Africa all over the world were stunned. Veteran South African journalist Allister Sparks remembers whispering to a colleague as de Klerk was concluding, "My God, he's done it all."

> **"The aim is a totally new and just constitutional dispensation in which every inhabitant will enjoy equal rights, treatment and opportunity in every sphere of endeavour – constitutional, social and economic."**
>
> F.W. de Klerk, from his speech at the opening of parliament, February 1990

Nelson Mandela was watching the speech on television in his house at Victor Verster prison. "It was a breathtaking moment," he said later, "for in one sweeping action he had virtually normalized the situation in South Africa. Our world had changed overnight." The changes he had spent the last fifty years fighting for and had said he was prepared to die for, were about to happen. His twenty-seven years and seven months in prison had not been in vain.

The UDF hastily put together a National Reception Committee to prepare for Mandela's release, led by **Cyril Ramaphosa**, secretary general of the mineworkers union and a shrewd politician and negotiator. They only had a week to organize – de Klerk wanted Mandela freed on 10 February – and asked for the release to be postponed by a day so they could finalize arrangements. The evening before the big day, committee members met with Mandela to discuss his first public address.

Free at last

Thousands of people lined the streets outside Victor Verster prison on the morning of 11 February, with hundreds of journalists and TV crews from all over the world jostling for position. It was a long wait, partly because, to the very punctual Mandela's great irritation, Winnie arrived late at the prison. And then at 4pm Mandela, in a grey suit with his hand in Winnie's, walked stiffly out of the prison gates. When the crowd started chanting "Amandla!" he cracked a smile and as he raised a clenched fist they went hysterical. If he or anyone else had had their doubts, they now knew that South Africa's road to democracy was irreversible.

Mandela was driven to Cape Town's historic **Grand Parade** and taken onto the balcony of the **City Hall**. The crowd surged forward to get a better look at the man very few of them had seen in the flesh before but who had come to embody all their dreams and anger. Some climbed on cars, trees and statues to get closer, a few youngsters even hanging from the balcony where he stood. When the noise had died down, Mandela pulled out his prepared speech – and then discovered he had left his reading glasses behind at Victor

Nelson and Winnie Mandela raise their fists in acknowledgement of the cheering crowds, shortly after his release from Victor Verster prison. (Alexander Joe/AFP/Getty Images)

Verster. He quickly borrowed Winnie's. Flanked by Ramaphosa, Walter Sisulu and with Winnie standing behind him, he addressed the excited crowd.

It was not a rousing speech, nor was it particularly reconciliatory or visionary. Foreign journalists expressed their disappointment and the speech was not welcomed by de Klerk nor by Western leaders concerned with South Africa – Margaret Thatcher expressed her discomfort with "the old ritual phrases". The armed struggle would continue, Mandela said, and sanctions against South Africa would be stepped up. "We have waited too long for our freedom. We can no longer wait. Now is the time to intensify the struggle on all fronts."

But the speech wasn't aimed at a foreign audience or at white South Africans. Mandela knew, and the previous evening Ramaphosa had concurred, that he had to address the ANC and UDF leaders and members who were very suspicious of his unilateral and mostly secretive talks with the apartheid regime. He wanted to put their minds at rest that he was still the old Nelson Mandela, freedom fighter and loyal member of the ANC.

Mandela spent his first night of freedom with **Archbishop Desmond Tutu** in the leafy white suburb of Bishopscourt. The next day he flew to Johannesburg, but his old Orlando house was surrounded by thousands of people and he had to spend the night elsewhere. On 13 February he addressed a hundred thousand followers in a Soweto stadium and that night returned to No. 8115 in Orlando West for the first time since going underground in 1961. He called the humble house "the centre point of my world, the place marked with an X in my mental geography". Here he faced a new challenge: how to get close to his children and try to heal the wide rift that had grown between him and his wife. Because of the hectic schedule he was to follow over the next few months, he wasn't especially successful.

Mandela did, however, succeed in getting closer to the whites and other minorities in South Africa in the weeks and months ahead. His decades-long interaction with prison warders and his many meetings with Niel Barnard's team had given him a good idea of the fears of white people and he knew how to address them. The white attitude towards him progressed from seeing him as a communist terrorist to astonishment that a man who had been in jail so long could be so void of bitterness or revenge, and ultimately to something close to hero-worship.

Mandela's first major concern was the bloody conflict for political turf between the supporters of the ANC/UDF and chief **Mangosuthu Buthelezi**'s Inkatha Freedom Party (IFP). Buthelezi was one of the first people Mandela phoned after his release, but militant ANC leaders in KwaZulu, the IFP's stronghold, prevented the two from meeting. Mandela flew to Durban where he urged a huge crowd to "throw your guns, your knives and your pangas [machetes] in the sea". But his words had no impact. The **conflict** continued for almost four years and it is estimated that over five thousand people were killed.

Another pressing concern was to pacify the ANC leadership in exile, especially the military men who were unhappy with all the reconciliatory talk. Mandela flew to Zambia, visited Zimbabwe and Namibia, flew to Tanzania and Egypt, and then on to Sweden, where his old partner and friend Oliver Tambo was recovering from a stroke suffered late in 1989. On his way back Mandela attended a rock concert in his honour in London. Once he was home he visited his **mother's grave** in his childhood village of Qunu, and then paid a visit to Robben Island to persuade 25 MK prisoners who distrusted the government to accept their freedom. After a meeting with de Klerk, he embarked on a further hectic six-week trip to Europe and the United States.

Everywhere Mandela went he was treated like an international hero, an **icon of freedom** somewhere between Che Guevara and the Dalai Lama. A new fad started among politicians, sports stars and celebrities that would go on until long after Mandela's retirement from politics: to meet and be photographed with the great man. In New York Mandela was given the biggest tickertape parade ever through the streets and he had a raucous welcome when he addressed the UN General Assembly. In Washington he addressed a joint session of the houses of congress and met President **George Bush**. On July 2 1990 Mandela was on the cover of Time magazine with the headline "A Hero in America". On the way home from the US he had lengthy talks with **Margaret Thatcher** and not long after visited Uganda, Kenya and Mozambique. Africa and the world had gone Mandela crazy.

The first ANC exiles started returning to South Africa in April. On 2 May 1990, delegations from the ANC, led by Mandela, and the government, led by de Klerk, met formally for the first time at the presidential residence in Cape Town, **Groote Schuur**. But it was all still "talks about talks": preparing the ground for negotiations; granting indemnity to ANC members; and establishing channels of communication between the two parties. The talks made a huge leap forward in August when the ANC, mainly at the instigation of militant communist **Joe Slovo**, announced that it was suspending all armed actions "in the interest of moving as speedily as possible towards a negotiated, peaceful political settlement". This was cemented formally in an accord with the government on 12 February 1991.

The negotiations proper only got underway on 20 December 1991 when the ANC, the government, the National Party and seventeen other organizations and parties met in a huge exhibition centre in Kempton Park outside Johannesburg. Collectively they were called **CODESA**, the Convention for a Democratic South Africa. It was an extremely hopeful start, but one that nearly ended in disaster. Speaking last, de Klerk criticized the ANC for breaking its word by not demobilizing its guerrilla army and questioned the ANC's ability to enter into binding agreements.

Mandela was livid and demanded a right to reply. De Klerk and most others present experienced Mandela's formidable wrath for the first time. He accused de Klerk of being underhand and breaking confidence on agreements between them. De Klerk turned crimson as Mandela coolly and in measured tones berated him: "Even the head of an illegitimate, discredited minority regime, as his is, has certain moral standards to uphold. If a man can come to a conference of this nature and play the type of politics he has played, very few people would want to deal with such a man." The political leaders present were holding their breath, but the two men realized they could not let the altercation slow down the progress of negotiations. They made peace, but would never have a cordial relationship.

The **negotiations process** moved from from crisis to crisis. The government and the National Party wanted "power-sharing" with the black majority but without really relinquishing power. They wanted the rights of white people to be protected in the constitution, almost to the extent that the white minority would be able to veto government decisions perceived to be against their interests. They aimed to draw out the process as long as possible, hoping the mystique around the ANC would wear off. And they wanted CODESA to negotiate a constitution before the first one person, one vote election. De Klerk's confidence was given a boost when he won almost three quarters of the vote in a white referendum on the negotiations in March 1992. The ANC, on the other hand, wanted a quick process and for the new constitution to be determined by those elected during the first elections. It refused to accept any constitutional solution based on race or group rights.

The biggest crisis came on 17 June 1992 when a group of armed Zulu migrant workers who supported the IFP launched an attack on residents of Boipatong township outside Vereeniging, killing 38 people. The ANC suspected that the IFP men were armed and supported by the police and announced that it was breaking off all negotiations with the government. The tensions in the country simmered for more than two months and were only broken when the two negotiating partners appointed Ramaphosa and the new Minister of Constitutional Affairs, Roelf Meyer, to act as a channel of communication. It became known as the **Cyril-Roelf Channel** and worked well, thanks to the warm personal relationship the two men developed. At the end of September 1992 the two parties signed the breakthrough **Record of Understanding** and resumed negotiations at the end of November. By this time, under the leadership of Mandela and de Klerk, the two parties understood that they were partners in a process that could not be allowed to fail.

NOBEL LAUREATES

If South Africans, with their deep divisions and long, brutal history of colonialism and apartheid, could make peace, then peace should be possible everywhere. That was what many were thinking as the negotiations proceeded in 1993. And that was the reason why **Nelson Mandela** and **F.W. de Klerk** were declared joint winners of the **Nobel Peace Prize** at the end of the same year.

Few people had a problem with Mandela being so honoured, but many, including South Africans, felt de Klerk – with his long service in various apartheid governments – did not. **Winnie Mandela** called it "an insult" to Mandela. The two men were clearly not at ease with each other when they appeared at the **Oslo ceremony** and in an interview afterwards Mandela held de Klerk responsible for the continuing violence in South Africa. When they appeared on the hotel balcony, as is the custom, **ANC supporters** below were heard shouting "Kill the Boer!" But Mandela did call the occasion "a milestone for two former enemies building a new South Africa".

The debate on whether de Klerk deserved the Nobel Prize still surfaces from time to time in South Africa. Those who thought he did, point out that his government had such strong defence forces at its disposal that he could easily have resisted a transfer of power for several more years. **Roelf Meyer**, de Klerk's chief negotiator, says that the then president deserved all the accolades: not only had he never backed down having started the negotiation process, but he had successfully convinced the majority of white South Africans to accept majority rule.

The next big crisis came when the hugely popular MK commander and Communist Party leader, **Chris Hani**, was assassinated outside his home on 10 April 1993. The country was now on a knife edge. Shortly afterward the assassin, a Polish anti-communist immigrant, Janus Walusz, and his co-conspirator, a right-wing Conservative Party member, Clive Derby-Lewis, were arrested. The police were tipped off by one of Hani's white neighbours who saw Walusz race away.

Something had to be done to lower the temperature. De Klerk agreed that Mandela should go on national television to calm emotions. "Tonight I am reaching out to every single South African, black and white, from the depths of my being," a sombre Mandela said. "A white man, full of prejudice and hate, came to our country and committed a deed so foul that our whole nation now teeters on the brink of a disaster. A white woman, of Afrikaner origin, risked her life so that we may know, and bring to justice, this assassin." From that moment on everyone in South Africa knew who the real leader of the nation was. There was an emotional funeral for Hani, but virtually no violence or revenge attacks, and within days South Africa was calm again.

On 18 November 1993 the parties in the negotiation process agreed on an interim constitution with a specially entrenched **Bill of Fundamental Human Rights** that would be in place until the newly elected parliament could draft a final constitution. In January 1994 forty-six years of white National Party rule came to an end when a **Transitional Executive Council** was established. The date for the country's first one person, one vote election was set for 27 and 28 April 1994.

But there was one more crisis. In March 1994 the former head of the South African Defence Force (SADF), **General Constand Viljoen**, led a force of armed men, many of them former soldiers, to protect Lucas Mangope, head of the Bophuthatswana Bantustan, whom the ANC wanted to unseat. The then current SADF commander, General George Meiring, confronted his former commander and warned him that his force would not be allowed to go against the decisions of the transitional government. When undisciplined members of the extreme right-wing group, the Afrikaner Weerstandsbeweging (AWB) under **Eugene Terre'Blanche**, also invaded Bophuthatswana and started firing on black pedestrians at will, Viljoen decided to withdraw and a day later registered to take part in the elections under the banner of the **Freedom Front**. The right-wing threat was finally neutralized. At the very last moment Buthelezi's IFP also decided to take part – so late that its name had to be pasted on to the already printed ballot papers. The end of the bloodiest internecine war in South Africa was coming to an end.

Election day

On 27 April 1994 the people of South Africa went to the polls, a day that must rank as one of the most remarkable in modern history. South Africa had never before organized an event of this magnitude and there were many delays and hiccups. On the day millions of South Africans stood patiently for hours and hours in long, snaking queues waiting to make their crosses. For many – perhaps even most – of them, it was the first occasion when they had met across colour and class lines on an equal footing; where they could observe each other's humanity. White and black, coloured and Indian shared stories and refreshments, joked and helped each other. For the majority it was a day of liberation, for whites a day of huge relief and the moment they were welcomed into the heart of the nation. And towering over all this was the unifying, reassuring figure of Nelson Mandela.

After a few days of counting, the results were announced. The ANC had won 63 percent of the vote; the National Party 20 percent; the IFP 11 percent; the Democratic Party 2 percent; the PAC 1 percent. On 10 May Nelson Mandela was inaugurated as South Africa's **first democratic president**, with Thabo Mbeki and F.W. de Klerk as his two deputies.

A hundred thousand people gathered in front of the **Union Buildings**, the seat of government in Pretoria, along with more heads of state and other dignitaries than had ever gathered in Africa. Air force jets flew overhead with the colours of the **new South Africa** trailing behind them; camouflaged helicopters carried the striking new flag underneath. The symbolism escaped few present or watching the live broadcast on television: not so long ago these very same aircraft were used to attack the people who fought against the apartheid state.

The imposing figure of Nelson Mandela was central to the celebrations. And then he spoke: "We enter into a covenant that we shall build a society in which all South Africans, both black and white,

Voters in the Western Cape queue up for miles waiting to cast their ballot in the 1994 election. (© Peter Turnley/CORBIS)

will be able to walk tall, without any fear in their hearts, assured of their inalienable right to human dignity; a rainbow nation at peace with itself and the world." He ended his address with a pledge that reminded many of his final statement during the Rivonia Trial: "Never, never, and never again shall it be that this beautiful land will again experience the oppression of one by another, and suffer the indignity of being the skunk of the world."

12 President Mandela

"We, the people of South Africa, feel fulfilled that humanity has taken us back into its bosom, that we, who were outlaws not so long ago, have today been given the rare privilege to be host to the nations of the world on our own soil."

Nelson Mandela, from his inaugural presidential address, 1994

Nelson Mandela was 75 years old when he became **president of South Africa**. It was a demanding role and the task was far more complex than his fifty-year struggle to overthrow apartheid and establish a democracy. On the one hand he had to reassure white South Africans and other minorities that they were appreciated as fellow citizens and would not be overwhelmed by the black majority, on the other he had to fulfil the expectations of black people that their new freedom would quickly reverse the conditions brought about by decades of apartheid and centuries of colonialism. A country designed to serve white interests at the expense of the black majority had to be completely redesigned while maintaining stability and stimulating economic growth.

The transition from white oppression and minority rule to democracy proved relatively smooth and peaceful, due in large part to Mandela's own efforts and personality. The spirit in the country, even among whites, was positive and upbeat and South Africa was now the darling of the world.

The new president inherited a country with modern cities and a sophisticated, **functioning infrastructure**. There were highly rated universities, efficient legal, financial and banking systems and a very rich mining industry, especially in gold, diamonds, manganese, platinum and coal. **Food security** was assured by some of the most successful farmers in the world. South Africa was by far the biggest and most advanced economy in Africa, and ranked among the top 25 economies in the world with the tenth largest stock exchange.

Inherited problems

On the downside, the overwhelming majority of black South Africans were living in **underdeveloped townships** or squatter camps. Half of them had no proper sanitation, a third had no electricity and a quarter had no clean water piped into their homes. Black schools were in a no less terrible state, with many unqualified teachers and two million children absent from school. More than a third of the black population was **illiterate**. Black shareholding in the private sector was negligible and about eight million people were classified as completely destitute. **Unemployment** was almost forty percent. The life expectancy of black citizens was much shorter than that of whites and the black infant mortality rate was more than double that of white infants. Under the 1913 **Land Act** black ownership of land was limited to about ten percent of the country's land mass.

The substantial **police force** was almost entirely led by white officers and had a huge legitimacy problem because of its use by successive governments to implement apartheid regulations and act against pro-democracy activists. Most of the state prosecutors, magistrates and judges were white, many of them tainted by their application of the apartheid laws. The **South African Defence Force** was the mightiest on the continent, but not only was it almost completely staffed by whites, it was also widely seen as a racist organization used to quell anti-apartheid protests and destabilize neighbouring states that had supported the ANC. The massive **state bureaucracy** was also mostly white and only accustomed to administering the apartheid system.

If these massive inequalities were not enough, Mandela also had to deal with the polarized mindset of the population, entrenched since white settlement started in 1652 and hardened by decades of legalized oppression and resistance. White South Africans had been conditioned to believe that black people were inherently inferior and fundamentally different, people who could not run a modern economy or democracy. This view was reinforced by the perceived failures, disasters and conflicts in much of the rest of Africa. Because whites made up only about ten percent of the population many thought the black majority would overwhelm them, and Afrikaners in particular were deeply fearful that their language and culture would be stifled.

Black South Africans were still full of resentment and anger – passed from generation to generation – at being robbed of their **ancestral lands**; about the strict measures that excluded them from most well-paid jobs and from gaining a stake in the economy; about being denied **full citizenship** outside the apartheid Bantustans; about the humiliation of **enforced segregation** and the pass laws; about the **inferior education** afforded them; about being treated as lesser human beings by "settlers" who came from Europe; about **police brutality** and the violent suppression of anti-apartheid campaigns.

No wonder black expectations were unrealistically high. Gaining political power was wonderful on a symbolic level, but black South Africans were impatient to be rescued from poverty and to start living like the rich whites they saw in the leafy suburbs.

Rebuilding the nation

Mandela was under no illusions about the challenges ahead, despite having been in jail for most of his adult life. His contact with policemen and prison warders and his long meetings with Kobie Coetsee, Niel Barnard and others had given him a good insight into the white psyche, while the angry young men sent to Robben Island after 1976 and the militant cadres who returned from MK's camps after 1990 made sure he realized the extent of growing black resentment.

Nation-building and **national reconciliation** became President Mandela's most important projects, with special emphasis on reassuring white South Africans. One advantage Mandela had was that his government was one of **National Unity**. As well as F.W. de Klerk and Thabo Mbeki as his two deputies, he had a cabinet that included Roelf Meyer of the National Party, and Mangosuthu Buthelezi of the Inkatha Freedom Party, all serving alongside ANC ministers – old foes ruling the country together.

Within a very short time Mandela's approval rating from white South Africans grew from five percent to over fifty percent. As a gesture to white Afrikaners and coloured Afrikaans speakers, he spoke Afrikaans on many occasions, despite a heavy accent and not being fluent in the language. In his opening address of the first parliament in 1994 he quoted a poem, "Die kind" ("The child"), by the liberal Afrikaans poet Ingrid Jonker.

A policy of forgiveness

Mandela was generous in his comments about P.W. Botha, calling him a gentleman and a reformer, and about de Klerk, whom he called "a great son of Africa", and had a warm relationship with Constand Viljoen, the army general who had threatened military intervention shortly before the 1994 elections. When he attended a service in the same Afrikaans church which several apartheid prime ministers had belonged to, he quipped that he needed bodyguards to protect him from "being killed out of love".

In 1995 he invited to lunch the widows and wives of prominent leaders from both sides of the conflict. These included the widows of former prime ministers John Vorster and Hans Strijdom and those of the anti-apartheid heroes Steve Biko and Moses Kotane. "We have fought our fights in the past," he said. "We have forgotten it now. We must build a new South Africa. By attending this occasion, each one is putting an important brick in the new building we are putting up."

Betsie Verwoerd, the widow of the much hated apartheid leader Hendrik Verwoerd, was also invited, but was too old to travel. Two weeks later Mandela flew by helicopter to Orania, the whites-only enclave in the Northern Cape, where Betsie was living, despite it being a self-proclaimed *volkstaat* (Afrikaner homeland). During his visit he had tea and *koesisters* (a traditional twisted doughnut) with the frail 94-year-old, and he even helped her with her speech, in Afrikaans, because she had forgotten her reading glasses. The townspeople, regarded as white supremacists by most South Africans, warmed to him and cheered when he spoke.

Demonstrating his remarkable ability to forgive and to embrace old enemies, Mandela invited the much-resented prosecutor at the Rivonia Trial, **Percy Yutar**, to lunch. Yutar was overwhelmed: "I wonder in what other country in the world you would have the head of the government inviting someone to lunch who prosecuted him thirty years ago. It shows the great humility of this saintly man."

Rugby World Cup triumph

Mandela's most astonishing act of nation-building occurred when South Africa hosted the **Rugby World Cup** in 1995. This was the first time South Africa had taken part in the competition because of the long-standing sports boycott of the country. Mandela understood the importance of rugby for Afrikaners: it was their favourite sport and an integral part of their culture. Well before the tournament began, he invited the team captain, **Francois Pienaar**, to his office and the two established a good relationship. The South African team are known as the **Springboks** and Mandela started wearing the team cap and encouraged black South Africans to "get behind our boys", despite the fact that there was only one black player in the team. Pienaar, in turn, made sure his team could sing the new national anthem, "Nkosi Sikelel' iAfrika", and the popular black folk song, "Shozaloza".

When the Springboks made it to the final against the New Zealand All Blacks at Johannesburg's **Ellis Park** on 24 June, Mandela visited "his boys" in the locker room before kick-off. As the president, smiling broadly, stepped onto the pitch wearing a green-and-gold Springbok jersey with the number 6 – Pienaar's number – on the back, the 62,000 spectators, almost all of them white, exploded in ecstasy. Then the chant started: "Nel-son! Nel-son! Nel-son!" For team manager Morne du Plessis, it was a "moment of wonder, a moment of magic"; Mandela showed he could forgive "and now they – white South Africa, rugby South Africa – showed in that response to him that they too wanted to give back."

Most experts agreed that the All Blacks were the better team, but the Springboks played out of their skins that day – for Madiba and for all the people of South Africa, Pienaar said afterwards. Still, after eighty minutes the score stood at 9–9 and the game went into extra time. It was extremely tense and physical, but the breakthrough came a few minutes before the end with a long-range drop goal by fly-half **Joel Stransky**. The 'Boks had won the Rugby World Cup.

As Mandela – still in his number 6 jersey – went onto the podium to hand the trophy to Pienaar, the crowd went wild and people all over South Africa, white and black, rich and poor, were delirious with them. With the world's televison cameras focused on him Pienaar was asked by an interviewer how it felt "to have 62,000 fans supporting

Springbok captain Francois Pienaar receiving the 1995 World Cup trophy from President Mandela. (David Rogers/ALLSPORT/Getty Images)

you here in the stadium?" He replied: "We didn't have 62,000 fans behind us. We had 43 million South Africans." Street parties broke out all over South Africa and, for the first time, even residents of the country's black townships celebrated a rugby victory.

In 2008 the journalist **John Carlin** wrote a book, *Playing the Enemy – Nelson Mandela and the Game that Made a Nation*, about the event and its significance. Carlin quotes the liberal Afrikaner politician Frederik van Zyl Slabbert, who attended the game, telling how he was surrounded by "classic Boers with their potbellies, shorts and long socks, real AWB (Afrikaner Resistance Movement) types", and how one of them with tears rolling down his face "kept saying, in Afrikaans, 'that's my president, that's my president'."

Mandela's handling of the World Cup tournament was a spectacular piece of **statesmanship**. As Carlin says, "Mandela mastered, more than anyone else alive (and, quite possibly, dead), the art of making friends and influencing people."

Dissenting voices

Inside his cabinet Mandela did not have so much success at reconciliation. His relationship with de Klerk remained strained and the resentment he harboured, that had surfaced when the two received the Nobel Prize, was still in evidence in renewed personal attacks on his deputy.

In May 1996 de Klerk withdrew the National Party from the Government of National Unity, on the grounds that they had too little influence on the ANC cabinet majority and because the ANC "was acting more and more as if they no longer needed a multi-party government". His party now went into opposition but, following de Klerk's retirement from politics in 1997, soon disintegrated with many of its members joining the liberal **Democratic Alliance**. Roelf Meyer, a National Party minister in the Mandela cabinet, thought

THE SOUTH AFRICAN CONSTITUTION

The South African Constitution, adopted in 1996 by the first elected parliament representing all citizens, is widely regarded as the most progressive constitution in the world. It has a strong emphasis on human rights and dignity, and entrenches freedom of speech and association as well as the right to housing, healthcare, education, access to information and access to courts. It is the only constitution in Africa that forbids discrimination on the basis of gender or sexual orientation. Gay and lesbian marriages are legal in South Africa.

The **Preamble** to the Constitution reads:

We, the people of South Africa,
Recognise the injustices of our past;
Honour those who suffered for justice and freedom in our land;
Respect those who have worked to build and develop our country; and
Believe that South Africa belongs to all who live in it, united in our diversity.
We therefore, through our freely elected representatives, adopt this
Constitution as the supreme law of the Republic so as to –

- Heal the divisions of the past and establish a society based on democratic values, social justice and fundamental human rights;
- Lay the foundations for a democratic and open society in which government is based on the will of the people and every citizen is equally protected by law;
- Improve the quality of life of all citizens and free the potential of each person; and
- Build a united and democratic South Africa able to take its rightful place as a sovereign state in the family of nations.

that withdrawing from the multi-party government was the biggest mistake of de Klerk's political career and had negative long-term effects on race relations.

But Mandela was also beginning to **encounter dissent** from within his own party. Black political commentators and columnists started complaining that he was spending too much energy appeasing whites and not enough on the plight of black South Africans. It was a criticism that was picked up by members of the ANC. **Thabo Mbeki**, Mandela's deputy president, did nothing to defend Mandela and later openly agreed with the criticism. Mandela was irritated by the attacks, responding that the allaying of white fears was crucial and in the interest of stability.

Impatience among black citizens was steadily surfacing and it soon became clear that the culture of **violent protest** had not disappeared. Black students, school pupils, nurses, prison warders, policemen and workers started engaging in the same lawless protests as during the turbulent 1980s. Hostage-taking, vandalizing property, looting and blockading public streets were all methods used to display anger. "Some have misread freedom to mean license to impose chaos," Mandela warned in parliament, adding, "the small minority in our midst which wears the mask of anarchy will meet its match in the government we lead".

Soon after he took office, Mandela had instituted **feeding schemes** for schoolchildren, and **free health care** for children and pregnant women, but his government struggled to cope with the huge backlog of housing, sanitation, electricity, clean water and hospital care needed for poor, mostly black, South Africans. Part of the problem was the decline in the economy during the years up to 1994. The servicing of **government debts** had taken up more than ninety percent of revenue, which left little to spend on much needed projects. The other, more complex, problem was the low skill levels and lack of experience of the new politicians, especially among the administrators and civil servants who had replaced those from the apartheid era.

On top of that, the old apartheid defence force and the guerrillas of both MK and the PAC's army (the Azanian People's Liberation Army) had to be integrated into a new South African National Defence Force. Similarly, the old "political" police force had to be rehabilitated under the command of new black officers into a new South African

Police Service. These processes were fraught with suspicion, hostility, insecurity and over-assertiveness.

Negotiating for a new order had been an easier task than governing the results of those negotiations.

Mounting criticism

Perhaps inevitably, three negative factors were cropping up with increasing regularity: a **culture of entitlement** among many who thought the new order meant "it was our turn to eat"; **corruption and fraud** in tendering for government contracts; and the **abuse of public funds** for personal enrichment. These were problems that Mandela struggled to deal with.

Soon after the first elections, members of parliament voted for massive increases in their, and ministers', salaries and allowances. Black newspapers and commentators were outraged. The "priest to the nation", **Archbishop Desmond Tutu**, declared that the new government had "stopped the gravy train only long enough to get on". Mandela launched an uncharacteristically vicious attack on his old friend, calling him irresponsible and accusing him of jumping on the bandwagon, saying Tutu should have spoken to him in private. Tutu responded sharply that he had in fact done so, adding that it was "very distressing that the president should behave like an ordinary politician" and that it was "beneath his stature".

It turned out that Mandela could be as **intolerant of criticism** as the next "ordinary politician" and had a tendency to put party loyalty and party interest above open debate. When black editors criticized him for acting in a dictatorial fashion, he attacked them for doing the dirty work for white newspaper owners.

When **Bantu Holomisa**, a deputy minister, publicly accused the Minister of Public Enterprises, **Stella Sigcau**, of accepting a bribe from casino magnate Sol Kerzner, Mandela dismissed him. No action was taken against Sigcau, who was a member of Xhosa royalty. He also stood by another of his ministers, Nkosazana Dlamini-Zuma, when she was found to have misspent European Union money on an anti-Aids play and to have misled parliament about it.

The **biggest scandal** to hit the post-liberation government had its origins in Mandela's time, though nobody has suggested that he was directly involved or benefited from it. In 1999 South Africa purchased three submarines, four corvettes, thirty helicopters and fifty-two military jets for about seven billion dollars. Despite rumours of financial irregularities and massive bribe-taking, there has never been an official enquiry. Revelations of malpractice continue to surface to this day. On top of this, the ANC was severely criticized for spending such a vast amount on military hardware while the country faced no foreseeable military threat and about half of all South African households lived below the poverty line.

The reality was that Mandela was everything but a hands-on head of government. "He was the big-picture guy, the father of the nation", is how one member of his first cabinet described him. Most of the day-to-day management of the government was handled by Thabo Mbeki, who functioned more as prime minister than deputy president. In 1997 Mandela even called Mbeki the "de facto ruler" of South Africa, and he was certainly the chief architect of **economic policy**. Mbeki's macro-economic plan, GEAR (for Growth, Employment and Redistribution), only appeared on Mandela's desk shortly before it was implemented, and for the last two years of Mandela's presidency Mbeki chaired all cabinet meetings.

One of the biggest criticisms of the Mandela administration was its slow and weak reaction to the **HIV/Aids pandemic** sweeping through the country. Mandela loyalists blame this on Mbeki, who later surfaced as a notorious Aids denialist. Others think that Mandela's status as a traditional African patriarch made him reluctant to talk about sexual matters, although he became much more open on the subject after his presidential term was over.

Foreign policy

Right through his term as president, Mandela had a strong presence on the world stage. "There was not a single head of state anywhere who would not immediately take Madiba's telephone calls," says a confidante who advised him on foreign relations, "even though he sometimes forgot about the vastly different time zones and called presidents at four in the morning."

But while he unashamedly made use of his charm and personal prestige, he was adamant that South Africa owed no allegiance to any power bloc and that **human rights**, as ensconced in the South African Constitution, should be the cornerstone of the country's foreign policy. He had a significant rider, though, which was continuing loyalty to old friends and supporters. When criticized for his warm relations with Cuba and Libya, Mandela said, "They are our friends and that is the moral code I respect above everything else." He used a similar argument to justify selling arms to Syria.

One result of this controversial stance was that Mandela scored what was seen, at the time, as one of his greatest foreign policy successes. Libya's **Muammar Gaddafi** was an old supporter of the ANC and the two men retained a good relationship. In October 1997 Mandela surprised the world when he met with Gaddafi in Tripoli and spoke glowingly about his moral leadership – this of a man who was accused of being a sponsor of international terrorism. From Tripoli Mandela went on to the Commonwealth summit in Scotland, and on his way back home returned to Tripoli, this time awarding Gaddafi South Africa's highest honour, the **Medal of Good Hope**. The Western powers, and many South Africans, were deeply disappointed by Mandela's stance. What they did not know was that Mandela had just launched a sensitive and complex diplomatic initiative aimed at the "rehabilitation" of Gaddafi and the lifting of sanctions against Libya. Mandela's chief of staff, Jakes Gerwel, and Saudi

Arabia's ambassador to the US, Prince Bandar bin Sultan, started a long, secretive and difficult process of liaising between Libya, the US, the UK and the UN. The end result was that Gaddafi accepted that the two Libyan agents suspected of blowing up Pan Am Flight 103 over Lockerbie in Scotland in December 1988, in which 270 people were killed, would be handed over to the authorities in Scotland to be tried under Scottish law. The arrangement also meant the end of Gaddafi's isolation from the West and of sanctions against his country.

Mandela's foreign policy was less successful in other parts of Africa. In 1995 his government failed to prevent the Nigerian dictator Sani Abacha from executing the activist and writer **Ken Saro-Wiwa**, and in 1997 failed to mediate successfully between Zairean dictator Mobutu Sese Seko and his successor, Laurent Kabila. Then in 1998 South Africa led a badly planned and chaotically executed military invasion of **Lesotho** to protect the government against a threatened coup. This led to much resentment in Lesotho towards its neighbour.

Healing the wounds

As South Africa was preparing to implement its negotiated political settlement, the question arose how the country should deal with its bitter past. There was a strong school of thought, both inside and outside the ANC, that apartheid politicians, soldiers and policemen should be hauled before tribunals and charged with war crimes. Mandela and others warned that this would seriously jeopardize the project of national reconciliation, but they also knew that not dealing with the past could be equally dangerous. The negotiating partners agreed that a form of truth commission would be a better alternative. The new parliament passed the **Promotion of National Unity and Reconciliation Act** in 1995, which created the Truth and Reconciliation Commission (TRC). Archbishop

Desmond Tutu (centre) and fellow commissioners listen to testimony during a TRC hearing in East London. (Philip Littleton/AFP/Getty Images)

Desmond Tutu was appointed chairman and the TRC started its activities in April 1996.

Truth and Reconciliation Commission

The TRC was made up of three committees: the **Human Rights Violations Committee** tasked with hearing the evidence of victims and survivors of gross human rights violations between 1960 and 1994; the **Rehabilitation and Reparation Committee** that had to attend to the plight of those found to have suffered directly from such violations; and the **Amnesty Committee** that would hear the applications of soldiers, policemen and politicians on all sides who wanted indemnity for politically motivated crimes like murder, torture and kidnapping.

Unlike most other truth commissions held before, the TRC's proceedings were open to the media and the public. For more than two years the people of South Africa were confronted on a daily basis with the heart-wrenching stories of the victims of political violence, and had the opportunity to look perpetrators in the face as they confessed their crimes and were quizzed by their victims and the TRC. In order to win an amnesty for their actions perpetrators had to convince the Amnesty Committee that their crimes were ordered or sanctioned by government or a recognized political party; that the acts were proportionate to the political aim; and that they had disclosed all relevant information. In this way several apartheid police generals, a number of officers and members of the former Security Police were granted immunity from any future prosecution for murder and torture.

The leaders of the National Party, the last apartheid government, the ANC and all other political parties were called before the commission to explain their role in the conflict. Former president **P.W. Botha** was summoned to appear before the TRC and was charged in court when he refused. After he succeeded in challenging the legality of the subpoena, the TRC abandoned the case against him. In its final report, the TRC declared that "by virtue of his position as head of state ... Botha contributed to and facilitated a climate in which gross violations of human rights could and did occur, and as such is accountable for such violations".

> **"Dear fellow South Africans, accept this report as an indispensible way to healing. Let the waters of healing flow from Pretoria today ... to cleanse our land, to cleanse its people and to bring unity and reconciliation."**
>
> Desmond Tutu, on presenting the TRC report to Mandela

Late in 1998 the TRC presented the summary of its findings to political parties to give them the opportunity to make inputs before the final report was released. At this point both F.W. de Klerk and Thabo Mbeki reacted angrily and tried to prevent publication of the report. De Klerk was livid because he was named as an accessory

JAIL HOUSE REPLICA

After his release from jail, the people of Nelson Mandela's ancestral village of **Qunu** in the Eastern Cape gave him a plot with the invitation to go and live with them. He had a holiday home built on the plot: an exact replica of the house at **Victor Verster Prison** where he stayed during the last two years of his incarceration. He explained that the prison house was the first comfortable house he had lived in and he liked its feel. Mandela kept up his prison routine of making his own bed every morning for years after his release, even when he became the president of the country and was staying in the best hotels in the world.

to the violations of human rights, while the ANC said that the TRC had "criminalized" the struggle against apartheid. Desmond Tutu was adamant, however, warning the ANC that South Africans "can't assume that yesterday's oppressed will not become tomorrow's oppressors". The TRC was even-handed, he said, and while the ANC's armed struggle was legitimate, some of the acts perpetrated during that struggle were not. Addressing all his critics, Tutu said, "reconciliation based on falsehood, on not facing up to reality, is not true reconciliation and will not last".

Once again it was Mandela who rose above the squabbles. He received the TRC's final report at a special function, thanked Tutu and his staff and said that the commission had "contributed to the work in progress of laying the foundation of the edifice of reconciliation". The South African Truth Commission was widely regarded as very successful and an example to other nations emerging from conflict.

Winnie under scrutiny

For Mandela, there was one chapter in the TRC process that he found particularly painful: the special hearing on **Winnie Mandela** and her

Mandela United Football Club (MUFC). Although Mandela and Winnie had separated in 1992, he remained supportive of her and, despite opposition from inside his party, appointed her as the deputy minister for arts, culture, science and technology in his first government. He came to regret his loyalty very soon afterwards.

The ghost of **Stompie Seipei** simply would not go away. In mid-1994 Winnie's former friend and confidante, **Xoliswa Falati**, was released from prison after having been convicted of criminal activities related to Winnie and the MUFC. Angry that Winnie had escaped jail, Falati started telling reporters that Winnie had been involved in several other murders, as well as kidnappings and assaults. Winnie obtained a court order against Falati to stop her making any more allegations and in parliament she fiercely defended herself, blaming the Stompie murder and other MUFC atrocities on circumstances created by apartheid.

However, Winnie had since become embroiled in new scandals, financial and otherwise, some of which involved abuse of her ministerial office and of the charities she had launched. She was later convicted of fraud and was given a suspended jail sentence. In February 1995 **Adelaide Tambo** (Oliver's widow) and ten other leaders of the ANC Women's League resigned in protest against her wayward behaviour.

Mandela's patience with his estranged wife finally snapped when she publicly attacked him and his government (of which she was a part) accusing them of doing more to appease white South Africans than to remedy the damage caused by apartheid. Mandela ordered a public apology but rejected her first attempt, at which point she was forced to sign a more grovelling letter.

Shortly afterwards she was at it again: "Nothing has changed", she told a public meeting in the Eastern Cape. "In fact, your struggle seems much worse than before, when the fight was against the Boers." She was fired from her post a few days later, on 27 March 1995, but remained a member of parliament.

Another divorce

Mandela had been trying for some time to get Winnie to agree to a **divorce**, because he wanted to avoid fighting for it in court. Despite their separation and her rather public relationship with at least one other man – what Mandela called her "brazen public conduct and infidelity" – Winnie resisted. In March 1996 the divorce case went before the court in Johannesburg.

Most South Africans were pained at the sight of their president having to be called as a witness at his own divorce case and admired his quiet dignity. His last court appearance had been at the Treason Trial in 1964. Mandela made it clear that he was desperate not to air the details of his private life in public, but Winnie had made that impossible. There was reference to a love letter Winnie had written to her young lover, the lawyer **Dali Mpofu**, given to Mandela by a newspaper. "The contents of the letter, My Lord, were incompatible with a marriage relationship and even if there was a possibility of reconciliation, it confirmed my decision never to reconcile with the defendant."

Mandela was annoyed at Winnie for obtaining an affidavit from **Kaizer Mantanzima**, his boyhood friend, onetime rival for Winnie's hand, and later political enemy. Mantanzima said that, according to Thembu custom, Mandela could not divorce Winnie without mediation by Thembu elders. Mandela's response in court was slow and clear: "I respect custom, but I am not a tribalist. I fought as an African nationalist and I have no commitment to the custom of any tribe. Custom is not moribund. It is a social phenomenon which develops and changes." When asked by his counsel, **Wim Trengove**, whether any intervention by Mantanzima could have saved his relationship, Mandela said, "Can I put it simply, My Lord? If the entire universe tried to persuade me to reconcile with the defendant, I would not." He added that he was "determined to get rid of this marriage".

Mandela then uttered the painful words that made a lot of people who still admired Winnie change their minds. "Ever since I came back from jail, not once has the defendant ever entered the bedroom whilst I was awake. I kept on saying to her, 'look, men and wives usually discuss the most intimate problems in the bedroom. I have been in jail for a long time. There are so many issues, almost all of them sensitive, I would like to have the opportunity to discuss with you.' Not once has she ever responded … I was the loneliest man during the period I stayed with her."

During his cross-examination by Winnie's counsel, **Ishmail Semenya**, an agitated Mandela repeatedly asked not to be pushed to "wash our dirty linen in public". He said, "I appeal to you not to put any questions which might compel me to reveal facts which could damage the image of the defendant and bring a great deal of pain to our children and grandchildren."

The judge granted Mandela a divorce and the financial settlement was made out of court – reportedly involving several million rand. Winnie now uses the surname **Madikizela-Mandela**.

Winnie and the TRC

In 1997 the TRC turned its attention to one of the most serious breaches of human rights from inside the liberation movement: the campaign of terror waged on the people of Soweto by Winnie Mandela's so-called **football club**. The TRC investigators wanted to confront her with eight murders and ten other serious crimes that she and her group of thugs were accused of.

The hearing was a media circus with dozens of foreign and local television networks and journalists jostling for position. Winnie arrived with several bodyguards and dressed extravagantly. Her approach to the hearing was simple: she **denied everything** and expressed her outrage that anyone could accuse her of anything unbecoming.

The witnesses painted a picture of a violent, abusive woman who used her "football club" as a tool of terror. A Soweto woman testified that Winnie savagely beat her for hours because Winnie was sleeping with her boyfriend; parents of some of the disappeared boys accused her of killing their children. The star witness was the "coach" of the club, **Jerry Richardson**, already in jail for killing Stompie Seipei. He said Winnie (who he called "Mummy") had instructed him to kill three young people – Kuki Zwane, Lolo Sono and Siboniso Tshabalala – and that he had reported back to her after doing so. Along with others, Richardson insisted that Winnie was present when Stompie was brutally tortured – some said she actively participated – and that she ordered Richardson to kill the unconscious boy. "Mummy never killed anyone but used us to kill a lot of people." Apart from denying everything, Winnie falsely claimed that she was in Brandfort at the time of Stompie's torture.

Desmond Tutu could not bear to see Winnie falling apart on the witness stand. He told her how much he loved her and begged her over and over again to apologize: "You are a great person, and you don't know how your greatness would be enhanced if you were to say: 'Sorry, things went wrong, forgive me'."

Winnie stood up and without acknowledging any part of the evidence before the commission, said she was sorry that so many people were killed. "I am saying it is true, things went horribly wrong. I fully agree with that and for that part of those painful years when things went horribly wrong, for that I am deeply sorry." Winnie still has her followers, especially in the ANC Youth League, but she lost all political clout after the TRC hearings.

The nation was relieved when news leaked out that Mandela had found a new love. A year after Winnie's TRC hearings he married **Graça Machel** (see box overleaf).

GRACE FOR MADIBA

"When I'm alone I'm very weak," Nelson Mandela once smilingly confessed in a television interview. After his release from prison, as his relationship with Winnie fell apart, he admitted to being very lonely. And then he met **Graça Machel**, widow of the former president of Mozambique, Samora Machel, and fell in love again. Completely.

The two met briefly when Mandela visited **Mozambique** after his release, but he really noticed her when she was awarded an honorary doctorate in Cape Town in 1992. The next year, when Oliver Tambo died, Mandela took over his role as a father figure to Samora Machel's six children, which meant seeing much more of Graça.

After his **divorce** from Winnie was finalized, Mandela started talking openly about his new love. He took her with him on foreign trips and the two were seen holding hands, even stealing a kiss at a state function in Zimbabwe. "It's just wonderful that finally we have found each other and can share a life together," Graça said in a radio interview. But they denied any talk of getting married. She still felt that she "belonged to Mozambique", but from 1996 began dividing her time between Mandela and her home in Maputo.

"I'm in love with a lovely lady," Mandela told a television interviewer. "I don't regret the reverses and setbacks because late in my life I'm blooming like a flower because of the love and support she has given me." In the end they couldn't bear to be apart and in 1998 bought a house together, getting married in July of that year. He was 78 and she was 51 years old. "Graça has made a decent man out of him," Archbishop Desmond Tutu said at the wedding. (He had previously complained that the two were setting a bad example by living together without being married.)

Graça could not be more different from Winnie. A dignified and thoughtful woman, she is highly educated and speaks French, Portuguese, Italian, English and Spanish fluently, as well as her native Tsonga. As a young woman Graça trained as a soldier in **FRELIMO**, the Mozambican liberation movement of which her late husband was the leader. After her country won independence in 1975, she was appointed minister of education, and since then has held several prestigious international positions. In 2007, along with Nelson Mandela, Desmond Tutu, Kofi Annan, Mary Robinson, Jimmy Carter and others, she launched **The Elders**, a group of world leaders of great experience and integrity who wished to play a role in international affairs, supporting peace initiatives and seeking ways to ease human suffering.

Nelson Mandela and Graça Machel celebrating his 87th birthday in Johannesburg in 2005. The event included the third Nelson Mandela Annual Lecture given, that year, by Kenyan environmentalist and Nobel Peace Laureate, Professor Wangari Maathai. (© Mike Hutchings/Reuters/Corbis)

Epilogue

Towards the end of his term as president, a **whispering campaign** was started by those around his deputy, Thabo Mbeki, that Mandela was actually too old to lead the country, and that most of the accolades for the achievements of his presidential term should actually go to Mbeki. But while some ambitious ANC politicians may have believed that, the people of South Africa continued to see him as their saviour, as the icon of their new freedom.

Looking back on his five-year presidency one can find many errors of judgement and even bad governance. But analysts and historians are agreed that it was Nelson Mandela's leadership that enabled the **peaceful transition** – from conflict and oppression to stable democracy – to take place, and that this would be remembered as one of the greatest achievements of a political leader in the modern era.

Mandela did not stand for re-election – one of very few African heads of state who willingly served only one term. After the general election in 1999, Thabo Mbeki became free South Africa's second president.

13 Retirement

"I'm confident that nobody present here today will accuse me of selfishness if I ask to spend time, while I'm still in good health, with my family, my friends, and also with myself ... My appeal therefore is: Don't call me, I will call you!"

Nelson Mandela, announcing his retirement to the press, 2004

Nelson Mandela made it clear that he was only available to serve one five-year term as president. After the 1999 general elections he was succeeded by **Thabo Mbeki**, once a confidante; now, increasingly, an enemy.

The ambitious Mbeki's resentment of Mandela's national and international standing had been brewing while he was still deputy president. The two men's personalities and styles were vastly different: Mandela was confident, charismatic and jovial, while Mbeki was terribly insecure, aloof and regarded himself as an intellectual. Physically, Mandela was larger than life, and strikingly tall and colourful in his trademark "Madiba shirts", while Mbeki was small of stature and rarely seen without a conservative suit and tie.

The source of much of Mbeki's irritation on becoming president was the often-asked question which hung over him like a dark cloud: how would he fill Mandela's shoes? It frustrated him so much that he once lost his cool and remarked sharply: "Yes, indeed. Mandela has much larger feet. I guess I could go back twenty-seven years and try going to jail, and then come out and wear funny shirts."

Mbeki takes over

Mbeki made it clear that Mandela's brand of reconciliation was "unsustainable and wrong" and that he was going to focus on **black advancement**, affirmative action and economic empowerment. In those companies partly or wholly controlled by the state – the airways, railways, arms manufacturing and electricity supply – he rapidly increased the replacement of white civil servants and bureaucrats with blacks. This was often done with little regard to qualifications or experience. He repeatedly talked about the "two nations" in South Africa: the one rich and white, the other black and poor. He even called white South African citizens "colonialists of a special kind".

Mbeki was soon **deeply resented** by most white South Africans; even whites within his own government and party started feeling uneasy. Inside the ANC he changed the culture from one that welcomed debate and discussion to one where his opinions mattered most, and criticism was seen as undermining.

Mandela tried very hard to stay out of his successor's hair and very rarely made any comments on the affairs of government. But when he felt compelled to give his opinion, he was more often than not informed that Mbeki was too busy to take his calls or meet with him.

The HIV/Aids controversy

It was the catastrophic **HIV/Aids pandemic** in South Africa that eventually forced Mandela into full confrontation with his successor. Mbeki, for reasons many have speculated about for years, decided to believe a tiny group of international **maverick scientists** who thought that the HI Virus either did not exist or, if it did, wasn't causing Aids. It was poverty, so the thinking went, that was killing the people of Africa, not Aids. Aids was less of a reality than it was a massive conspiracy by Western pharmaceutical companies to make huge profits. **Antiretroviral drugs**, Mbeki argued, were toxic and would kill hundreds of thousands of Africans while making their manufacturers rich.

He was supported by his loyal minister of health, **Manto Tshabalala-Msimang**, who launched her own campaign promoting the use of garlic, lemon and beetroot as a treatment for Aids. Mbeki told parliament that there was no link between HIV and Aids: "Aids is Acquired Immune Deficiency Syndrome. I don't believe it is a sensible thing to ask: does a virus cause a syndrome? It can't. A virus will cause a disease." In a 2003 interview with *The Washington Post* he claimed that he didn't know anyone who had died of Aids. By then, close to a million South Africans had died of Aids-related illnesses, and many in the field – including the prominent immunologist Professor Malegapuru Makgoba, and Aids lobby group, the **Treatment Action Campaign** – felt that Mbeki's denialism was tantamount to genocide.

Mandela tried to lobby the government and its ministers privately, but in 2001 he came out in public with direct criticism of Mbeki's Aids policies and his refusal to introduce antiretroviral drugs, saying the pandemic was a war that was killing more people than in any other war. "We must not continue to be debating, to be arguing, when people are dying."

Mandela increased his HIV and Aids activism and made it abundantly clear that he thought Mbeki was wrong and irresponsible. At this point Mbeki decided to put him in his place. The occasion was the annual meeting of the **ANC's national executive**, the party's most senior decision-making body, in March 2002, which Mandela attended.

Senior members of the national executive, eager to please Mbeki, lined up to launch unprecedented and vicious attacks on Mandela – he was undermining the president, breaching party discipline and "trying to rule the party from the grave". Six years later one of those present, Ngoako Ramatlhodi, wrote how "Madiba was being violated in the most brutal manner by junior leaders of the movement". He said no one "had the courage to stand up and defend an innocent old man, our former president and icon of the struggle. They must have been genuinely afraid of Mbeki, a president who somehow turned out to be the ANC itself. He has become larger than the movement."

Mandela was stunned and deeply disappointed, but it did not affect his involvement in fighting the scourge of Aids. He spoke

GATEKEEPER AND HONORARY GRANDDAUGHTER

It is as unlikely a combination as one can imagine: a black revolutionary leader and international icon of liberation and a humble *Boeremeisie* (Afrikaner maiden) from a right-wing white background, whose childhood nightmare was that blacks would massacre her and her family. That is the story of **Zelda la Grange**, Nelson Mandela's closest confidante besides his wife. After the end of his presidential term, anyone who wanted to see Mandela had to get past Zelda first.

When Mandela was released from jail in 1990, Zelda was nineteen years old. She was in the family swimming pool in **Pretoria** when her father told her the news of his release. "The terrorist is being freed," he said, "now we're in trouble." Zelda was barely aware of Mandela's existence at that point.

After school she studied to be an executive secretary and her first job, in 1994, was as a typist in the civil service. Shortly after, Mary Mxadana, Mandela's private secretary, recruited her to the president's office. When she met Mandela for the first time, two weeks later, she was shaking with fear that he might humiliate her. "My people sent this man to jail", was the thought that crossed her mind. She started crying, but Mandela took her hand, spoke to her in Afrikaans and calmed her down.

One year later, before a state visit to Japan, Mandela invited her to serve as his **secretary**. When he left office, he asked her to continue working for him. It did not take long before she virtually ran his life. She was gatekeeper, adviser, companion and manager. Even heads of state and international celebrities who wanted to see Mandela – and there were many of them – had to convince Zelda first, and she proved to be fiercely protective. It helped that she was a stickler for punctuality, as Mandela was, and had the **Calvinist work ethic** of many Afrikaners. When his schedule became less hectic, she spent more and more time working with the Nelson Mandela Foundation and his charities. But right until his health scare in early 2011, Mandela would almost always be seen in public leaning on Zelda's arm.

powerfully at the 2002 international UN conference on Aids in Spain and on his return was photographed wearing a T-shirt with the slogan "HIV Positive" on it. From 2003 he used his prison number, **46664**, as the name of a series of international charity concerts to raise awareness of HIV and Aids.

Madiba has his hearing aid adjusted by his personal assistant, Zelda la Grange, at a Nelson Mandela Foundation event in 2008. (© Siphiwe Sibeko/Reuters/Corbis)

Zelda calls her employer *khulu*, granddad. He likes it, and says she's his granddaughter. She says he's changed her life and outlook completely – she laughs when she tells of family members who thought it was humiliating for a white Afrikaner girl to serve a black man. She struggles to find the right words to explain her *khulu*, and ends up saying he is "a very, very special, extraordinary human being".

When Mandela's son **Makgatho** died on 6 January 2005, Mandela announced at a press conference that he had died of Aids-related factors. He made this unusual announcement because he believed it would help to break the stigma surrounding HIV and Aids, especially in Africa; he wanted it to be seen as a normal illness, just like cancer or tuberculosis. The Treatment Action Campaign, South Africa's foremost Aids lobby group, praised Mandela for disclosing the cause of death "in the national interest of raising awareness and destigmatising Aids during a time of great personal pain and loss".

When Thabo Mbeki was dumped as leader of the ANC in December 2007, and shortly afterwards sacked as president, the tide began to turn. His replacement and former deputy, **Jacob Zuma**, completely reversed both the ANC and the government's policies on HIV and Aids, and rolled out the biggest programme of antiretrovirals in the world.

Elder statesman

Mandela continued to remain active in **international affairs** after leaving office. From December 1999 he acted as the facilitator between Hutu and Tutsi movements in **Burundi**, where some 400,000 people had been killed in tribal violence since 1996. This was two years after the genocide of almost a million Tutsi by Hutu militia in neighbouring Rwanda. Mandela replaced former Tanzanian president **Julius Nyerere**, who had had no success in getting the different groupings to agree on a negotiated settlement. Drawing on his South African experience and using his unparalleled moral authority and international standing to the full, Mandela succeeded in getting the Hutu and Tutsi to sign an accord in August 2000.

Mandela did not hesitate to raise his voice about other international developments after he had left office. In 1999 he sharply criticized the NATO intervention in **Kosovo** and had harsh words for US President

George W. Bush's foreign policy and the US **invasion of Iraq**. "What I am condemning is that one power, with a president who has no foresight, who cannot think properly, is now wanting to plunge the world into a holocaust," he said. He didn't spare the British Prime Minister **Tony Blair**, whom he once called "the foreign minister of the US".

Mandela announced his retirement from public life in 2004. He was 84 years old, and the fourteen years he had spent outside prison had aged him considerably. He started spending more time at his wife Graça's beautiful **Maputo** home overlooking the Indian Ocean, and with his many grandchildren. But visiting government leaders, international dignitaries and celebrities from the music, sports and

THE MADIBA SHIRT

Before he went to jail, Nelson Mandela was known for his smart suits and tasteful ties. But as a free man he abandoned the Western suit and introduced the world to the **Madiba shirt**, a loose-fitting, brightly coloured shirt that he elevated to "formal attire", even wearing it to international state banquets.

The Madiba shirt is now popular all over sub-Saharan Africa, but not everyone approves. Mandela's old friend Archbishop Desmond Tutu, who mostly wears a purple cassock, says, "It's all right when he teases me and says he can't understand a man who wears a dress in public being fussy about his own sartorial habits, but I still don't think too highly of his sartorial taste."

Such is the style's success, that 46664 (the Nelson Mandela Foundation's charity organization) has announced plans to launch a global clothing brand that will include versions of the Madiba shirt.

The origin of the shirt is contested. **Yusuf Surtee**, the owner of a chain of men's clothing shops, says Mandela was given a loose, colourful shirt by President Suharto of Indonesia and liked it so much he asked Surtee to design and make more of them. However, clothes designer **Desré Buirski** says she made a hand-painted silk shirt for Mandela and gave it to his bodyguards in 1994. Mandela wore the shirt at the rehearsal of the opening of the first democratic parliament, and since then she has made many more for him.

Mandela was once asked by a child why he liked the shirts and explained, "You must remember I was in jail for twenty-seven years. I want to feel freedom."

film worlds kept on visiting him, in many cases clearly for that special trophy – a photograph with Madiba. Every year his office turns away many thousands of requests for meetings with him.

One meeting he did make was **F.W. de Klerk**'s seventieth birthday party in Cape Town in 2006. He jokingly said he was in reality the same age as de Klerk, because he had "spent thirty years idly relaxing on islands and other resorts" while de Klerk had to deal with the politics of the time. He used the occasion to publicly credit the former president for his important role in bringing about democracy in South Africa.

Charities and foundations

After Mandela's retirement in 1999, the **Nelson Mandela Foundation**, was founded, its mission to lead "the development of a living legacy that captures the vision and values of Mr. Mandela's life and work". Through its Centre for Memory and Dialogue, the foundation aims to contribute "to the making of a just society" by promoting dialogue around critical social issues. In 2009 the foundation launched **Mandela Day**, the 18 July, as an international day of humanitarian action: "It is a call to action for people everywhere to take responsibility for making the world a better place, one small step at a time, just as Nelson Mandela did." The Foundation also manages Mandela's public schedule and issues statements on his private life and health.

The **Nelson Mandela Children's Fund** was founded four years earlier as an international fundraising organization for schools and hospitals in southern Africa. It's a charity that has always been very close to Mandela's heart and business leaders came to dread the inevitable call from him – both during and after his presidency. His tactic was to invite top business people for lunch or dinner, at the end of which he would say that he wanted them to finance the building of a specific school for township children. No one ever declined the request. In

2003 the Nelson Mandela Foundation and the Rhodes Foundation established the **Mandela Rhodes Foundation**, which offers scholarships to African students undertaking postgraduate studies.

Squandering the legacy

From 2007 onwards, deep divisions and power struggles rocked the ANC, with new and **rampant populism** manifesting itself for the first time in the party's history. Allegations of corruption, tender fraud, nepotism and living the high life were directed at the ANC government on an almost weekly basis. Mbeki's successor, Jacob Zuma, was facing serious corruption and fraud charges that were controversially dropped just before he became president. The leader of the ANC Youth League and foremost Zuma supporter, **Julius Malema**, blatantly threw Mandela's reconciliation project out the window by calling all white South Africans "criminals" and singing a song with the words "Kill the Boer" at public rallies. When the Afrikaner civic movement **AfriForum** took Malema to court, charging him with hate speech, Winnie Madikizela-Mandela demonstrated her support for the Youth League leader and told a crowd outside court that it wasn't Malema who was on trial, "but the revolution".

As his health deteriorated, Mandela spent less time at Graça's Maputo residence and more at their home in **Houghton**, Johannesburg. Though described as "Mandela's rock" by a Nelson Mandela Foundation spokesperson, **Graça Machel** is an international political heavyweight in her own right and a sought-after speaker all over the globe. In April 2010, she was recognized as one of the world's hundred most influential people by *Time* magazine, who called her "a born freedom fighter".

Although the Mandela clan's private lives are kept confidential, reports of tension between Graça and Winnie and her daughters surfaced from time to time, suggesting an upcoming battle over the Mandela legacy.

Mandela's grandson **Mandla**, the eldest son of Makgatho, is one person positioning himself as heir apparent. Since becoming the traditional chief of Mvezo, Mandla calls himself Nkosi Zwelivelile ("the nation has appeared"). A wealthy businessman and ANC member of parliament, he recently sold the television rights to Mandela's funeral to the **South African Broadcasting Corporation** for three million rand, and has repeatedly come into conflict with the Nelson Mandela Foundation. According to Mandla, the Foundation is "profiting from my grandfather's name but they give nothing to his people". In 2010 he defended traditional marriages with underage girls, saying, "When a man sees this one is ripe for marriage, then she is taken and she is put through a ceremony and then she's ready. Don't bring in white people's things such as her age." Unlike his grandfather, Mandla has two wives.

Waiting for the inevitable

In January 2011 Nelson Mandela had a serious **health scare** and spent several days in intensive care with a respiratory infection, but recovered sufficiently to be able to vote at home in the May local government elections. The chairperson of the Independent Electoral Commission, **Brigalia Bam**, personally went to help him vote and said he was in good health and spirits. "Mandela looks fine and handsome as he always does," she said. She added that he was mildly irritated when officials wanted to help him make his cross, saying he could manage on his own. Photographs of the occasion were the first published since his hospitalization four months earlier.

Right-wing extremists in South Africa are predicting that a mass killing of whites will follow Mandela's demise. The opposite is much more likely: Mandela's funeral will probably be a rare moment of national unity across all racial, ethnic and class boundaries in South Africa as the people of his "rainbow nation" mourn the passing of the one person they all loved in equal measure.

PART TWO

MANDELA, SOUTH AFRICA & THE WORLD

14 A man of Africa

Nelson Mandela is viewed by many worldwide as a unique, spectacular individual with an extraordinary personality and charisma. In Africa, he is seen more as the best possible product of the continent's history and wisdom, surfacing at exactly the right time.

There is no denying that Mandela the international icon cannot be divorced from his South African context. Someone with the same personality type and attributes in another society or at another time may not have soared so far above the ordinary.

The same applies to the two other leaders who rose to prominence with Mandela, **Walter Sisulu** and **Oliver Tambo**. There are South African scholars who believe that if there had been no Mandela, Sisulu may well have blossomed even more as a national leader and played a similar role to the one his younger colleague ended up playing. But there is no knowing if Sisulu – or anyone else – would have had the stature, charm, vision and chutzpah to initiate negotiations with the apartheid regime and sell his vision to fearful whites and angry blacks.

Africa, with its particular history of colonial exploitation, has indeed produced other Mandela-like figures, such as the nineteenth-century chiefs Mohlomi, Sekhukhune, Sobhuza and Kgama. The most notable example is **King Moshoeshoe**, who was born 130 years before Mandela in modern-day Lesotho.

King Moshoeshoe

Moshoeshoe was the young chief of a minor Sotho-speaking clan in central South Africa when the *difaqane* started, the devastating period of conflict and warfare between 1815 and 1840 in the central and eastern parts of the subcontinent that killed or traumatized hundreds of thousands of people.

Unlike the other leaders of the time, such as **Shaka** of the Zulu and **Mzilikazi** of the Matabele, whose armies were doing most of the damage, Moshoeshoe decided on a completely different strategy. He chose an impenetrable flat mountain fortress as the location from where he would defend rather than attack. At a time of great famine, he accumulated a vast herd of cattle and planted crops to feed his own people, and then started inviting the starving, the refugees and even his attackers to join his kingdom, regardless of their tribal or ethnic affiliation. So the **Basotho nation** was formed.

When the first European missionaries reached him in 1833, Moshoeshoe embraced them, not as masters or teachers, but as allies, treating them as his fellow Basotho, and he used them to help deal with the new threat of the Boer settlers and the British colonialists who were beginning to invade his land.

Moshoeshoe proved himself as a supreme diplomat, pragmatist and nation-builder during one of southern Africa's most difficult periods. If he had followed the violent actions of the other African, white settler and British colonial leaders of the time, it is arguable that South Africa would not have developed into the beacon of stability and progress it is today. In fact, a figure such as Mandela would have been impossible a century later. Which is why Moshoeshoe has been called the Mandela of the nineteenth century.

As well as being a charismatic leader, a visionary and a humanist, Moshoeshoe also had the insight to anchor himself in the wisdoms and traditions of the African chiefs and philosophers who came before him, while at the same time embracing change and modernization.

Like Mandela, he overcame his own **tribal instincts** and sought strength in diversity; like Mandela he realized the value of inclusivity, human dignity, stability and peace. (And not unlike Mandela, he had a love of good clothes, a black top hat and tails being his favourite after his leopardskin cloak. He also had a love of women – he married more than a hundred of them.)

But Moshoeshoe's main attribute that made him stand out as an extraordinary, trend-setting leader of his time was his **counter-intuitive** thinking. When it was clear that he had to build the strongest army in the region and annihilate his enemies, he had his able-bodied men raise cattle and plant maize. When logic dictated that this was a tribal war and enemy tribes had to be wiped out, he invited them to join his kingdom.

Mandela's counter-intuitivity

Aguably, it is Mandela's similar talent for counter-intuitive thought that has made him a great leader rather than just a good one. In one of the most insightful pieces on leadership in Africa and the world, South African author and intellectual **Professor Njabulo Ndebele** highlights this quality in Mandela. He tells the story of Mandela's secret 1993 meeting with three old-order Afrikaner generals who were threatening an armed intervention. He told them that if they went to war, the ANC would not have the resources to stand up to them on the battlefield. But, he said, the generals and their followers could not win either because of the overwhelming numbers of black people and because the international community would side with them. The generals had to agree and face the fact of their mutual dependency.

Ndebele then suggests that "Nelson Mandela's supreme gift to us is to expose us to the notion of counter-intuitive leadership and its immense possibilities. The characteristic feature of this type of leadership is in the ability of a leader to read a situation whose most observable logic points to a most likely outcome, but then to detect

MANDELA, CHRISTIANITY AND COMMUNISM

Is Nelson Mandela a Christian? An atheist? A communist? Many people – not least South Africans – asked such questions when he was released from prison and became the first president of a free South Africa. His mother, **Nosekeni**, was a devout Christian, and he was baptized and attended two **Methodist** missionary schools where he had a strongly Christian education. While a student at Fort Hare University, Mandela regularly attended church services, joined the **Students' Christian Association** and even taught Sunday school classes. He still retains his Methodist Church membership cards from 1929 to 1934. However, doubts about his faith were raised when he blamed his estrangement from his first wife, **Evelyn Mase**, on her Christian fervour and also because of his closeness to many communists aligned to the ANC.

In a 1977 letter from prison, written to his daughter Maki, Mandela mentioned his Christian activities at Fort Hare. "Even here I attended all church services and have enjoyed some of the sermons," but he added: "I have my own beliefs as to the existence or non-existence of a **Supreme Being** and that it is possible that one could easily explain why mankind has from time immemorial believed in the existence of a God." Mandela also referred to the fact that less than a third of people polled in England were believers. "I'm making no comment on the matter … except to say that, from experience, it's far better, darling, to keep religious beliefs to yourself. You may unconsciously offend a lot of people by trying to sell them ideas they regard as unscientific and pure fiction."

Following his release, Mandela never publicly talked about his religious beliefs and shunned questions on the subject. However, in 1990, he had a number of meetings with his friend and fellow Robben Island prisoner **Ahmed Kathrada** to discuss the draft of his autobiography, *Long Walk to Freedom*. In the manuscript, **Richard Stengel** (Mandela's American ghost-writer) stated that: "He [Mandela] felt some pangs at abandoning his Christian beliefs which had fortified his childhood." According to a transcript of the conversation, Kathrada asked him: "Now, is it correct wording to say you

in that very likely outcome not a solution but a compounding of the problem. This assessment then calls for the prescription of an **unexpected outcome**, which initially may look strikingly improbable. Somehow, it is in the apparent improbability of the unlikely outcome 'abandoned your Christian beliefs'?" Mandela: "No, never." Kathrada: "It would be wrong, isn't it?" Mandela: "I say it is absolutely untrue. I never abandoned my Christian beliefs."

Referring to his early contacts with **Communist Party** members, Mandela remarks in *Long Walk to Freedom*: "I was also quite religious, and the party's antipathy to religion put me off." **Dr Stanley Mogoba**, a Methodist minister who later became president of the PAC, was a fellow prisoner of Mandela on Robben Island and he remembers the two of them receiving Holy Communion there. Mandela's biographer and friend **Anthony Sampson** thought he was "not a formal believer like Tambo: he did not quote the Bible, or discuss theology. His interest in the Sunday services was more political than religious."

Successive apartheid governments insisted that Mandela was a communist. During his early years as an activist in the ANC Youth League he was in fact virulently and publicly **anti-communist**, but later became close to some of the party's leaders and sanctioned cooperation between the ANC and the Communist Party. At the Treason Trial in 1960 he was asked by his counsel whether he was a communist. His response was: "Well, I don't know if I did become a communist. If by communist you mean a member of the Communist Party and a person who believes in the theory of Marx, Engels, Lenin and Stalin and who adheres strictly to the discipline of the party, I did not become a communist." At the Rivonia Trial he said, "From my reading of Marxist literature and from conversations with Marxists, I have gained the impression that communists regard the parliamentary system of the West as undemocratic and reactionary. But, on the contrary, I am an admirer of such a system."

Mandela told Richard Stengel that he was never "a Party man" and thought Marxism was "something that actually was subjecting us to a foreign ideology". According to the South African Communist Party's own records, Mandela never became a member

that we can derive principles for its sustainability. A leader then has to sell the unexpected because he has to overcome intuitive doubts and suspicions that will have been expected. In this act of salesmanship is the content that crucially counts."

> "Men of peace must not think about retribution or recriminations. Courageous people do not fear forgiving, for the sake of peace."
>
> Nelson Mandela, talking to Anthony Sampson

It can be argued that it was within Mandela's grasp to enforce a different kind of settlement with the white government of South Africa, and then proceed to punish whites for their role in his and his people's suffering, and in doing so to satisfy the desire for retaliation felt by most black South Africans. In Zimbabwe, following independence in 1980, **Robert Mugabe** started off as a great reconciliator like Mandela, but soon found it politically expedient to mobilize against the white minority in order to create a new common enemy he could rally black Zimbabweans against.

Nelson Mandela revisiting his cell in Robben Island in 1974. (© Jürgen Schadeberg)

Instead, Mandela risked the wrath of his own party's radicals and many of the former oppressed by embarking on a remarkable **charm offensive** that not only disarmed white intransigents and ensured the end of right-wing militancy, but ensured stability and economic continuity. And he sold this risky endeavour to the nationalists, the communists, the workerists, black consciousness disciples, and to the entire country, both young and old, through the sheer force of his own personality and moral authority.

Former US President **Bill Clinton** recalls Mandela's response when he asked him whether he felt an anger at the moment of his release: "I said, 'Come on, you were a great man, you invited your jailers to your inauguration, you put your pressures on the government. But tell me the truth. Weren't you angry all over again?' And he said, 'Yes, I was angry. And I was a little afraid… But when I felt that anger well up inside me I realised that if I hated them after I got outside that gate then they would still have me.' And he smiled and said, 'I wanted to be free so I let it go.' It was an astonishing moment in my life. It changed me."

Leadership exemplar

Perhaps if leaders elsewhere in the world had been capable of the same kind of counter-intuitive vision, risk-taking and leadership as Mandela, then the Middle East might not still be a powder keg, the genocide in Rwanda and the Balkan states (taking place as he became president) might have been prevented and the wars in Afghanistan and Iraq avoided. During and after his presidency of South Africa, right up until his retirement in 2004, Mandela has been the closest thing the world has had to a political leader with a truly global appeal.

In part his stature as an international statesman has been built on his 27 years in jail. Politicians, leaders and ordinary people everywhere asked themselves how they would have survived such an experience, and they marvelled at the way it seemed to have deepened Mandela's resolve to effect not only freedom, but peaceful transition from apartheid to democracy; how it seemed to have strengthened his humanity and his capacity to embrace his enemies and turn them into friends and allies.

Surviving such a long period of detention and emerging from it undiminished gave Mandela a licence to be bold and adventurous – how does one challenge such a person's magnanimity, how can anyone ever call him a "sell-out" or "soft" on his former enemies? How could senior Western leaders actually take him on when he publicly criticized them or argued the case of his old friends who were regarded as enemies of the West?

> "He is a symbol and he is good at projecting what he represents, his values. But at the same time you have to look at him as a human being who has strengths and weaknesses. I want him as a human being. He is a symbol, that's correct, but he is not a saint."
>
> Graça Machel, talking to Anthony Sampson

Mandela himself has said several times, as has his wife **Graça Machel** and many close friends, that he isn't a saint and shouldn't be treated as one. His womanizing tendencies as a younger man, his failings as a father, his vanity, his stubbornness, his occasional fierce temper and his sporadic lapses of judgement all underline this rather obvious statement. But even when these weaknesses are revealed and the notion of him as a living superhero is abandoned, Mandela still emerges as much more than an ordinary politician. Here was a man who was more of a humanist than an ideologue, who took a pragmatic approach to defeating apartheid and – having done so – displayed a unique capacity for forgiveness and reconciliation, delivering his country from near-civil war almost single-handedly, and inspiring millions of people around the world.

15 International icon

In the eyes of much of the rest of the world, **Africa** is a dark, dangerous land where civil war, disease, poverty and corruption are rife – the continent of Idi Amin, Mobutu Sese Seko, Charles Taylor and Robert Mugabe. A place with more failed states than successful democracies; of constant ethnic and tribal conflict – in Rwanda, Burundi, the Democratic Republic of Congo and Nigeria; of chaos, illiteracy and superstition.

From this land of conflict emerged a man of rare integrity and moral authority, a sophisticated political philosopher, an almost messianic figure who overwhelmed the world with his humanity, tolerance, capacity to forgive and ability to unite people. He was living proof that good can prevail over evil, that there does exist some kind of shared humanity.

Within a decade of his release, after twenty-seven years in prison, Mandela was widely regarded as the **greatest world leader** of the modern era. In the minds of billions of people, he rated higher than Mahatma Gandhi, Winston Churchill and Franklin D. Roosevelt; something between Che Guevara and Mother Teresa, Karl Marx and the Dalai Lama. His image was on more T-shirts than Michael Jackson and on more fridge magnets than diet mantras. Presidents, prime ministers, billionaire industrialists, rock and sports stars clamoured to meet and have their picture taken with him.

Perhaps what makes Mandela's African roots more relevant is the knowledge – subconscious or otherwise – that Africa is the **Mother Continent**, the birthplace of the human species. Could it be that this made it easier for people from the Americas, Europe and Asia to associate with and adopt as their idol an elderly black man from a relatively insignificant country in the far south of the southern hemisphere?

Our Madiba

To Africans, African-Americans and black people all over the world, Mandela's emergence as a revered statesman and humanitarian was a powerful rejoinder to the colonialist idea – prevalent in the world since the days of slavery – that black equals inferior.

African-Americans particularly regarded Mandela as a sort of messiah. Many prominent black Americans made the pilgrimage to South Africa and many more gathered to meet him when he visited the US: Oprah Winfrey, Harry Belafonte, Jesse Jackson, Morgan Freeman, Randall Robinson, Walter Fauntroy, Alfre Woodard, Danny Glover and Maya Angelou to name just a few. Winfrey promised Mandela in 2001 that she would build a school for disadvantaged girls in South Africa and in 2007 she opened the prestigious **Oprah Winfrey Leadership Academy for Girls** near Johannesburg. Chido Nwangwu, founder of USAfricaonline.com and *The Black Business Journal*, says Mandela has "shattered a number of ancient bogeys to smithereens" and "made nonsense of the strings of quasi-racist mythologies" put forward by right-wing Americans like radio talk show host Rush Limbaugh.

American actor **Sidney Poitier**, who played Mandela in the film *Mandela and De Klerk*, says, "Of course he has made a contribution to the status of black people, but I can't imagine there are too many people in the world for whom Mandela would not be a hero. Although we are characterized by differences of religion and culture, we are one family and he has made a contribution unlike any other. When an individual astounds with his greatness, when he puts his life on the line, it serves to strengthen all of us."

It could be argued that Mandela rekindled the kind of pride and commitment to social justice in many African-Americans that they last felt when **Martin Luther King Jr.** was alive. And, arguably, Mandela's high status in American public opinion was a contributory factor in the election of the first black US president in 2008. In many ways **Barack Obama** projected the same promise of integrity, justice and reconciliation as Mandela had.

Stuart Hall, a British cultural theorist born in Jamaica, says that the fact that Mandela is black is very significant. "Although there are many important black and Asian leaders, there are very few who command that kind of universal respect and no one else who has that capacity not only to embody and speak on behalf of the interests of the rising nations of the south but to represent a kind of consciousness which 'includes people other than my people'."

In Africa itself, Mandela has inspired the idea that the continent could be reborn as a democratic, peaceful and prosperous place. He had overcome **tribalism**, the scourge of so much of Africa, and found a balance between pride in roots and tradition and embracing modernization and globalization.

In the Annual Nelson Mandela Lecture in Johannesburg in 2008, President **Ellen Johnson-Sirleaf** of Liberia talked of how Mandela's election to the presidency of South Africa had enabled Africans to dream. "Africans dreamed of the end of the exploitation of the

> "He was no longer our cause, our battle cry, our inspiration, our mythical brother/father. He became our Madiba. And we could touch him and know our own potential, our own strength and possibility."
>
> Alfre Woodard, tribute on Mandela's 92nd birthday

past. They dreamed of having dignified economic opportunities to provide for their families. They dreamed of sending their children to decent schools. They dreamed of an end to gender disparities. They dreamed of competent governments that were accountable to the people. They dreamed of national reconciliation and national unity. And they dreamed of living in peace and security with their neighbours."

Anti-colonialist symbol

A large part of the international power of Mandela as icon is the fact that South Africa, with its bitter history of **European colonialism** and white domination, is seen as something of a pilot project for the rest of the world. In 1973 the United Nations declared apartheid to be a crime against humanity. The **Anti-Apartheid Movement** rallied many thousands of people from across the world to the cause of ending racial discrimination and enfranchising the black majority. Between the mid-1960s and the late 1980s, few other places on earth were viewed with such contempt and pessimism as apartheid South Africa. This was a country where ten percent of the population dominated the rest with an iron fist and an odious ideology. Most whites were rich or comfortably off; most blacks were poor or destitute. And the whites saw themselves as Westerners or even Europeans, being mostly of Dutch, German, French and British ancestry.

Apartheid was an assault on the sense of decency and fairness of most people in the world – and an unspoken itch on the consciences of white-skinned people everywhere, many struggling with their own demons of racial prejudice. Nelson Mandela and his comrades not only defeated apartheid and racism and **restored black dignity** and pride; they did it without driving the whites into the sea or killing them. In fact, white South Africans sat down and willingly negotiated themselves out of power and embraced the black revolutionary who played such a crucial role in ending their domination. In Mandela's own words, the oppressed not only liberated themselves, they liberated their oppressors.

Mandela is the architect and symbol of this unlikely win-win solution. In a world divided between developed and developing societies, between black and white, north and south, rich and poor, this was an extremely rare bit of good news. If divided South Africa can do it, it should be possible everywhere. "Mandela will remain a great icon," says former British Prime Minister **Tony Blair**. "The fact that a black man is the most respected figure in the world is also part of what he has brought about. The fall of apartheid was not only important for South Africa and for the world, but it also symbolized the last bastion of all that terrible bullshit you used to get about genetics."

> "When apartheid fell, it was as if racism all round the world was suddenly put in the past. It's not that racism doesn't exist today, but it isn't countenanced as part of respectable society."
>
> Tony Blair, in *Mandela, the Authorised Portrait*

Mandela and the British

The British – in particular those on the left – embraced Mandela's cause probably more than any other nation and were key participants in the international Anti-Apartheid Campaign. It was reciprocal – Mandela has always admitted to being something of an **Anglophile**. He had a polite relationships with British prime ministers Margaret Thatcher and John Major, even though their party, the Conservatives, regarded the ANC as, in Thatcher's words, "a typical terrorist organisation." He received greater support from the **Labour Party** and was very close to Tony Blair, who became Prime Minister in 1997. This did not stop Mandela from blasting Blair for his decision to join the US in the invasion of Iraq in 2003.

Mandela is one of only three foreign leaders to address a joint sitting of both houses of the British parliament – in 1993 and 1996

– the other two being Mikhail Gorbachev and Shimon Peres. The only other South African to address the House of Commons was General Jan Smuts in 1942. Mandela's statue was erected in London's Parliament Square in 2007, a few yards away from that of Smuts which was put up 51 years earlier.

London was also the scene of a number of concerts staged in support of Mandela which helped raise global awarness about his imprisonment. Following the huge success of the UK hit single "Free Nelson Mandela" in 1984, the song's writer, **Jerry Dammers**, organized an Artists Against Apartheid concert on Clapham Common in 1986. Two years later he helped to set up one of the biggest rock concerts ever, to commemorate Mandela's seventieth birthday and demand his release. The event took place on 11 June 1988 at **Wembley Stadium**: it was attended by some 70,000 people and was broadcast to more than 750 million people in 67 countries. Performers included Stevie Wonder, Roberta Flack, Whitney Houston, the Bee Gees, Dire Straits, George Michael and Sting, as well as the South African musicians **Hugh Masekela** and **Miriam Makeba**. Two years later, the same venue was filled again to celebrate Mandela's release, and in 1996 the Queen attended a concert in his honour at the Royal Albert Hall.

The common touch

Mandela's common touch, unmistakeable *joie de vivre*, joviality and inner warmth cannot be matched by any other international statesman. He also possesses a brilliant sense of showmanship and timing. There are those who have criticized him for the way he seemed to court celebrity, and – with his cool shirts and "Madiba jive" dance routine – there was certainly something of the rock star about him. But by his presence at the various concerts held in aid of his charities, he reached more people – and the widest range of people – than he could have done in any other way.

When Nelson Mandela first visited London in 1962, he and Oliver Tambo wondered whether a statue of a black person would ever be erected in Parliament Square to stand near that of General Smuts. On 29 August 2007 a bronze statue of Mandela was unveiled there in the presence of the former president and his wife Graça Machel. (© Lewis K. Bush)

At the same time, Mandela's huge global appeal means there is always a danger that people, especially those outside of Africa, will reduce him to a cuddly mascot, a secular saint, a face on a T-shirt, rather than a great African leader and product of South African society. "When we talk about Mandela as an international icon," insists **Thabo Mbeki**, "he is not only an individual, he is an individual with fundamental perspectives who represents a movement, a country, a process which is dealing with some of the most basic challenges facing humanity."

While Mandela constantly tries to bring an African perspective to political leadership, as the South African poet **Antjie Krog** points out, that's usually not what people want to hear: "We want to see him as an exception, so that we can all claim him." The world, she suggests, takes *him* seriously, but not what he stands for. "All his actions are rooted in the notion that he can only become his fullest potential if his community becomes their fullest potential. By the end of the twentieth century black people had put on the table a fundamentally different but important alternative on how to deal with a past of injustice and racism. And yet the world persists in regarding Mandela as an icon rather than a great leader. The want to hold his hand … take his photograph, but never, never to understand what he is trying to convey. There is a universal refusal to accept his soul."

16 What would Madiba do?

More than a decade after he stepped down as president and long after disappearing from public life, Nelson Mandela remains the **moral compass** of the South African people. Government and opposition politicians and leaders of civil society still regularly invoke his name and example in public debates. When depression about the state of the nation surfaces, opinion leaders almost always remind South Africans that they should remember Mandela and how he had led South Africa out of what was generally perceived to be an **impossible stalemate** – and how much better off the country was in virtually every respect compared to the apartheid era.

And yet the country has lost most of the **momentum** of what was Mandela's primary agenda after his release from prison: tolerance, national reconciliation and honest, accountable and caring government. "Madiba would be ashamed of this" is a refrain often heard in the public discourse.

Attacks on immigrants

Among the most alarming type of behaviour to have arisen since the end of Mandela's presidency is the **xenophobic violence** against African immigrants, which surfaced after 2000 and reached bloody

May 2008: Protesters march through downtown Johannesburg in protest against the violent attacks on foreigners that left many dead and injured and thousands displaced. (© Jon Hrusa/epa/Corbis)

proportions in 2008 and 2009. **Immigration control** basically broke down, especially when the police took over border protection from the army in 2004. The numbers of economic and political **refugees** in South Africa from countries such as Zimbabwe, the Democratic Republic of Congo, Somalia, Mozambique, Nigeria and Sudan are estimated at between three and five million (out of a population of 49 million), a large percentage of them without working or residence permits.

The immigrants are referred to as *makwerekwere*, slang for foreigners, and are accused of stealing South African jobs and being involved in crime. Township dwellers have turned on them and burned down their shops and houses, with more than eighty foreigners killed and thousands left homeless or robbed of their livelihood since 2008. Photographs of a Zimbabwean man burning to death after xenophobic violence east of Johannesburg in May of that year caused shock around the world.

African immigrants complained that the **South African police** were reluctant to come to their aid and sometimes even participated in the attacks. They also charged the government with treating them inhumanely in the "immigration centres" and accused the ruling ANC of complicity because of its initial denial that a problem existed and its weak condemnation of the attacks.

Archbishop Desmond Tutu repeatedly condemned the violence and pleaded for tolerance. He pointed out that many South Africans fighting apartheid were welcomed as refugees by other African states, and that some of these states allowed the ANC to have military bases on their soil even at the risk of being attacked by the forces of apartheid.

Unbuilding the nation?

Mandela's nation-building project also lost momentum. His successor, **Thabo Mbeki**, switched the priorities to **black empowerment** and assertiveness, some say at the expense of reconciliation. White political leaders accused him of "re-racializing" the country and effectively alienating minority groups. Mbeki regularly referred to the "two nations" problem in South Africa, "the one white and rich, the other black and poor". On more than one occasion he referred to white South Africans as "colonialists of a special kind" and often blamed the outrage at the horrific crime wave in the country on "racist whites" expressing their discomfort at living in a black-ruled state. White journalists, he said, liked to portray blacks as barbaric savages prone to raping and killing.

Desmond Tutu accused Mbeki in 2004 of **suppressing public debate** and of only promoting the interests of a small black elite. Mbeki reacted sharply, implying that Tutu was merely an icon of the white elite who had never been an ANC member. "One of the fundamental requirements for the rational discussion suggested by the archbishop is familiarity with the facts relevant to any matter under discussion." Tutu replied: "Thank you, Mr President, for telling me what you think of me. That I am a liar with scant regard for the truth, and a charlatan posing with his concern for the poor, the hungry, the oppressed and the voiceless. I will continue to pray for you and your government by name daily, as I have done and as I did even for the apartheid government. God bless you."

The Mbeki administration was engulfed in several corruption cases and scandals, notably the **arms procurement scandal** (see p.208). In 2005 Mbeki fired his deputy president, Jacob Zuma, after serious allegations of corruption related to the arms deal. But Mbeki's leadership style, his **Aids denialism** and his proximity to a small black elite annoyed the trade union federation COSATU, the SA Communist Party, the ANC Youth League as well as others in the ANC. When he insisted on standing for a further term as leader of the ANC, he was defeated in humiliating fashion at the national conference in December 2007 and **Jacob Zuma** became the new party leader. Under highly suspicious circumstances, all charges against Zuma were then dropped. In September 2008 Mbeki was forced to resign and after the 2009 general election Zuma became president.

Zuma was so beholden to all the different forces that saved him from prosecution and propelled him to power that he was like a leaf blown by the wind. Riddled with infighting and power struggles, his party had little time and energy left for running the country properly or efficiently. At most party functions, Zuma sings his controversial signature struggle song, "Awuleth' Umshini Wam" (Please bring me my machine gun), a chant that has been taken up by xenophobic mobs since 2008.

A smiling Mandela is supported by Mbeki (right) and Zuma (left) at an ANC rally held in August 2008 to celebrate his 90th birthday. A month later the ANC forced President Mbeki to resign, paving the way for Zuma – his former deputy – to succeed him. (© Siphiwe Sibeko/Reuters/Corbis)

Rampant populism

From 2007 the ANC has been engulfed in a wave of **populism** that it had not experienced before. Reckless statements – seldom repudiated by the ANC leadership – became the formula for winning power in the party.

The new populism quickly developed into a new, narrow **black nationalism** and **ethnic chauvinism** where the minority groups are defined out of the mainstream. While this had been the position held by firebrand Youth League leaders (Mandela, Lembede and Sisulu) in the 1940s, it was abandoned in favour of the non-racialism embodied in the Freedom Charter of 1955. When the ANC government's chief spokesman, **Jimmy Manyi**, said in March 2011 that there was "an oversupply of coloureds" in the Western Cape and that "Indians had bargained their way to the top", the most senior member of Zuma's cabinet, **Trevor Manuel**, called him "a racist in the mould of Hendrik Verwoerd". But instead of supporting Manuel, the government instead rallied around Manyi, who kept his job. When the local elections of May 2011 took place, the overwhelming majority of the minority groups abandoned the ANC and voted for the **Democratic Alliance** instead.

Foremost among the current populists is **Julius Malema**, leader of the ANC Youth League, who vowed to "kill for Zuma". Malema called **Helen Zille**, leader of the official opposition and premier of the Western Cape, "the racist madam" and a "dancing monkey", and claimed that she was sleeping with all her male cabinet colleagues. Malema's campaign to have all mines and banks **nationalized** has led to the ANC instituting an official investigation into the pros and cons of such a policy. In 2009 he started singing at rallies and meetings a song with the chorus line "Kill the Boer", which led to white civil action groups taking him to court. During the campaigning for the 2011 local elections, Malema declared from an ANC platform (as a silent Zuma sat next to him) that all white South Africans were criminals and should be treated as such and demanded a Zimbabwe-type **forced redistribution** of white-owned land. Malema warned black people that they would cause Mandela's death if they voted against the ANC.

Cronyism and corruption

The ANC leadership and government have come under sustained pressure for their **lavish lifestyles** and wasting of money in the face of the severe poverty in the country. Nearly every week newspapers report on a new instance of cabinet ministers or members of provincial or local government buying expensive cars, staying in five-star hotels or splashing out on foreign trips. The post-Mandela culture of public functionaries driving in fast-travelling convoys with blue lights flashing and pushing other traffic off the road has become increasingly unpopular with ordinary citizens.

Many local governments have virtually collapsed due to tender fraud, corruption and weak governance. Most analysts blame the ANC's policy of "cadre deployment", whereby loyal ANC members are rewarded with public positions, often regardless of qualifications, skills or experience. According to **Dr Mamphela Ramphele**, vice-chancellor of the University of Cape Town and former MD of the World Bank, "The culture of impunity with respect to the abuse of power and public resources in our public institutions has reached alarming levels. Even parliament is not immune. It comes as no surprise that after fifteen years of watching how those in positions of power have enriched themselves at their expense, poor communities have taken to the streets to demand attention."

Local government breakdowns have led to a phenomenon called "service delivery protests" – violent protests in black townships across the country almost on a weekly basis protesting against the lack of housing, electricity supply, water and sanitation. It was during one such protest, in the Free State province of **Ficksburg** on 13 April 2011, that teacher and community activist **Andries Tatane** was savagely beaten and shot to death by police. The whole incident was shown on national television, proving that Tatane was neither armed nor resisting. Tatane's killing has led to renewed uproar against **police brutality**, which according to non-governmental organizations and watchdog bodies (such as the Institute for Security Studies and the Centre for the Study of Violence and Reconciliation) is definitely on the increase in South Africa.

Silencing the critics

A growing tendency under the Zuma administration is to target the media, especially newspapers, and to rewrite the law books to limit the **freedom of speech** guaranteed in the South African constitution.

In 2011 the ANC was steamrolling a **Protection of Information Bill** through parliament that would, if it became law, allow any organ of the state to classify any information as secret "in the national interest", and to impose heavy jail penalties on people found in possession of such information. This could lead to the end of virtually all **investigative journalism** and the practice of **whistleblowing**. The ANC has also decided to propose to parliament that a statutory Media Tribunal be formed to regulate newspapers.

In June 2011, former president **F.W. de Klerk** launched a stinging attack on the ANC government. For de Klerk the country was "balanced between success and failure and the fulcrum on which South Africa's future will pivot is our constitution. If the forces of history come down on the side of constitutional values we can all look forward to a positive future. However, if the balance tips in the other direction, the consequences for all South Africans could be very dire." He felt that the ANC was "obliterating the constitutional borders between the party and the state; it is undermining the independence of key constitutional institutions and it is opening the way to large-scale corruption and government impunity." He believed "Whites, Coloureds and Asians would be corralled into demographic pens in all aspects of their economic and professional lives according to the percentage of the population they represent. The prospects of South African citizens would once again be determined by the colour of their skins."

The good news

Not everything is doom and gloom. The dark predictions of South Africa becoming a "banana republic" or of the large-scale oppression of whites – of becoming "another Zimbabwe" – have been proved utterly wrong. Despite the many challenges, South Africa is still a **beacon of stability** and, in terms of social cohesion, the envy of many other multicultural societies.

In economic terms, the way South Africa survived the **worldwide recession** and the massive crisis hitting financial institutions was admired by most international economists. South Africa's **economy** is still sound, growing and generally well-managed, and its infrastructure has developed. Africa remains the most promising growth point in the world for the future and South Africa is the gateway to that growth. The invitation, in December 2010, for South Africa to join **BRIC**, the four-member grouping of fast-growing markets (comprising Brazil, Russia, India and China) is a great opportunity to strengthen its international voice and influence and advance its economic interests.

There have been forward strides in other areas, most notably in stemming the devastating tide of **HIV infections** and **Aids**, both by the increased use of antiretrovirals and by a wave of media campaigns that have successfully raised awarness of the disease and how to combat it. In legal matters, the **Constitutional Court** (which safeguards the constitution) and the judiciary are still demonstrably independent and functioning well, although the increasingly strict **racial quotas** for the appointment of new judges is widely criticized. Unlike most of Africa, South Africa's regular national and local elections are run smoothly and credibly and the integrity of the **Independent Electoral Commission** has never been questioned. Most promisingly, there are signs of a reawakening of **civil society** with vibrant popular campaigns against the government's attempts to curb press freedom and for the strengthening of the constitution. In 2010 the country hosted a very successful Football World Cup which – despite the national team's exit in the first round – momentarily united the citizens in what was called a "Mandela moment".

Mandela's example and philosophies are still often evoked in the South African political discourse, by the opposition parties and political commentators, but also by the ruling ANC. "What would Mandela have done?" is a question frequently asked.

> "We became too dependent on the 'Madiba Magic' and on leaders in general to drive the building of the future. We allowed leaders to live our lives for us."
>
> Mamphela Ramphele

Mamphela Ramphele echoed the feelings of many when she wrote, in an opinion piece of October 2009, that South Africa had been blessed with Nelson Mandela as its first democratic leader. "He had the ability to lead in a way that inspired confidence in our ability to transcend our past and build a future where, together, we could become a great nation." But, she went on to warn of the "many among our fellow citizens, inside and outside government, who have a different understanding of what constitutional democracy means… The tendency to conflate the person of the leader of the governing party, the party, the government and the state is a worrying feature of our political system at all levels of government… It may be that we idealised President Mandela too much and paid too little attention to our role as citizens to build our future together alongside our leaders."

There is an old African saying that where a big tree once stood, new trees struggle to grow. That was true of King Moshoeshoe and it seems to be true of Nelson Mandela.

PART THREE

RESOURCES

17 The Mandela trail

Since Nelson Mandela's release in 1990, several of the key South African locations where he spent time have become popular destinations for anyone fascinated and inspired by his life. Some of them, such as Robben Island and the Mandela House in Soweto, have been turned into museums and are both visitor-friendly and reasonably accessible. Others are more difficult to reach and recommended only to the most intrepid travellers.

The Eastern Cape

All of Nelson Mandela's early life (see Chapter 1) was spent in the Transkei in the villages of **Mvezo**, **Qunu** and **Mqhekezweni**, near to the capital Umtata (now called Mthatha). **Mthatha** itself is a bustling, dusty town, comprising a small grid of streets lined with dull office buildings, interspersed with the odd older architectural gem. On the corner of Owen and Nelson Mandela Drive, housed in the old parliament, or *bunga*, built in 1927, is the **Nelson Mandela Museum** (Mon–Sun 9am–4pm; free; 047 532 5110, www .nelsonmandelamuseum.org.za). As well as some fascinating displays tracing Mandela's life in photos, the museum offers **free guided trips**

The Nelson Mandela Museum at Mthatha. (© David Larsen/Africa Media Online)

to Qunu and Mvezo and is in the process of restoring Mandela's home at Mqhekezweni – for more information, contact the museum or the tour coordinator, Zimisele Gamakhulu (047 538 0217).

Thirty kilometres south of Mthatha are the scattered dwellings of **Qunu**, where Mandela grew up. The N2 highway thunders through the settlement, but his large house (not open to the public) is clearly visible on the roadside, to the left as you head south. At Qunu the women still wear traditional clothing and you can see boys herding the family cows. Places you can visit include the remains of Mandela's primary school, the rock he used to slide down with friends, and the graveyard where his parents, son and daughter are buried.

Mandela's secondary education took place at two Methodist missionary schools: the **Clarkebury Boarding Institute** at **Engcobo** (not far from Mqhekezweni) and **Healdtown** at **Fort Beaufort** some 200km southwest of Mthatha. Following the Bantu Education Act of 1953 both establishments became increasingly dilapidated and prey to vandalism. Clarkebury has been badly damaged by fire and is not worth visiting; Healdtown (now Healdtown Comprehensive School) was also damaged during the apartheid era but has managed to re-establish itself. Several of its original Victorian buildings have been restored, although the hostel where Mandela lived is still a ruin.

Not far from Fort Beaufort, near the town of **Alice**, is the main campus of the **University of Fort Hare**, where Mandela was a student from 1937 to 1939. Established as a multiracial college by missionaries, it became the country's first institution to deliver tertiary education to blacks, and was attended by many distinguished South Africans (see p.21). The university library has an extensive archive of original ANC documents; its School of Law is named after its most famous alumnus, and the Chair of Human Rights after Oliver Tambo. The university houses the **De Beers Centenary Art Gallery**, a treasury of contemporary black southern African art, and Fort Hare's **ethnographic collection**, a major museum of traditional crafts and artefacts. Tours of the university must be booked in advance by contacting Vuyani Booi (078 158 9631; vbooi@ufh.ac.za). Fort Hare is a couple of kilometres east of Alice on the R63 and 64km west of King William's Town. Minibus taxis travelling between the two towns can drop off passengers at the university gates. It's best visited on a day-trip as there's virtually no accommodation in Alice.

Johannesburg

After leaving university, Mandela headed for Johannesburg (see Chapter 2), to begin his career as a lawyer. On arriving, he lived briefly with his cousin in George Goch township, before moving to the desperately poor township of **Alexandra** (commonly known as Alex) in the northeast of the city. Here he lodged first with the Reverend Mabutho at his home on **Eighth Avenue** and later with the Xhoma family at **no. 46 Seventh Avenue**. The latter house still stands, marked by a blue plaque naming it as "Mandela's Place".

About a year after getting married to Evelyn Mase, Mandela moved to Orlando, a township in **Soweto**. Initially the couple lived in Orlando East, but soon moved to **8115 Vilakazi Street** in **Orlando West**. After his divorce from Evelyn in 1957, Mandela lived there briefly with Winnie before going underground in 1961. On his release, Mandela insisted on returning to his old home, but its small size and lack of security proved too much of a strain, and he moved out of Soweto, eventually settling in the affluent suburb of **Houghton**. He donated his old house to the Soweto Heritage Trust in 1997 and it is now the **Mandela House Museum** (Mon–Fri 9am–5pm, Sat & Sun 9am–4.30pm; R60; 011 936 7754; www.mandelahouse.com). Tours of the old bungalow reveal some fascinatingly mundane memorabilia, including original furnishings and a collection of family photographs, alongside audiovisual displays describing conditions in Soweto at the time. Vilakazi Street is the only street in the world to have had two resident Nobel Prize Laureates – Desmond Tutu's house is across the street, but it's not open to visitors.

Within walking distance on Maseko Street is the **Hector Pieterson Museum** (Mon–Fri 10am–5pm, Sat & Sun 10am–4.30pm; R25 adults, R5 concessions; 011 536 0611), commemorating the Soweto Youth Uprising of June 1976 and named after the twelve-year-old boy who was the first to be shot. Displays focus on the events surrounding and leading up to the uprising, using video and photographic images including the famous photo by Sam Nzima of the dying Pieterson. There's a memorial to Pieterson at nearby **Khumalo Street**.

The **Walter Sisulu Square of Dedication** (011 945 2200, www .waltersisulusquare.co.za), also known as **Freedom Square**, in **Kliptown**, now a suburb of Soweto, was built on the space where delegates to the 1955 Congress of the People gathered to accept the Freedom Charter. Mandela's movements were legally restricted at

Walter Sisulu Square, Kliptown. (© Graeme Williams/South Photos/
Africa Media Online)

the time, but he managed to watch the proceedings in secret. The
monument complex now has a large paved area for gatherings, stalls
for informal traders, an art gallery, a community hall and the four-star
Soweto Hotel. Ten columns represent the ten clauses of the charter
and a cylindrical brick tower contains a round stone tablet with the
charter etched into it.

In 1952 Mandela established South Africa's first black law firm with
Oliver Tambo. Their offices were on the second floor of the recently
built **Chancellor House**, at the corner of Fox Street and Gerard
Sekoto Street in the central business district (CBD) of Johannesburg.
The practice was almost directly opposite the **Magistrate's Court**,
where many of their cases were heard. Virtually derelict for the last
ten years, Chancellor House has been restored by the Johannesburg
Development Agency and reopened in May 2011. A small **museum**,

recording the achievements of the Mandela and Tambo law firm, is located on the ground floor – originally the site of Kosi's Café. Close by, at no.11a Kort Street was the legendary **Kapitan's Restaurant**, a favoured eating place of the partners, famed for its curries.

After the decision to go underground in 1961, Mandela spent much of his time at the secluded **Liliesleaf Farm** in **Rivonia**, now a northeastern suburb of Johannesburg. The leaderships of the ANC and Communist Party met frequently at this relatively secluded location, and it was where many of them were arrested on 11 July 1963. In 2008 it was opened by the Liliesleaf Trust as an interactive museum and study centre (Mon–Fri 8.30am–5pm, Sat & Sun 9am–4pm; 011 803 7882; www.liliesleaf.co.za), focusing not just on Mandela, but on all the members of the liberation struggle who met there.

Since 2003, **Constitution Hill** in the suburb of **Braamfontein** has been the home of South Africa's highest court, the Constitutional Court. Right beside it stands the **Old Fort Prison** complex (tours hourly Mon–Fri & Sun 9am–5pm, Sat 10am–3pm; R30; 011 381 3100; www.constitutionhill.org.za). Built by Paul Kruger during the second Anglo-Boer War, the fort was subsequently converted to a prison and used to incarcerate black men who broke racial laws or fought for their repeal. You can visit the spine-chilling **Number Four prison building**, where Gandhi and PAC leader Robert Sobukwe were both held, and the cell where Mandela was kept briefly after his arrest in 1962. The **Women's Jail**, built in 1910, is a grand Edwardian building which held black and white women prisoners in separate sections. Major political leaders Winnie Madikizela-Mandela, Albertina Sisulu, Helen Joseph and Ruth First all spent time there.

Johannesburg's **Apartheid Museum** (Tues–Sun 9am–5pm; R55; 011 309 4700; www.apartheidmuseum.org), located at Northern Parkway and Gold Reef Road in the southern suburb of **Ormonde**, is a world-class museum, delivering a sophisticated visual history that is both distressing and inspiring. As well as a permanent exhibition of photographs by Peter Magubane of the 1976 Soweto Uprising, there's a short documentary on the State of Emergency during the mid-1980s, when a wave of mass demonstrations and riots shook the resolve of the regime. The museum also helps to explain the persistence of poverty and racial tension in the new South Africa.

Pretoria

A mere 50km north of Johannesburg, **Pretoria** is the most architecturally impressive of South Africa's three capital cities. During the apartheid era it acquired a hated reputation among the country's black population, its Supreme Court and prisons being notorious for enforcing the many racial laws and regulations. Its significance for Mandela is that he was tried here on three separate occasions (see Chapters 4 and 9).

In 1952 the government purchased the **Old Synagogue** in Paul Kruger Street for use as a courtroom. It was here that Mandela, Walter Sisulu and others were tried for treason between 1958 and 1961. After his acquittal, Mandela was tried again and this time sentenced to five years on Robben Island (see p.269). The synagogue, which opened in 1898, was largely paid for by local Jewish entrepreneur Sammy Marks. Despite talk of turning the building into a cultural centre or museum, it remains in a dilapidated state.

The Rivonia Trial, which took place in 1963–64 and resulted in life sentences for Mandela and eight of his co-defendants, was held at the **Palace of Justice** on the northwest side of **Church Square**, Pretoria's historical core. Designed by Dutch architect Sytze Wierda, in a grandiose neo-Renaissance style, the building was used as a hospital during the second Anglo-Boer War and only completed in 1902. Recent restoration work has revealed a splendid turreted facade, although the new court is now located in an adjacent street. The only parts of the building left untouched are the **underground holding cells** where Mandela and his fellow defendants were kept while the trial was in progress.

During both of these trials, Mandela spent sustained periods in **Pretoria Local Prison**, part of a complex of prisons on Potgieter Street. The cells where he was held are no longer standing, but for an insight into South African prison life, the chilling **Correctional Services Museum** at **Pretoria Central Prison** (Tues–Fri 9am–3pm; free; 012 314 1766; www.dcs.gov.za/AboutUs/Museum.aspx) is well worth a visit. You can see the notorious prison, where many famous political prisoners were held (and many executed) as well as artworks made by prisoners. Other exhibits include knives concealed in Bibles and shoes, files in cakes and so forth. Most alarming by far are the group photos of various forbidding-looking prison warders through the ages.

Across from the prison, Skietpoort Street is the turn-off for **Freedom Park** (tours Mon–Fri & public hols at 9am, noon & 3pm; R45; www .freedompark.co.za), which sits atop **Salvokop Hill**. Begun in 2000 in response to the Truth and Reconciliation Commission's call for new symbols to resolve past conflicts, the park is a courageous and successful attempt to create a memorial that speaks to all sections of society. Visits are by guided tour only and take you past **The Wall of Names**, inscribed with the names of 75,000 victims of various South African conflicts, an eternal flame to the unknown soldier and boulders representing important moments in the history of the country's nine provinces.

The **Presidential official residence** – Mandela's home from 1994 to 1999 – is located in the **Bryntirion Estate**, along with several other government residencies. Originally called Libertas, the name of the house was changed to **Mahlamba Ndlopfu** (meaning "new dawn" in Tsonga) in 1995. It was built in 1940 in the Cape-Dutch style to a design by the architect Gerrit Moerdyk, and is surrounded by beautifully landscaped gardens with a stunning view of the Magaliesberg, the mountain range to the north of Pretoria.

Robben Island & Cape Town

After Mandela was sentenced to life imprisonment in 1964, he spent the next 27 years in prisons close to Cape Town, most famously Robben Island (see Chapter 10). Cape Town's City Hall is where he made his first public speech following his release in 1990 (see Chapter 11).

Lying only a few kilometres from the commerce of the Cape Town waterfront, **Robben Island** is a key site of South Africa's liberation struggle. The apartheid authorities saw the prison as a way of silencing its domestic critics; instead it became the international focus for opposition to the regime. The last political prisoners left the island in 1991 and the remaining inmates were moved off in 1996. On 1 January 1997, control of the island was transferred from the Department of Correctional Services to the Department of the Arts,

Robben Island prison perimeter fence and watchtower. (© Lewis K. Bush)

Culture, Science and Technology, which established it as a museum. In December 1999 the entire island was declared a **UN World Heritage Site.**

From the Pierhead at the Victoria and Alfred Waterfront in Cape Town you can use the swing bridge to cross to Fish Quay, the Clock Tower Precinct and the **Nelson Mandela Gateway** (daily 7.30am–5.30pm; free). The embarkation point for ferries to Robben Island, this two-storey building also incorporates a restaurant with a great view and a small museum with hi-tech interactive displays, featuring a history of the island, the voices of prisoners and resistance songs. The catamaran from the waterfront (see box opposite) takes 30 to 45 minutes to reach the island, where ex-prisoners and ex-warders work as guides.

After arrival at the tiny **Murray's Bay harbour**, you are taken on a bus tour around the island, stopping off at several historical landmarks, the first of which is the *kramat*, a shrine in memory of **Tuan Guru**, a Muslim cleric from the Maluku Islands who was imprisoned here by the Dutch in the eighteenth century. The tour also passes a leper graveyard and church designed by Sir Herbert Baker, both reminders that the island was once a place of exile for leprosy sufferers.

Robert Sobukwe's house is where the leader of the Pan Africanist Congress was held in solitary confinement for nine years. Initially sentenced to three years, he was regarded as so dangerous that the authorities passed a special law – the "Sobukwe Clause" – to keep him on Robben Island for a further six years.

Another stop-off is the **lime quarry** where Mandela and his fellow inmates spent countless hours in hard labour and which later became a place of study and debate among the prisoners. The bus tour also takes in a **stretch of coast** dotted with shipwrecks and abundant bird life, including African penguins and the elegant sacred ibis. You may also spot some of the island's recently expanded antelope population.

ROBBEN ISLAND TOURS

A number of vendors at the waterfront sell tickets for cruises which may go close to Robben Island, but only the official ones sold at the **Nelson Mandela Gateway** will get you onto it (R220, children R110, including boat trip, island entry and 3hr 30min tour). **Bookings** must be made well in advance with a credit card (021 413 4263, www.robben-island.org.za) as the boats are often full, especially around December and January. Be sure to present your booking reference number and arrive at least half an hour before departure to collect your ticket. Boats leave daily at 9am, 11am, 1pm & 3pm. All trips are dependent on the weather.

The **Maximum Security Prison** is a forbidding complex of unadorned H-blocks on the edge of the island. This includes **B-Section**, a small compound of tiny rooms, of which Mandela's cell has been left exactly as it was. The rest of the cells are now locked and empty. In the nearby **A-Section**, the "Cell Stories" exhibition evokes the austerity of prison life. The tiny **isolation cells** feature personal artefacts loaned by former prisoners, plus boards bearing quotations, recordings and photographs. Towards the end of the 1980s, cameras were sneaked onto the island and inmates took snapshots of each other, which have been enlarged and mounted as the **Smuggled Camera Exhibition** in the **D-Section** communal cells. Finally, there's the **Living Legacy** tour in **F-Section**, in which the ex-prisoner guides describe their lives here and answer questions.

In 1982 Mandela and Walter Sisulu were moved from Robben Island to **Pollsmoor Prison**, in the Cape Town suburb of **Tokai**; five years later, during ongoing discussions about his release, Mandela was transferred to the **Victor Verster Prison** (renamed **Groot Drakenstein** in 2000) in the town of **Paarl**, northeast of Cape Town. This was his last place of imprisonment and he was housed not in a cell but a spacious bungalow, complete with garden and swimming pool. The working jail looks rather like a boys' school, fronted by rugby fields beneath hazy mountains and surrounded by vineyards. In 2008 a **bronze statue** of the prison's most famous inmate was unveiled outside the prison; it shows Mandela striding purposefully forward with his clenched right hand raised in salute.

A few hours after his release on 11 February 1990, Mandela addressed a crowd of 100,000 people – and millions of televison viewers around the world – from the balcony of Cape Town's **City Hall**. A monumental building in the Edwardian Baroque style, it dominates Grand Parade, the main public square of the city.

Not far from City Hall, in the shadow of Devil's Peak, is a vacant lot shown on maps as the suburb of **Zonnebloem**. This was once an inner-city slum known as **District Six**, an impoverished but lively community of 55,000 predominantly coloured people that harboured a rich cultural life in its narrow alleys and crowded tenements. Then in 1966, apartheid ideologues declared District Six a White Group Area and the bulldozers moved in, taking fifteen years to drive its presence from the skyline, leaving only the mosques and churches.

On the corner of Buitenkant and Albertus streets, the **District Six Museum** (Mon 9am–2pm, Tues–Sat 9am–4pm; R120; 021 466 7200; www.districtsix.co.za) occupies the former Central Methodist Mission Church, which offered solidarity and ministry to the victims of forced removals and served as a venue for anti-apartheid gatherings. The museum houses a series of fascinating displays that include everyday household items and documentary photographs evoking the lives of its inhabitants. Covering most of the floor is a huge map of District Six as it was, annotated by former residents, who recall memories and events associated with places and buildings that no longer exist. Tours of the site must be booked in advance.

18 Books, films & websites

Since Mandela's release from prison and the collapse of apartheid, there has been a torrent of books about both him and the liberation struggle in general, many written by those directly involved. The drama of these historic events has also inspired attempts by filmmakers and TV producers to capture the Mandela myth, from earnest documentaries to Hollywood biopics. Below are some of the best known and critically regarded books and films, plus the pick of the most helpful websites.

Books

Anne Marie du Preez Bezdrob *Winnie Mandela: A Life* (2008). Winnie biography with lots of new insights and revelations. Bezdrob has also written an accessible, honest but rather uncritical biography of Mandela himself.

Elleke Boehmer *Nelson Mandela: A Very Short Introduction* (2008). Overview of various aspects of the Mandela phenomenon. In some respects its compartmentalized approach yields dividends,

especially on topics such as Mandela's dress sense, image and masculine persona.

John Carlin *Playing the Game: Nelson Mandela and the Game that Made a Nation* (2008). Filmed as *Invictus* (see p.276), this is a detailed account of how Mandela shrewdly grasped the importance of rugby to white South Africa and seized the moment of opportunity to build bridges.

Eddie Daniels *There and Back: Robben Island 1964–1979* (2002). Fascinating autobiography of a Robben Island prisoner and friend of Mandela, with many anecdotes – this was the man who hatched the most ambitious plan to help Mandela escape from the island.

Harriet Deacon *The Island: A History of Robben Island 1488–1990* (1992). Written by one of South Africa's foremost historians, it tells the story of an island which in microcosm can be read almost as the story of South Africa itself.

Stephen Ellis & Tsepo Sechaba *Comrades Against Apartheid: The ANC & the South African Communist Party in Exile* (1992). Ellis is the former editor of *Africa Confidential* and now professor at Leiden University, Sechaba is the alias of a SACP insider. Contains rare insights into the interaction between the ANC and SACP, and into Umkhonto we Sizwe.

James Gregory *Goodbye Bafana: Nelson Mandela, My Prisoner, My Friend* (1995). Gregory, a Robben Island prison guard, tells the story of how his relationship with Mandela forced him to question his hardline apartheid beliefs. Some critics have accused him of sensationalizing his account of events.

Heidi Holland *The Struggle: A History of the African National Congress* (1989). A succinct overview of the first 77 years of the ANC, outlining its changing ideology from passive resistance to armed struggle and eventual power. Like Martin Meredith (see p.275), Holland has also written about Zimbabwe's Robert Mugabe, who led his country in a rather different direction.

Joel Joffe *The State vs Nelson Mandela: The Trial That Changed South Africa* (2009). The inside story of the Rivonia Trial by Mandela's attorney at the time was first published in 1995 as *The Rivonia Story*. Joffe went on to chair Oxfam and become a Labour peer in the UK's House of Lords.

Ahmed Kathrada *Memoirs* (2004). This wide-ranging life story of a major anti-apartheid activist, who was one of Mandela's fellow prisoners on Robben Island, provides sharp insights into the early years of the struggle. His prison letters and Robben Island notebooks have also been published.

Alf Kumalo & Zukiswa Wanner *8115 A Prisoner's Home* (2010). A photographic record of life in Mandela's Soweto home, from the 1950s to the 90s, by renowned photographer and family friend Alf Kumalo. Combines images of everyday domestic incidents with scenes of police harassment.

Tom Lodge *Nelson Mandela: A Critical Life* (2006). By no means as critical of Mandela as Smith's book (see below), this is nevertheless a solid overview of his life, with a special emphasis on its place within the context of South African politics.

Mac Maharaj and Ahmed Kathrada (editorial consultants) *Mandela: The Authorised Portrait* (2009). An attractive book of rare photographs of Mandela with the basic story of his life alongside tributes from South African and international luminaries, including Desmond Tutu and Bill Clinton.

Nelson Mandela *Conversations With Myself* (2010). Long-awaited private letters, jottings, journals and other previously unpublished material. This set of collected personal documents was hailed as candid and moving, though some regretted that they were not more revealing of Mandela's feelings about his ex-wives and his children.

Nelson Mandela *Long Walk to Freedom* (1995). This autobiography, published early on in his term as South African president, reveals Mandela's character in his homely turns of phrase and in his generosity. As he was a serving politician when the book was published, it is not surprising that criticisms of contemporaries are comparatively muted.

Nelson Mandela with Chris van Wyk and Paddy Bouma *Long Walk to Freedom* (1995). Short, colourful and deliberately simple 64-page rendering of the Mandela story designed for children.

Nelson Mandela *Nelson Mandela by Himself: The Authorised Book of Quotations* (2011). Over 2000 quotations gleaned from speeches, correspondence recordings and Mandela's own archive of private papers.

Nelson Mandela *No Easy Walk to Freedom* (2002). A short collection of speeches and miscellaneous writings from the key period of 1953–1964. The voice of the writer here is that of the original

Mandela, the courageous and principled political activist. A welcome antidote to later idolatry and a necessary reminder of why he matters.

Fatima Meer *Higher than Hope: The Authorised Biography of Nelson Mandela* (1988). First biography of Mandela by his old friend and comrade, with a foreword by Winnie. Meer had access to many letters Mandela had written to friends and family in prison, as well as to Winnie and their children.

Martin Meredith *Mandela: A Biography* (1997). This ambitious biography features extensive research by an experienced Africanist, offering a critical look at Mandela's childhood, friendships, and his accomplishments and failures as an armed revolutionary and a father.

Anthony Sampson *Mandela: The Authorised Biography* (2011). The standard one-volume biography first published in 1999 has been updated for a paperback re-release by South African journalist John Battersby. Sampson's account is suitably intimate and readable but doesn't idolize its subject.

Elinor Sisulu *Walter & Albertina Sisulu: In our Lifetime* (2002). Exhaustive biography of Mandela's best friend and adviser, and his wife, written by their daughter-in-law. Tells the story of the early years of the ANC Youth League, the Rivonia Trial and Robben Island through the eyes of Walter Sisulu, and provides Albertina's perspective on what was going on inside the country while her husband was in prison.

David James Smith *Young Mandela* (2010). Hyped as a "warts and all" exposé, Smith's book emphasizes the sacrifices Mandela and his family made for the cause. Much is made (with gossip aplenty) of Mandela as a womanizer and an authoritarian patriarch who found it easier to express his feelings for the masses than for his own children.

Allister Sparks *Tomorrow is Another Country: The Inside Story of South Africa's Negotiated Settlement* (1995). As the title suggests, an account of the delicate negotiations (many in secret) between the Nationalist government and Mandela which paved the way for the peaceful transition to full democracy. Sparks is a former editor of the *Rand Daily Mail* and regarded as the doyen of South African journalists.

Richard Stengel *Mandela's Way: Lessons on Life* (2010). The author, who worked with Mandela on his autobiography, sets out to explain the leader's unique moral vision and explain what everyone might learn from him. More self-help than biography, it's nonetheless revealing because of the author's connection to Madiba, here presented almost as a "secular saint".

Patti Waldmeir *Anatomy of a Miracle: The End of Apartheid and the Birth of a New South Africa* (1997). Behind the scenes of South Africa's negotiated settlement. Covers the same ground as Sparks's book but with more journalistic detail.

Winnie Mandela *Part of my Soul Went With Him* (1985). This powerful indictment of apartheid is Winnie's autobiography written (with help) before things "went wrong". The book was edited by Anne Benjamin and adapted by Mary Benson, both struggle veterans.

Film and TV

Endgame (dir. Pete Travis, 2009). Journalism meets conspiracy theory in this dramatic TV thriller. For once Mandela is upstaged onscreen by successor Thabo Mbeki (Chiwetel Ejiofor) taking the lead for the ANC in secret negotiations that were to usher in the new South Africa. Clarke Peters (*The Wire*'s Lester Freedman) plays Mandela.

Goodbye Bafana (dir. Billie August, 2007). Dennis Haysbert plays Mandela but the focus is the white South African worldview in the form of resentful prison guard James Gregory (Joseph Fiennes), who gradually comes to understand and sympathize with his famous prisoner but at significant personal cost.

Invictus (dir. Clint Eastwood, 2009). Morgan Freeman makes probably the most memorable Mandela: he and Matt Damon (as rugby captain Francois Pienaar) gained Oscar nominations for their roles in this stately and stirring rendering of Mandela's "rainbow" nation-building masterclass.

Malcolm X (dir. Spike Lee, 1992). A unique but tiny cameo by Mandela as a Soweto schoolteacher reciting a section of a Malcolm X speech (filmed not long after his release from prison) rounds off this momentous biopic which links the apartheid and American civil rights struggles.

Mandela (dir. Philip Saville, 1987). Made before Mandela's release, this film is now best viewed as a historical curio. Activist and oftimes comedy actor Danny Glover probably never had a prouder moment than in this starring role.

Mandela (dir. Angus Gibson and Jo Menell, 1996). Conventional film biography with an educational rather than polemical slant. It now feels rather dated but remains one of only a handful of Mandela documentaries readily available in the worldwide English-language market.

Mandela and De Klerk (dir. Joseph Sargent, 1997). Odd couple Sidney Poitier and an undeniably English Michael Caine negotiate a famous peace aided by the hand of history in this made-for-TV drama.

The Man Who Drove with Mandela (dir. Greta Schiller, 1999). Unsung hero Cecil Williams was a gay theatre director who helped Mandela conceal his identity; the dangerous political activist posed as his chauffeur. An unconventional documentary which casts an unusual light on those revolutionary times.

Mrs Mandela (dir. Michael Samuels, 2010). Sophie Okenodo as Winnie received all the plaudits in this provocative BBC TV drama. It shows the high price of Winnie's own freedom-fighting and how it eventually lapsed into bitterness, controversy and then divorce from her husband whom she refused to be overshadowed by.

The 16th Man (dir. Clifford Bestall, 2010). Fifty-minute documentary, produced and voiced by Morgan Freeman, about the real story of Mandela and the 1995 Rugby World Cup. Like *Invictus*, this was based on John Carlin's book, *Playing With the Enemy*, but is best viewed before the earlier film.

Winnie (dir. Darrell Roodt, 2011). *American Idol*'s Jennifer Hudson was a controversial choice for this biopic of "A Young Woman's Voyage of Discovery"; neither she nor Terrence Howard (Mandela) have South African roots. Loosely based on Anne Marie du Preez Bezdrob's biography, the prospect of the film caused Winnie Madikizela-Mandela to threaten legal action, describing it as an "insult".

Young Mandela (working title) (dir. Peter Kosminsky). At the time of writing in 2011 news broke of a feature film depicting Mandela's time as head of Umkhonto we Sizwe, the armed wing of the ANC. Not a "hatchet job" according to the director, the film is expected to depict Mandela's early days as a "terrorist" before he turned to peace.

Websites

www.46664.com Mandela's Robben Island prison number was the inspiration for the name of this worldwide Aids/HIV awareness and prevention campaign. Many of its ambassadors are musicians, from all parts of the globe. 46664 have organized several concerts, including one at Hyde Park in London for Mandela's ninetieth birthday in 2008 – a DVD was subsequently released.

www.nelsonmandelachildren sfund.com and **www.mandela -children.org.uk** Official websites of the Nelson Mandela Children's Fund, with information on programmes, projects, reports and research.

www.nelsonmandela.org Lovingly created and well designed, the Nelson Mandela Foundation's site is an obvious first port of call with lots of information, resources and links to other sites of interest. For instance, there is a intriguing overview of three of Mandela's prison warders to download – very much an example of reconciliation in action. The site is organized around the three themes of memory, dialogue and the institution itself, and is the best place to learn about initiatives like Mandela Day.

www.radiodiaries.org/mandela A brief series of US national public radio broadcasts, called "Mandela: An Audio History", can be streamed from this site.

These feature the voices of many involved in the historic events, Mandela included. There are text transcripts too.

www.sahistory.org.za Topic-based resource covering a huge range of wider South African history topics. As you'd expect from a national online archive, much of the emphasis is towards educational use.

www.saho.org.zag An independent archive of material covering past struggles for justice in South Africa and current history in the making. Though a lot of material is online, much of the archive's work has been printed in book form. To visit the archive at the University of Witwatersrand, Johannesburg, you need to make an appointment.

www.theelders.org Founder and honorary elder Mandela is one of twelve senior statesmen and stateswomen who use their high profile to encourage dialogue and peace in troubled areas of the world and to support humanitarian causes such as the alleviation of poverty and disease, and equality for women. His third wife Graça Machel is a prominent member, with a particular brief for gender equality and children's issues.

http://tiny.cc/7uobg Extensive transcripts of interviews and anecdotes from the two-hour PBS documentary *The Long Walk of Nelson Mandela*.

Index